CARESHARING

A Reciprocal Approach to Caregiving
and Care Receiving in the Complexities
of Aging, Illness or Disability

CARESHARING

MARTY RICHARDS

Walking Together, Finding the Way ®
SKYLIGHT PATHS®
PUBLISHING
Woodstock, Vermont

Caresharing:
A Reciprocal Approach to Caregiving and Care Receiving in the Complexities of Aging,
Illness or Disability

2010 Quality Paperback Edition, First Printing
2009 Hardcover Edition, First Printing
© 2009 by Martha Richards

For information regarding permission to reprint material from this book, please mail or fax your request in writing to SkyLight Paths Publishing, Permissions Department, at the address / fax number listed below, or e-mail your request to permissions@skylightpaths.com.

Scripture quotations are from the New Revised Standard Version Bible, © 1989 by the Division of Christian Education of the National Council of the Churches of Christ in the USA. Used by permission. All rights reserved.

The stories shared in this book are true, but the names of persons and any identifying details have been changed to protect the privacy of each individual.

Library of Congress Cataloging-in-Publication Data
Richards, Marty.
Caresharing : a reciprocal approach to caregiving and care receiving in the complexities of aging, illness, or disability / Marty Richards.
p. cm.
Includes bibliographical references.
ISBN-13: 978-1-59473-247-8 (hardcover)
ISBN-10: 1-59473-247-7 (hardcover)
1. Caring. 2. Charity. I. Title.
BJ1475.R525 2008
259'.4—dc22

2008041299

ISBN-13: 978-1-59473-286-7 (quality pbk.)
ISBN-10: 1-59473-286-8 (quality pbk.)

10   9   8   7   6   5   4   3   2   1
Manufactured in the United States of America
Cover design: Melanie Robinson
Cover art: Melanie Robinson

SkyLight Paths Publishing is creating a place where people of different spiritual traditions come together for challenge and inspiration, a place where we can help each other understand the mystery that lies at the heart of our existence.

SkyLight Paths sees both believers and seekers as a community that increasingly transcends traditional boundaries of religion and denomination—people wanting to learn from each other, *walking together, finding the way.*

SkyLight Paths, "Walking Together, Finding the Way," and colophon are trademarks of LongHill Partners, Inc., registered in the U.S. Patent and Trademark Office.

Walking Together, Finding the Way®
Published by SkyLight Paths Publishing
A Division of Longhill Partners, Inc.
Sunset Farm Offices, Route 4, P.O. Box 237
Woodstock, VT 05091
Tel: (802) 457-4000 Fax: (802) 457-4004
www.skylightpaths.com

To my beloved Aunt Toni,
who died at 102½ as I was writing this book.
She indeed has been, and continues to be,
my teacher and "the wind beneath my wings."

CONTENTS

Contents

Contents

PRELUDE

Most likely you picked up this book because, in one way or another, you are caring for a person who needs assistance, whether it's due to a physical, mental, or emotional concern. As a daughter or son, a husband or wife, a sibling, a long-term partner, or a good friend who is "like family," you are on a journey. It is also possible that you are part of an intentional network that has been drawn together as a care team of supportive friends and acquaintances. You may be doing hands-on care or providing it from afar. You might be emotionally, materially, or spiritually supporting someone by carrying out daily tasks, or it may fall on you to be solely responsible.

Whatever your role, you may be seeking support or information. You may feel overloaded, lonely, and isolated. My hope is that *Caresharing* will open the door to help you feel more connected and empowered. You are not alone, even though it may feel that way at times. Many are on a similar journey, and many more will be following the same path in the future.

In my career as a professional caregiver in social work and gerontology, I have been privileged to work with many families who have taught me a great deal. In long-term care facilities and the community, I have shared their lives and spiritual paths. Even in their struggles and when things seemed bleak, those "being cared for" and those doing the "caring" have taught me many lessons. My hope is that you will find their stories helpful as you walk the caregiving path.

In recent years, I, too, have been a family caregiver. I supported a brother in another state who provided support to my 102- and 89-year-old aunts, who resided at home with a caregiver and then in a small nursing home. I helped support my mother-in-law, who lived a few miles from me. My husband and I assisted her, both in her own home and then in a long-term care facility until her death at age 99. From these older "saints" in my family and work, I have learned much about aging, survival, love, and gratitude—and about nurturing and sustaining people as they age. I hope to share their wisdom with you as well, as you face your own challenges.

There is one other thing you need to know: I was not, and am not, a "perfect" caregiver. In coming to realize that I do the best I can, I try to forgive myself when I fail. And in so doing, I have experienced how important it is to reach out. Providing care is not a solitary journey, but a relational one.

THE CONCEPT OF CARESHARING

I was first introduced to the concept of caresharing some years ago when I spoke at a Parkinson's caregivers' retreat. I heard people who were caring for their partners with Parkinson's disease stress the importance of sharing care between the one giving care and the one receiving care. It struck me that, though they were all partners in marital relationships, the concept holds in all caregiver and care-receiver relationships.

When you care for someone who is dealing with the complexities of aging, illness, or disability, you share intense emotions and form deep bonds. You each have the opportunity to recognize what is most deeply human—and most deeply divine—in the other. You both have a chance to give and receive, to honor and learn from each other. This sense of reciprocal sharing—between the caregiver and the care receiver, and with others around you— is the essence of the dance of caresharing.

THE SPIRITUAL DIMENSION OF CARESHARING

While caregiving is never an easy task, I believe it is always sacred. Throughout this book, I will be examining ways that the spiritual figures in coping and caring. Although "spiritual" and "religious" are intimately connected, they are not synonymous. For the purposes of this book, I use the term *religion* to denote a formalized set of tenets, theology, values, philosophy, and institutional rites and rituals. Religion may include a sense of connection to God, a Higher or Sacred Power, Supreme Being, or Transcendent Power. Religion may encompass the beliefs that provide a compass for a moral life, a faith that is an integral facet of our existence.

The word *spiritual,* on the other hand, although it may be included as part of religion, has broader connotations. Spirituality may help us ponder questions about life's meaning and purpose, and find guidance in life's difficult choices. The spiritual can offer a larger story context in which to make sense of the world and our experiences. Our stories are connected to others' stories and, ultimately, to the stories of the greater universe.

The ways I look at spiritual aspects of sharing care have evolved from my own upbringing and beliefs from a liturgical Lutheran heritage. My professional experiences have been within the Jewish and Christian traditions, so, for the most part, the stories in this book flow from those backgrounds. But I have also come to appreciate spiritual wisdom in beliefs different from my own and honor these perspectives as well.

THE INVITATION TO CARESHARING

As you reflect on the spiritual aspects of sharing care and listen to the stories other people have to tell about their journey, I invite you to consider how you might shift from caregiving to caresharing so you will feel less alone, more connected, and more hopeful.

In the pages ahead we will explore ways that caresharing can be structured to your benefit and, at the same time, preserve the well-being of the person for whom you are caring. I'll teach you a few new moves and steps in the dance of caresharing that may be well worth your time and energy. And, most important, I'll invite you to enter into the dance of a richer, spiritual connection with your care partner.

Because this book is conversational in tone, I have used the word *they* (and its relatives, *their, them, themselves*) as a singular pronoun. In conversation, we might say, "No one in their right mind would do that." This phrasing is so natural that we are hardly aware of it. And everyone understands what we mean. Given the alternative of switching back and forth between "he" and "she," "they" *singular* is a reasonable way of dealing with the gender issue. An occasional use of "he or she" is one thing, but in every paragraph and on every page, it becomes far too cumbersome. So I am following a long-established precedent, going back as far as the fourteenth century, of adopting "they" as a singular pronoun. For those who might disagree with this usage, I would simply quote Jane Austen's line from *Persuasion*: "Everybody has their taste."

1

THE DANCE
OF SHARING CARE

AN INVITATION TO SHARE CARE

Caring for someone who is struggling with chronic illness or a disability is difficult. If you feel you have to handle every aspect of caregiving by yourself, it is easy to feel quickly overwhelmed. You might believe (and society reinforces this notion) that you are totally on your own. Yet no one lives in a vacuum or is completely self-reliant. The reality is, throughout our lives, each of us has to depend on others; it's not possible to survive totally by our own skills and wit.

Yet I have seen many caregivers who believed the myth of independence ... until the circumstances of caregiving totally pressed them to the wall. They thought they could handle the daily ups and downs, but they found themselves disintegrating emotionally and spiritually—sometimes even physically—before they faced up to their need for assistance. It was only when they realized they could not manage everything on their own that they were finally able to explore a broader meaning of "independence." Caregiving turned out to be a disguised blessing. In their vulnerability, they were enabled to reach out to others and discover *inter*dependence.

1

If you're like most people, you probably have some ambivalence about the idea of "interdependence." It's not hard to say that you need and want other people in good times, to share the joys of graduations, weddings, births of children, new jobs, and so forth. But acknowledging that you need someone's help because your loved one is disabled or facing a terminal diagnosis—or because you yourself are ill—that's another story altogether.

I hear people say, "I don't want to bother my family or friends with this," or "I never want to become a burden to others." If you're thinking along these lines, it makes reaching out to others tough to do and leaves you pretty isolated in your journey. Here's a question I've heard people ask that may strike a chord with you: "Does it make me less of a person if I ask for assistance?"

Offering help, asking for help, and receiving help is a delicate balance. It is a dance where you move back and forth to the rhythms you sense for yourself and for the one receiving your care. It is a dance with multiple partners, including caregivers and care receivers alike, friends and family, the community of faith, and healthcare professionals.

I invite you to consider a new way of thinking: What if you were to approach care*giving* not as a two-step dance ("I give and you receive"), but as a dance of care*sharing* with multiple partners where each person is giving and receiving? What if you were to shift your thinking from, "The person I'm caring for needs me" to "We need each other"?

A NEW VISION FOR SHARING CARE

Caresharing is quite different from the traditional view of caregiving. A caresharing relationship has some very distinct qualities. For example, in a traditional view of caregiving, a person who has a problem, such as ill health or dementia, is cared for by a caregiver who is stronger physically. By contrast, in caresharing the care partners build on each other's strengths rather than focusing solely on the challenges, concerns, or problems. Although there is an emphasis on physical, mental, and emotional health in traditional caregiving, caresharers are very aware that keeping their spirit alive is integral to their well-being. Those who share care grow spiritually and emotionally to stand together in their efforts to deal with what life has handed them.

Unfortunately, in traditional caregiving, there is so much emphasis on the person's illness or disability that, at times, the care receiver forgets who they have been and that their story is uniquely their own. This happens not out of neglect, but because in the press of everything else, the person's story is way down on the list of priorities. In caresharing, the narratives and stories are a meaningful part of shaping care and enlivening the day-to-day experience of each care partner.

Most of all, in caresharing people are flexible in the moment with one another and work out plans for the future with each other's input. There are several very important aspects of the dance of caresharing that contribute to its unique way of approaching care.

SHARING ON AN EQUAL FOOTING

In a caresharing relationship, there is a sense of reciprocity, of give-and-take. Even though, on the surface, it might seem that the carer is "better" than the one being cared for, emotionally and spiritually you are on an equal footing. You each have your strengths and resources. One of you may possess more skills and abilities, and one might have to do more for the other physically or mentally, but both of you can share love and caring. Each of you may have particular concerns, but neither is more or less valuable.

In her wonderful book *My Grandfather's Blessings,* Rachel Naomi Remen discusses what it means to be a blessing and explores how we "serve" each other. The perspective of "serving" rather than "helping" is an important distinction in caresharing. In the role of servant, you as a carer are not greater than, better than, or more important than the person you are caring for. You and your care partner are both children of God who are journeying on a long path together. This rebalanced approach to caring enables each of you to have a sense of connection to the best of your abilities and not be limited by a label that makes one "less than" the other.

LEARNING FROM EACH OTHER

In caresharing, a carer can learn a great deal from the one being cared for, such as life skills, survival techniques, resiliency, and valuable internal resources. As a carer, you might learn much from your care partner about coping methods or about their worldview. The person receiving your care might, in fact, become a mentor. I am reminded of the stories of Jesus in the Christian tradition. He often assisted those who were seen as "less than" by society, just as those with dementia, developmental disabilities, or chronic illness are often labeled as "not whole" by our society. He aided people in very concrete ways, just as you might be doing in the mundane tasks of daily care. And he always added to their spiritual life. Among the questions you might ask yourself are these: "How is my caring, and my relationship with the person for whom I am caring, adding to my spiritual life? What spiritual lessons am I learning from the person who is receiving my care?"

HONORING WHAT IS WHOLE

Caresharing means never having to do it all! It means encouraging your care partner to do what they can still do, and honoring what is still whole in them. Too often I have seen well-meaning carers try to take over all activities of daily living once there has been a diagnosis of some chronic illness. Or carers with good intentions take over the decision making. But just because a person with dementia, for example, may not be able to legally sign checks because of poor judgment, that doesn't mean that they cannot choose the color of the clothing they wear. Or just because a person is feeling in poor health, it does not mean that they can no longer express their feelings and opinions in some way. Many people being cared for, who can speak for themselves, have told me that others are "running their lives."

The next time you feel compelled to take over, remember that people receiving care did not get where they are by being "wimps." They are survivors. Encourage your care partner to direct their care and make choices to the extent that they are able to. If their verbal expressions are hindered, help them work out an alternate means of communication. The important thing, as a caregiver, is not to take over what your care partner can still do. Honor what is still intact in your care partner by reaching out to what is whole in them.

PRESERVING THE RESPECT AND DIGNITY OF ALL INVOLVED

This is perhaps the most intricate and important step of caresharing. Working out reasonable alternatives in caring is a big part of this. Even though there may be constraints imposed by the illness or disability from which your care receiver suffers, it does not need to impose limits on respect.

Make a special effort to involve your care partner in conversations about their care. Too often care receivers tell me that they feel other people are dictating what their life is going to be. Speaking to the person you care about with gentleness and kindness, and including them in decision making, are signs of respect. This may have to be limited, given their understanding, but the message you are sending is that they are part of the whole picture.

You can build on the dignity and respect for your care partner by adjusting and adapting situations so they can succeed. Issues revolving around eating are good examples. If, for instance, your care partner has difficulty holding a spoon steady to manage soup, you might choose soup in a cup or get them a spoon with adaptations so they can manage more effectively on their own. In social situations you can make food or pick food from a menu that they can eat without too much fuss.

This idea of respect goes both ways: You also need to make sure that you treat yourself with respect by taking care of yourself. As you treat yourself, you treat the person you care about.

SEEING THE SENSE OF THE SACRED IN EACH OTHER

Caresharing is a practice of treating all as persons of value. It means seeing the image of God or the sense of the sacred in each other, and responding in a way that honors this holiness, no matter what a person's physical or cognitive limitations or strengths may be. I am reminded of an intergenerational conference that I participated in years ago, where we practiced a nontraditional form of what liturgical churches call the "sharing of the peace." One person turned to the other and said, "I see the image of God in you," and the other responded, "I see the image of God in you." This is something similar to the Hindu *Namaste* greeting, "The Spirit in me meets the Spirit in you," which acknowledges the divine spark in each of us. Picture how this might affect the way you think about care, not as a task to be done but as an offering of respect and reverence.

In the dance of caresharing, both you as a carer and your care partner will struggle with uncertainties and difficulties. In no way do I mean to minimize these. Loneliness may swamp you at times, and frayed nerves may erupt because of the changes in your relationship. Each of you may feel periodically frustrated or discouraged because of the nature of the illness or the complexity of the problem. But if you can see the Spirit within yourself and in each other, you will be better able to face the future together, not as separate entities but as partners. If you can stay grounded in your deep belief in the other person, and figuratively stand side by side, you will be stronger than any one person alone. And both of you may be more open to accepting others who have offered to join you in your journey. The caresharing dance is an exchange of learning and an honoring of interdependence among a growing, multigenerational network of family, friends, and faith communities.

THE BASIC STEPS
OF THE CARESHARING DANCE

There are three basic steps in the caresharing dance that you may need to learn, or rehearse a bit, if you're out of practice. The first, offering help to your care partner, may seem like an old, familiar step. But there are a few nuances in this move that deserve some new consideration. The other two steps—asking for and receiving help—may never be easy for you or your care partner, but each time you ask and receive, the task will become less daunting. It may take practice to be comfortable with these steps of the dance, but as you move through them over and over again, your experience of caresharing will expand in depth and wholeness.

OFFERING HELP
Perhaps you have been taught all your life to "help others." So it may seem obvious to you: "Someone needs my care, I want to help, end of discussion." It's natural to want to lend a hand to someone who is having difficulty. However, this can soon become a problem if you do *more* than your care receiver needs. Sadly, I've seen this kind of "overcaring" when caregivers come to believe that they need to do *everything* for their care partner at the first signs of "weakness" in physical or mental abilities. I've seen caregivers totally take over making meals for their care partner when there are things their partner might still be able to do to help prepare them. Or dressing a person when they might be able to do some things

on their own, such as buttoning their shirt. A social work colleague calls this "Help strikes again." This puts the cared-for person in a "less than" position and becomes a barrier to building on their strengths. While they might have to struggle a bit to do these things, it is well worth the effort for them.

In reciprocal caresharing, helping someone means building on their capabilities and preserving their dignity and self-respect. Even when a person's abilities or mobility are limited, you can still offer "bounded choices." For example, you may not be able to offer the choice to bathe or not bathe, but you may be able to offer the alternative of bathing in the morning or in the evening. This would give your care partner a chance to decide what might work best for them and give them the respect they deserve. Or perhaps your loved one needs help navigating around their home. They might be very reluctant to use a walker, yet the doctor and the physical therapist have strongly suggested its use. The "bounded choice" might not be whether or not to use a walker at home, but to consider different styles of walker and help them pick the one that might work best for them.

Learning how your care partner is thinking and feeling can go a long way toward ensuring that you won't smother them with your good intentions. Your role as a care partner is to encourage and enable them to do and be all they can, to respect both their limits and their strengths, not to take over their life. Together, you and your care partner can consider an array of possibilities that they could realistically do, and they can pick from among those choices. Together, you can plan what will work for both of you to make the quality of life better.

ASKING FOR HELP

Underlying the entire text of this book is this basic message: *It is okay to ask for help*. In fact, I believe that asking for help is a sign of emotional and spiritual strength. I am reminded of the theme of a conference I attended for older adults and carers, "Independence is knowing when to ask for help." This might seem contrary to what you believe, especially if you equate independence with self-sufficiency or if you take a certain pride in being able to do what you need to by yourself.

If you have been a "giver" and a "doer" most of your life, perhaps the most basic step of the caresharing dance that you will need to practice is getting your heart and your head around the idea that the person receiving your care isn't the only "receiver" in this dance. You can be a receiver of assistance from others as well. Learning this step requires knowing three things: when to ask for help, how to ask for help, and how to let someone say "no."

When to ask for help. Maybe you are the kind of person who puts off asking for help until things get critical. This all changes when you are in a caresharing relationship. The time to ask for help is *now*. My ninety-seven-year-old friend Bill put it simply: "I have learned to ask for an arm when I need it. That way I can get around better."

Perhaps your tendency is to feel as if you've somehow failed if you have to ask for help. When someone asks you how you are doing, you may automatically respond, "I'm okay," when, really, you are exhausted, hurting spiritually and emotionally.

Or maybe you just don't want to be a "burden" to others. Have you ever thought that asking for help might make you a role model for someone else? Your honesty might give someone who is new to the caregiver role courage to ask for themselves.

By asking for help along the way, you will not only be allowing others the opportunity to give, but also, by learning where and what kind of help is available, you will be building up your "reserve" for future challenges.

I think of the unlikely people who have appeared in my life when I have needed them, and from whom I received help to get "back on course." I remember those faithful friends who have loved me through thick and thin, when I've been in need and when I've stumbled. As an older woman who became a mentor to me taught me when she was a hundred years old, "Friends are those who love us with our warts." I have come to see friends as God's nurture in my life, and I am forever thankful for their love and care. This is all a part of the interdependence of depending on each other.

How to ask for help. How many times have well-meaning folks—including close friends and relatives, and people in your community of faith—said to you, "Just let me know what I can do," or "Call me if you need me." Maybe you freeze in the moment and can't come up with anything. But you could turn this into a valuable opportunity for yourself, and for them, if you do some thinking ahead. Consider how and in what circumstances you could realistically use some help. Ask yourself, "What activities or tasks could someone else assist with?" and make a list.

Then, when a potential helper inquires, you can respond with a specific suggestion, such as, "It would really be helpful if you could shop for me on Friday mornings," or "I could really use someone to stay with my dad on Thursday nights so I could go to the support group at the library." Be as clear as you can about what you are asking another to do. Dropping hints rarely is as effective as a clear request: "I need help getting John to his doctor's appointment next week."

Being prepared with a suggestion or two can bring you needed relief, and it also lets people who want to be useful (but are not sure how to help) know exactly what they can do to help. Some people are uncomfortable with a commitment that seems to have no end, so your concrete and limited task would make it easier for them to do what they really want to do—help!

Honesty is a crucial component of asking. If someone inquires about how you are doing, this might be a good time to say, "I'd like to tell you, if you have a few minutes." When you can tell the "real story" of your life to those who ask, you open the door to a straightforward conversation, as well as the potential to ask for the help you need. While there will be some who won't want this level of information, or who will not understand your feelings and requests, there will be others who genuinely care about you and your loved one, and who will respond gladly. When you are honest with them about what is really happening in your life, they will not have to second-guess how you are feeling or what you need, and they will be able to more realistically assist you.

How to let someone say "no." When you ask someone for assistance, it is important to give them the chance to say no. For many reasons, they may not be able to assist you just then, but they may be able to help with another task later on. If you give them a way to opt out, it will also feel less like you are imposing. Although each situation is unique, there are some things you can do to facilitate this. You can acknowledge to the other person that you may be asking for more than they can do. You can ask them if they can help you develop a team of people to assist you with a specific need, such as rides to treatment. And you can thank the person for considering your request.

Also, be aware that some people may have financial concerns about giving help that they are not comfortable raising with you, but these concerns may cause them to be reticent about offering assistance. Although their hearts are willing, their finances may not allow them to be as generous as they would like. There are some ways to make this better. For example, you could offer to fill up their gas tank or give them a few dollars for what they bring. This may get a little tricky because some people may be offended that you offered, but at least they will know you understand that helping has its financial costs.

There is one other important aspect to making room for "no"—*your* "no." Sometimes very well-meaning friends and relatives offer something that is not going to be really useful, and you'll need to be gently honest in declining their offer *at this time*. Or you may experience a flood of help all at the same time, and you may reach a point of one-too-many casseroles or one-too-many visitors. This, too, requires being gently direct. It's important to thank them for their caring and let them know how much you appreciate what they are doing, while at the same time explaining that you need some quiet space or some time alone with your care partner.

RECEIVING HELP

One of the corollaries of learning how to ask for help is learning how to be a gracious and grateful receiver. The theme "It is more blessed to give than to receive," or some variation, is foundational to many religious traditions, and you may well have been taught this principle from an early age. But when you or your care partner are no longer the "giver," there are no clear guidelines for how to negotiate the blessings of *receiving*.

Issues of feeling vulnerable and dependent abound for care partners. Certainly the person you are caring for has to deal with these issues. But what about you as a caregiver? What is your comfort level with receiving—receiving gratitude, blessings, and help? Caresharing invites you to reexamine how you feel about being on the receiving, rather than the giving, end.

Giving yourself permission to receive is a fundamental step in this caresharing dance, and it requires a new openness to receiving. You might need to widen your circles to include people with whom you have had little contact before. You might need to "let go" of those who can't help you. You might need some practice in learning to receive aid graciously.

If you think you're being "a burden," or being "selfish," you might try thinking of receiving this way: When you allow others to give to you, you are helping them be "more blessed." Asking allows others the blessing of serving you. In your worries about being a burden, you may have lost sight of this, especially if you have always been the giver.

This is your opportunity to learn to receive. There is a beauty in reciprocity, in the give-and-take of the caresharing dance. It can be freeing and empowering to recognize that you cannot do it all yourself and that you are not alone. And it is also a lesson in reality: Although you are the caregiver today, you may be the care receiver tomorrow.

Even after considering your present realities and the possible benefits of asking for help, it can still be difficult to ask. My recommendation is both simple and difficult at the same time: *Take one step at a time.* Take a deep breath. All your concerns do not have to be solved at once. You might build up your courage by asking for something small to begin with. You may need to practice allowing another to do what you cannot. With practice, it can get easier to ask for and receive the blessing of assistance from those who care about you and your care partner.

EXPANDING THE CARESHARING NETWORK

Perhaps you are fortunate enough to have a ready network—within your own family and/or your community of faith—who will travel this caresharing journey with you. But there may be times when no one is nearby or available, or when people you might usually turn to have struggles of their own that prevent them from helping you.

Recognize that there are others who can offer assistance. Options do exist outside of your known network. Knowing *who* to ask is as important as knowing *what* to ask for. Sometimes people you never could have imagined can become part of your caresharing community.

FAITH COMMUNITIES

I am always saddened when people tell me that their community of faith, or their pastor, priest, rabbi, or spiritual advisor, is the last place they would look for help on their caregiving journey. At the same time, clergy tell me that they cannot "read the minds" of their church members, or that congregants sometimes hide the realities of their caregiving situation from them.

I saw this illustrated when I was leading a congregation's adult education class. A woman in that seminar poignantly told the story of moving her mother to more supportive care just the day before. Class participants sat in stunned silence, as this was the first they knew of her troubles. Together we talked about the pain and sadness she was feeling, with others lending their experiences in an encouraging way. As I was leaving the church, I was stopped in the restroom by an anxious woman who blurted out, "I am a deacon in this church, and I had no idea Joan was having trouble." She was horrified that this member of her parish could have so much pain without anyone being aware of it. When Joan was able to share her story, she received much support. It was indeed sad that she took so long to do so.

A faith community can be especially sustaining to you as a care partner. Some congregations can provide people to fill in with tangible tasks where needed. Clergy can offer the rites, rituals, and spiritual counsel. Many religious groups have parish nurses or Stephen Ministry programs* that offer educational programs or direct counseling and spiritual support. Stephen

---

*Programs for training and organizing laypeople to provide one-on-one care to people in need. Stephen Ministry is rooted in the Christian faith tradition.

Ministry visitors receive careful training and are especially sensitive to preserving confidentiality and setting reasonable boundaries, and they can be important allies who can help you gain not only a better understanding of the physical aspects of an illness or disability, but also the emotional and spiritual aspects.

A community of faith might have a prayer network that will regularly pray for you and your concerns. Some who are praying might be people struggling with their own physical or mental challenges, and you might want to participate by praying for them as well. A certain understanding exists among those who practice intentionally praying for one another. Knowing that you are being prayed for can help you feel powerfully upheld, and praying for others can add meaning and purpose to your life.

Some communities of faith have telephone trees or social ministry committees set up to handle special requests. Inez, a middle-age woman struggling at home with multiple sclerosis, did the phoning for volunteer chore services for people in her church, even as she herself received services. As the phone "point" person, she felt that she was a contributing part of her congregation, connecting those who had specific needs with those who had particular resources. She and her congregation truly understood the dance of interdependency.

SUPPORT GROUPS

Over the years, a number of support groups have evolved for caregivers and people with chronic illnesses that might be valuable resources for both you and your care partner. Although each individual group has its own personality, support groups generally offer a place where people with similar situations can gather together on a regular basis to discuss issues, offer understanding, and give each other encouragement. In general, the purpose of a support group is to help people derive strength from each other in facing the daily realities of coping, not to solve a concern. Confidentiality is a governing principle, so you will not need to worry about your story being inappropriately shared outside the group.

The group may be led by a professional (such as a social worker, clergyperson, nurse, or doctor), or by a layperson, or some combination of both, and can exist under the sponsorship of many different entities. Alcoholics Anonymous is perhaps one of the best known of such groups. In the 12-step program, people who are struggling with the effects of alcohol abuse band together to provide mutual help so each person can work toward their recovery. This principle of mutuality is fundamental to most support groups.

I've seen some amazing relationships develop in support groups among people who have faced or are experiencing similar situations. I've seen widows reach out to other women who are grieving the death of their husbands. They may not have known the deceased or the bereaved, but they offer much-needed tangible, emotional, and spiritual comfort. They have walked this path, and they understand. And for the new widow, there is something very encouraging about not having to recount extensive details. The empathy and support is there because of shared experience.

People have told me that, as a result of their group experience, they are better able to view their care partner as they are *today*, not just as who they were at another time. (This is especially important in families, as roles may change or have to be adapted. I'll delve into this more deeply in chapter 3, "Families Sharing the Care.") Support groups might offer useful suggestions for working out difficulties in relationships, such as how to be protective of a loved one in a nurturing, not smothering, way; looking realistically at what can and cannot be expected of the other person, given their physical or cognitive limits; and dealing with overwhelming losses.

Some carers discover a new network of care among those they have gotten to know in such groups. Some find people who "understand without judgment" when those within their own circle of friends have not grasped their situation. Some value that they don't have to constantly retell the story of their circumstances. Some find that when they do share their personal concerns with others who have "been there," they not only help themselves but other group participants as well. Verbalizing what's happening for them helps them feel less alone and empowers them because they are able to help someone else. There is often a real sense of give-and-take in a support group, and out of that comes a sense of hope.

A retired minister, who was describing his early stage Alzheimer's support group, put it this way: "I don't have to pretend." Displaying a wonderful sense of humor, which was one of his greatest coping skills, he jokingly noted, "I still play tennis and golf; they just don't ask me to keep score." This man found a sense of comfort with others who shared his illness, and they provided an anchor to keep him going.

I do want to add a word of caution, however. Despite my strong belief that support groups are very helpful, they are not for everyone. You may not feel comfortable sharing with others in a group. But my advice is to at least check it out. The information, fellowship, and understanding that you are not alone are some of the valuable gifts you might receive from a support group.

There are many ways to find a support group. If you are connected to a congregation, your spiritual advisor, parish nurse, church secretary, or Stephen Minister may be able to assist you. Perhaps your community of faith has its own support groups or has opened the doors to larger community support groups.

Another way to look for a support group is to contact the Senior Information and Assistance Services agency in your area. (The names of these agencies vary from region to region; see the "Other Options" section below for further information on how to find resources in your area.) Also, because many groups have been formed around particular diseases, such as Alzheimer's disease or cancer, it might be helpful to look in the phone book or search the Internet for these specific groups as well.

Many different groups exist for the person facing a specific condition, for their carers, or both together, and it is important to find a group that will work for you and for your loved one. And, please, do not be afraid to look for another group if the one you first attend is not a good fit.

IN-HOME CARE

If you're considering bringing "outsiders" into your home to help with the tasks of daily living, you might be struggling with your need for privacy, and you may not be sure that it is worth the bother of bringing helpers in. The thought of "strangers" in your home can be upsetting. You may also be feeling guilty that you can't do it all. One of the things that I tell people in these circumstances—and I hope you will consider this carefully—is that respite and support from "outsiders" may keep you and your loved one where you want to be longer and with a better quality of life. If you need to, read this statement again. I'll also say more about this when we talk later about self-care.

OUT-OF-HOME CARE

Out-of-home care in nursing homes, assisted-living facilities, adult family homes, or hospice may be a lifesaver, both for you and the person you are caring for. Yet it may also be your greatest fear. The truth is, we fear what we do not know, or our fear is based on preconceived notions. My suggestion is that you look into what is available *before* you reach the point of needing these services. When you are in a crisis brought on by an acute illness or other problem, this is *not* the moment to begin thinking about these options. Check out these resources at a time when they will not be so threatening to you. A relatively easy way to do this is to visit a member of your church or a neighbor who happens to reside in one of these alternatives.

If you and your loved one are facing the time when you can no longer live together, it is important to remind yourselves that there will still be many ways to stay connected, to share love and care. I've seen some care partners actually have a closer relationship when the care receiver gets help from someone else. Having another person to do the hands-on care for your loved one will allow you to attend more to their emotional and spiritual needs.

PEOPLE OF OTHER GENERATIONS

Another source of help that you might have overlooked is people of younger generations. If the network you count on is all of the same age, or is working through the same challenges that you are, they may not be available to you on a practical level (though their understanding and empathy can be significant). They may be so overwhelmed by their own problems that they cannot really be helpful to you at this time. A wise person leading a retreat once reminded me, "We all need at least one friend who is fifteen years younger than we are, or we will all be dying or chronically ill at the same time." These are important words to remember. Cultivating friends from many generations throughout your life can be of real benefit, but if you find yourself without this kind of ready support, you may find that grandchildren or younger people from your community of faith may be able to assist you and your care partner.

OTHER OPTIONS

There are many professional and volunteer agencies that serve families and care partners. Understanding what is available and how such programs work is important both for your self-care and for the best possible care for your loved one.

There are so many print and Web sources that it is impossible to list them all here. However, I will name a few that offer "one-stop shopping" or are primary referral agencies. They can open doors to help you let go of the nitty-gritty details of care, and free you to be a more comfortable person in caring. This may, in turn, give you time to reflect on your inner life and pay attention to self-care so you can better serve your loved one.

The most prevalent resources across the United States are Senior Information and Assistance Services, Area Agencies on Aging, or some name similar to that. These agencies receive basic funding through the national Older Americans Act and offer a wide range of services. At times, individual communities, regions, or counties organize them. To find these in your area, or to become aware of services in other regions, you can contact Eldercare Locator, a service of the federal government. At the time of this publication, information was available at 1-800-677-1116 or at www.eldercare.gov. To access the pertinent information, you will need to know the zip code of the person cared for so the agency can direct you to resources available in that vicinity.

Another program that works closely with the federal government is BenefitsCheckUp (www.BenefitsCheckUp.org). This service, provided by the National Council on Aging, can help you learn which benefits you may be eligible for at the federal, state, and local levels. By giving specifics about your situation, you can access directories to determine the availability of services to meet your needs. This has proved to be a very valuable asset to people across the country, carer and cared-for alike, and might be able to help alleviate some of your caregiving stresses so you can feel more ready for the future.

If your care partner has a disability not associated with aging, you can often find services through your local Department of Health Services, Department of Human Services, or Department of Social Services. There are also many national organizations devoted to a particular illness, such as multiple sclerosis or Parkinson's disease, that are good places to begin looking for resources. One website that is chock-full of resources is www.disabilityresources.org (a nonprofit organization established to help make information accessible). If you click on the

"States" tab, you'll get a pretty good picture of what is available in your location.

I'll close this section by telling you a story of one parish that took the idea of interdependence and the dance of caring seriously. It involves a woman who had been a "professional helper" in her job and had become a full-time carer for her husband with Alzheimer's disease. Her parish decided to give her the gift of Thursday nights off, with "no strings attached." While a team of several volunteers visited with her husband and made sure that he was safe, she got much-needed time to rejuvenate her body and spirit, and ultimately was better able to be wholly present for her spouse. When the congregational leaders first approached her to offer this respite care, she had to learn how to receive the help graciously. This solution became a win-win situation for all concerned.

As you consider what your options are for expanding your network of resources, remember that these communities, groups, and programs exist to sustain you and the one you are caring for, to help both of you thrive by maintaining the highest quality of life with the fewest restrictions or changes to your life that can be managed.

THE BODY/MIND/SPIRIT CONNECTION

In a caresharing partnership, one of the fundamental principles is to honor and build on what is whole in every person. If we are to honor wholeness, we need to see the "whole" person—their body, mind, and spirit. There has been considerable research about how these three aspects of our lives are integrated, and medicine is now at the point that we need to consider health not just as a physical function but also as an interdependency among all three. In the caresharing process, all three aspects of each care partner's lives are affected, and it is important to consider how we are tending to each and how the partnership among them is working.

SELF-CARE

I'll say it straight up: Self-care is a necessity, not an option. To care for another, you need to care for yourself. It is as simple and difficult as that. Yet if you have always seen yourself as a "giver," it may seem "selfish" to focus on your personal care.

The truth is, time and again I have seen situations where carers did not care for themselves and there is a break of some sort, and both care partners end up in crisis. I know that you don't want to collapse while caring for someone you love, so it is essential that you keep your own spirit alive. Exercising, eating right, doing spiritual rituals and practices, and finding something to be grateful for on a daily basis can all be part of this.

Consider what you have done to keep your spirit alive throughout your life. What are you doing now? What works for you? What have you *not* been doing because you do not have the time? Finding the time to do whatever works, or to adapt a way that has helped you keep whole in the past, is essential to self-care.

As a caregiver, you need to be especially aware of warning signals that may be red flags that you are not doing so well physically, emotionally, and, ultimately, spiritually. For example, exhaustion, not sleeping, gaining or losing too much weight, not eating or having no appetite, or using alcohol or medications (legal or illegal) to get you through the day are all signs that you need relief from caregiving. You may find yourself becoming so angry that you fear you could do harm to your care receiver. Or you may be isolating yourself and your loved from others, or loudly professing, "I can do it," when you are actually struggling in your tasks. Neglecting spiritual practices that have sustained you in prior difficult times can also be a warning that you may be entering into emotional and spiritual distress.

If a friend, family member, or church acquaintance tells you that they are worried about you and your loved one, *listen!* Although we often underestimate the value of friends, I think the old Beatles lyrics had it right: "I get by with a little help from my friends." Friends can point out what you are doing to yourself even when you yourself cannot see what is happening.

When you are actively caresharing, you especially need others to reflect how you are doing and to extend a helping hand. Although this is true all of your life, it is especially important when your world has begun to shrink down to you and the person you are caring for. Because you are so close to the circumstances, you cannot be objective. But if you listen to your heart when someone close to you calls you to account, you can begin to get back on track.

EMOTIONAL CARE

There are many kinds and levels of hurts that need attention in a caresharing setting. Amid all the physical needs that require care, it is crucial to tend to the emotional needs as well. There may be small emotional hurts, just "scratches," while others are more like "gaping wounds," that take on even greater primacy in the confines of care or the limits on life.

Sadness, for instance, is almost always omnipresent, whether it is visible or simmering just below the surface of daily tasks and routines. When you are doing very basic tasks for someone, you may feel grief that the person you are caring for is not "who they used to be." This grief is heightened if that person cannot remember who you are, or strikes out verbally or physically because of lack of recognition. (Feelings of sadness can be very intense in this journey of caresharing, and I will be discussing this in more detail in chapter 5, "Sharing Grief.")

Fear also often accompanies the caregiver role. You might be asking yourself whether you can do this job of caring, whether you can do it well enough, or what will happen if you're not able to do it. You may be asking, "Will my health hold up long enough for me to be a caregiver?" These kinds of fears can be immobilizing.

Anger can be another companion in the caring process. You may find yourself angry at the situation in which find yourself, at the dwindling resources being drained off for medical needs, at others in the family who appear not to care, at the seeming end-lessness of the situation, or at the loss of plans and dreams. You may be frustrated that those who are at a distance seem to be judging you for not doing enough or making poor choices. Anger is a normal feeling. I'll say it again: *Anger is a normal feeling.* But if you've been taught to push your anger down, to not say something if you can't say something "nice," you may end up with pressure-cooker anger. Bottled up anger can come out in very destructive ways, while giving voice to your anger appropriately can prevent you from saying or doing something harmful to yourself or to the person for whom you are caring.

Guilt is another tricky emotion that is often present in care-giving. You may feel that you are not doing enough. Or you may feel guilty when you get angry with your care partner. Or you might feel guilty about needing time away from the situation once in a while so you can find a better balance.

To complicate these feelings, you might feel ambivalent. You may greatly respect and love the person you are caring for and, at the same time, feel incredible frustration at the circumstances causing them to require care. Or you may feel grateful for the help you are getting from health and social services professionals, yet at the same time resent that they are in your house or in your life. You may feel grateful for all the medical support you are getting but frustrated that you seem to be getting mixed messages about the prognosis or about treatment.

The sense of hopelessness and helplessness, and the loss of power and control, can be overwhelming, and you may feel a real sense of impotence about not being able to make things any better for your care partner.

The person you are caring for has many strong feelings, which will affect the caresharing relationship as well. Sadness is also a companion for them. They probably have a strong sense of not wanting to be a burden to others, and they may feel almost despondent about being dependent and not able to take care of their own needs. The loss of their plans and dreams is also difficult, as they see their chronic physical or mental illness dissolving those dreams.

Your care partner may also feel understandable anger. If they're feeling frustrated about what they cannot do, they may lash out at your "incompetence" at caregiving. Because they are experiencing many losses in their life, they may express a great deal of negativity toward you. As a caregiver, try your best not take this personally; realize that their anger is an understandable feeling and that you simply happen to be "in the line of fire."

Fear is another strong emotion that care receivers face, especially fear of becoming too much for a loved one to deal with and then needing assistance from someone outside the trusted family. Your care partner may worry about needing a long-term care facility as their health declines.

Impotence and loss of control, and the sense of not being able to change anything, are also common feelings. Your care partner may feel that they have no say in how the caregiving will be done or about other decisions being made about their life. They may have a great sense of vulnerability because their whole life is on view to another, even down to the daily personal tasks with which they need help. When people need assistance with very private facets of life, they can feel less worthwhile.

Feelings of worthlessness and "I don't matter to anyone" are all too common. Because they are constantly on the receiving end of care and not able to do things for anyone else, they may feel both helpless and hopeless. This is especially difficult for someone who has always been a giver and a "doer."

All these feelings are common and normal. It is very important for you and your care partner to name them, share them, and discuss them. This will not take the feelings away, but it will make it easier for both of you to cope. If you are in a situation where verbal communication is not possible, it will take a special effort to share the feelings in your relationship. This can be especially true with those who have dementia, where verbal sharing may be somewhat limited or not make sense, yet your care partner still has many feelings and frustrations. These feelings may have to be accessed in different ways than you are used to. (I'll explore this in depth when we get to chapter 4, "Sharing 'Soul to Soul.'")

Another roadblock to sharing feelings that I see in caresharing partnerships is a discomfort about revealing personal emotions. If you grew up in a family or a religious tradition that emphasized keeping feelings private, or "between you and God," you or your care partner may feel uncomfortable telling people how you feel. Yet acknowledging and dealing with your feelings is essential for this caresharing journey. If you "stuff your feelings inside," you may become depressed and end up being more of a hindrance than a helping influence. Or, worse, you may find yourself thinking about acting on your feelings or in some way hurting the very person you are caring for. Sharing your feelings with a counselor or support group can make a helpful difference in how you deal with your feelings.

When you do share how you feel, you will need to be gently honest. The goal is not to hurt or blame anyone, but to have a level playing field where these feelings can be examined and worked through. Both you and your care partner may already sense that something is wrong, and gently verbalizing feelings can be healing. Many people have shared with me a sense of accomplishment when they have been able to be open about their feelings; they've learned something new, even experienced something spiritual. Perhaps more than any other single experience in the dynamics of caring, this deep exchange of feelings has the potential to shift the relationship from caregiver/care receiver to mutual partners in the caresharing dance.

I also want to add a word here about positive feelings. The emotions of caresharing are not all negative! In spite of all the complexities, there can still be laughter, love, and joy in your caresharing. Humor is a way that many get through the hard times of caring, and when you and your care partner can laugh together, you will feel better. Love is also a deep, connecting emotion, and it can still be strong even when severely tested by illness or disability. And then there is joy. Just when you might think that joy doesn't stand a chance, along it comes in the small things in life. The essence of caresharing—sharing a connection with someone you care about—leaves the door wide open for enjoying each other's company. Even when the day gets long or the prognosis looks dim, there is still the chance for a grin at a funny joke or a smile about a shared memory. In the middle of caring, it is important to make room for the full range of human emotions.

SPIRITUAL CARE

Although there are many dimensions of caring, the physical aspects might be the most obvious or of immediate concern, with the emotional aspects often being more invisible. But perhaps the most underidentified dimension, and the one that affects the quality of life and care the most, is the spiritual component.

When I use the word *spiritual,* I'm talking about what gives your life meaning and purpose, what guides you in your difficult choices. This may be part of a formal religion that you practice, but it is also the very deep level where you experience connection with a Power beyond yourself. This is where I believe the interdependency of caresharing becomes complete, when we accept that we are interdependent not only on each other but also on our God.

Too often in the press of caring for another, the spiritual component seems to be optional, or at best, something like a distant relative who comes to visit for a while. I believe, however, that the spiritual aspect is integral to caresharing and cannot be neglected. As a carer, when all is not well with your spirit, other more visible aspects of the caregiving relationship suffer, and you may suffer what is often referred to as "burnout." Not only can refilling your inner spirit assist you in making sense of your situation, but it can also help your care partner feel spiritually alive.

Each individual has their own unique way to keep the spirit alive. Many care partners find comfort in the awareness that God or a Higher Power walks beside them. Others feel supported by the intercessory prayers of their family or faith group members. Still others find that reflecting on nature helps them maintain a balance of their emotions and spirit. Some feel spiritually connected when they can share the "quality of a moment."

Making spiritual nurture a part of care—for both you and your care partner—is an important element in the dance of caresharing. You might share verses, hymns, prayers, or rituals with your care partner or, depending on their needs, you may need a more intentional approach. Putting a Bible at the bedside of someone for whom this has always provided spiritual nurture may not be enough if they are limited in their ability to reach it. You may need to place it in their hands. If they are no longer able to read, you might ask about their favorite passages and read these selections aloud so they can still experience this facet of their spiritual life. Even if the person you are caring for does not have full cognition or speech, they can still feel that God or a Higher Power cherishes them. And both of you may find that you share a deep sense of connection when you share in this spiritual dimension.

At times, the idea of God or a Higher Power may seem like a distant reality. You or your care partner may find yourselves asking, "Where is God in all this?" My suggestion is to take a long, careful look around you. The love and concern of the people whom you have invited into your caresharing partnership might well be a reflection of a God who walks with you, even in times of great distress. The people who listen to your story without judgment and provide tangible help and support may be part of your spiritual nurture. Those who can be quiet with you may be part of the Spirit's presence.

It is especially important for you, as a person giving care, to take in spiritual nurture wherever you find it. While you are attending to the important aspects of physical and emotional needs in giving care, your spiritual care can be integral to staying whole and keeping a sense of balance. Your inner self needs tending as much as your physical self needs food, rest, and exercise.

Take a moment to reflect on what the word *spiritual* means for you. I offer the following questions to help you focus your responses and get in touch with what matters for you. You might want to write your thoughts in a journal, in a notebook, or on your computer.

- What is your personal definition of *spiritual*?
- How does the person you are caring for define it?
- Is your sense of the spiritual helping or hindering you right now?
- How might you build on the spiritual to cope and stay strong in caring?
- What is important to you in your spiritual life at this time?
- Is there someone to whom you could turn to walk with you in keeping your spirit strong?

As a carer, taking stock of how you are doing physically, emotionally, and spiritually is crucial to keeping your spirit alive. And keeping your spirit vibrant will, in turn, enrich your care partnership. And taking care of the partnership will help keep the spirit alive for both you and your care partner. This marvelous interdependency is, indeed, a synergistic process, and it is a core part of the dance of caresharing.

WHEN THINGS GET COMPLICATED

This dance of caresharing has some tricky steps, and it is ever evolving. At times, it may seem as if the steps are moving in a direction that you cannot follow. Or they may be going so fast that you feel dizzy trying to keep up with all that is happening. When things seem very complex and overwhelming, it is important to take a deep breath and take one step at a time as much as you can.

WHEN YOU FEEL "PRESSED INTO SERVICE"

Perhaps, like many, you have not given much thought to the idea that you could be in this position of intensive caring for another; somehow that happens to "other people." Or you may have imagined that it might happen someday with a close family member, but somehow that seemed like a long way off. But if a distant relation or person who is "like family" is now needing help, you may have been "pressed into service" because no one else was available. The situation may require assistance that only you can give, either because you're the closest one geographically or the one with the most flexible job, or simply the one whom your family seems to turn to in a crisis. Even if the person needing help is someone you care about, you may still feel frustrated and angry that, somehow, you got "stuck" with the job. This is a normal reaction, given the circumstances, but you may find it helpful to talk with someone outside the situation, such as a pastoral counselor or a social worker, to help you work through specific issues and feelings.

WHEN YOU FEEL OTHERS HAVE FAILED YOU

If you've had the experience of being turned down when you reached out to someone for help, you know how much that hurts. Maybe someone from your family or your community of faith has told you that they're "there for you," but when it was "crunch time," and you asked for their help, they weren't there. You may have felt that they failed you, and this may well be true.

The hurt we feel when someone whom we have depended on does not respond to our requests and expectations for help is very disheartening and frustrating. I hear this often as people exclaim, "You'd think that my [sister ... son ... grandson ...] would visit our mother more often. Mom has done so much for them." I have seen many situations where people just could not get over the indelible hurt of feeling let down or disappointed by someone they thought they could count on.

What I have learned as well, often the hard way, is that at any particular time people may have myriad, sometimes hidden, reasons why they are not able to carry out a specific task, or act in a way that would be most beneficial for all concerned. They may quietly be struggling with their own problems. Or they may harbor their own fears about disability and mental changes. Becoming part of the life of a caregiver or care receiver brings these anxieties into sharp focus. Still other people may say that they may want to remember a care receiver "the way they were, and not as they are now."

Such concerns may have little to do with you as the carer or with the one you are caring for. These concerns most likely reflect people's fears about their own aging and inevitable disabilities. Even though you "know" this, you can still feel isolated and not cared about. But being aware of these possibilities can ease some of the pain and keep you from taking the seeming lack of compassion personally.

This became clear to me in an early, unforgettable experience when I was the new mother of a premature baby with some physical

31

problems. My beloved aunt, who had always "been in my corner" emotionally, did not write or call to see how I was doing, or even inquire about how the baby was progressing. I was very hurt, and I felt neglected by her seeming lack of support. I remember being in tears, feeling that she "did not care about me."

Later, I learned that she had her own issues about disability, stemming from the sad circumstances of my grandfather's death a few years earlier. As a result, she could not face her worries that my daughter might not live. When I discovered what had been at the bottom of her seeming neglect, I felt better about our relationship, and we worked through it. Though I had initially felt shut out because she was not able to be there for me when I needed her, understanding her perspective changed how I felt about her.

If someone has "let you down" and you are feeling hurt, give yourself some time to consider these options:

- *Find out the deeper meaning* underlying their lack of response. There are many reasons why someone might seem to fail you, and if you can understand the reason for their seeming lack of interest, it can mitigate some of your feelings of rejection.

- *Depersonalize* the perceived lack of response as much as possible. It may not have any connection to you personally.

- *Be flexible and forgiving,* not just frustrated or mad. While it is difficult to forgive people who seemingly "won't" assist you, forgiving them can provide an escape valve for you and enable you to move on with your life.

- *Ask someone else for help.* If you turn one rejection into an overriding fear that *everyone* will disappoint you, you may not venture to ask anymore, and you will miss out on the comfort of others who might be willing to be part of your caring network.

WHEN YOU FEEL AS IF YOU'VE FAILED

Somewhere in the caregiving partnership, there may come a time when you need to ask others to take over some or most of the care. It could be because of your own ill health, or because the needs of your care partner have become too great, or some other event forces you to face that you cannot be the primary carer any longer. While all the "reasons" for turning over caregiving to another may be rational and true, you might still feel as if you've failed. And not only may a feeling of failure keep you from being totally honest with yourself about your limits, but it may also keep you from staying in touch with others.

If you've come to the point where you realize that you can't do everything by yourself and have begun the process of looking for home care or a long-term care facility, read these next two sentences slowly and carefully: *When you need others to take over the physical caregiving, you have NOT failed. You may be doing the most loving and important thing that you can for your loved one.*

You can still be involved in caregiving at the most elemental levels—emotional and spiritual. You can still offer love and connection to your care partner. Despite the changes in the structure of the caring, you still are "family." In fact, having others relieve you of the hands-on care may allow for more quality in the relationship emotionally and spiritually because you are not "on duty" twenty-four hours a day.

You may need to remind yourself over and over again, "I am doing the best I can, even though I am not perfect." Or you may need to say to yourself—and to others—"I am doing the best I can with the information, energy, and resources I have at this particular time." If you are feeling the weight of "might haves, could haves, or should haves," forgiving yourself is key. You may need to work on forgiveness with others in the family or caring network to allow caresharing to happen in the most beneficial way for all concerned. (Forgiveness is such an important topic that I've devoted all of chapter 6 to it.)

WHEN THE UNEXPECTED HAPPENS

There's one reality we all know: We can't predict what is going to happen. But I've talked with many people who spend a lot of time and energy worrying about what *might* happen without taking any steps to prepare in advance. Being prepared for future possibilities in caregiving can add to your peace of mind today. In order to be prepared for the "what ifs," for the eventualities in caring, you need to do some contingency planning *pre-need*.

I think of Vera, who struggled with depression. She described her life as a state of "do-lessness," and her family consulted with me and asked me to visit her. After some polite conversation, this very independent lady stated that she did not need my services. However, when she died, her daughter found my business card taped next to her phone. Even though she never did call me, I was a lifeline nonetheless. Vera's story is a reminder that having such information close at hand may be a lifeline. You never know when something you put in place before it is needed will, in fact, be exactly what is needed at a future time.

Although it is not a foolproof process, planning ahead can be invaluable. Here are just a few pre-planning strategies you can put in place now that may help when the unexpected happens:

- Have emergency numbers by the phone, as well as the address of the location where help might be needed, so if a crisis arises, you can read the information to emergency responders.

- Keep the phone numbers of your friends, support network, and spiritual advisors close at hand so you can call on them when you need to.

- Draw up legal papers, such as a durable power of attorney for health care and a living will, and have these readily available.

- If your care partner has papers that emergency responders might need (their wishes about resuscitation, for example), it is a good idea to put a note about where to find such papers where it can be easily seen. I know people who keep a note on their refrigerator or have a note on a window near the entrance. And I've known people to keep their papers in the freezer!

- Discuss with your care partner what they might want for future care, if circumstances change. Include decision making about future medical treatment and choices about living situation options. It is important that you both understand and share the same perspective on caring and the future.

There are many difficult aspects to the caresharing relationship, and I do not mean to minimize them. At the same time, you and your care partner have internal abilities or gifts that may get all but forgotten in the stresses of caresharing. You may find that you have more "true grit" than you thought. Or your strong faith and beliefs may sustain you when it all begins to feel "too much." Perhaps you will find that you can tap into previously unknown resources. Or maybe your organizational skills or communication skills will bridge some especially difficult gap. Most of all, your willingness to address tough issues and to ask for assistance may produce surprising and rewarding results. To keep the spirit alive in caring, you can build on all these strengths and inner resources.

Working on steps to *inter*dependence in caresharing can be both challenging and rewarding. My hope is that you will be able to hold in your heart and mind, and put into action, these essential points about caresharing:

- Let go of the barriers you might have once put up against asking for assistance. Others have trod this caresharing path before; you are not alone. Help is available.

- Talk with the person for whom you are caring. By discussing the underlying concerns and problems you each have, you can make real sharing in care possible.

- Take some time to ask yourself: What are the things that keep me going? How can I utilize them to increase my ability? What do I need to do take care of myself? Reflecting on your abilities and limits, and celebrating your resources, are important facets of the caresharing dance.

- Tap into your spiritual strength. I have heard caregivers say many times, "I need to remember that God loves me, and God is leading me through this difficult time." Your spiritual strength is an important resource in your caresharing partnership.

- Celebrate your blessings—for your care partner, for yourself, and for those who reach out and care about both of you.

- Hold on to hope—even in the most difficult of times.

SHARING WISDOM

What the Frail Teach the Well

INNER WISDOM

Our society categorizes people throughout life. As people age, they are often classified as "strong" or "weak," "well" or "frail." Society also touts those who are "productive" and devalues those who are not contributing materially in some manner. Many of those not "working" are elders or people struggling with chronic illness, and there is a general assumption that there is something wrong with not "doing." Culturally, we are uncomfortable with the idea of just "being" because the adage "work has worth" has infiltrated our lives so thoroughly.

At the first signs of "weakness" in physical or mental abilities, of not being able to "do" or "produce," we tend to downgrade our perception of people's abilities to think and act for themselves, to contribute anything of worth. All too often I've seen cases where people begin to treat someone receiving care as mentally frail because their bodies are ailing, or as not capable of making the smallest decision on their own.

Yet any measure of "well" or "frail," "more than" or "less than," "abled" or "disabled," disappears when we get down to the bedrock of a reciprocal caresharing relationship where the fundamental belief is that every person is a person of value. Although some people do change with disability or illness, their core self—and value—remains the same. This belief is not a "new" perspective; it's really quite old. It is one of the basic tenets of most religious traditions.

From this perspective, *every* person has wisdom to share, including those who are chronically ill, disabled, or struggling with dementia. There is much insight to be uncovered in interacting with someone who might be considered "frail." There is much knowledge to be gained from care partners who, traditionally, might be thought of as "less than."

I invite you to look with "new eyes" at your own caresharing situation. Seeing your care partner on a level field is at the core of learning from each other. If you are intentional about looking, you will be open to your care partner's wisdom, even while understanding the real limits of their frailty.

A chaplain in a long-term care facility recounted visiting a man who said to him, "Thanks for not having pity on me." The chaplain responded, "Why should I pity you? You are my hero. I want to be like you, not only when I am also ninety-two and in a wheelchair, but right now." The chaplain was responding to that which was alive in this older man.

This is precisely what I mean by looking with "new eyes." If you only feel sadness about your care partner's frailty, if you only feel heavyhearted for them, you will be closing your eyes to the very real positives that they have to share with you. Even as I say this, I am by no means minimizing the problems that you and your care partner are facing. But I have also seen, time and again, that the reciprocal nature of caresharing gives care partners a chance to mentor each other, to discover new understandings, and to grow.

CLEARING THE WAY

Facing what it means to be sick, frail, or weak can be very upsetting for everyone involved. We all fear being vulnerable. We all harbor concerns about being frail or losing our productivity and independence. And when these fears are not examined, they impede our ability to truly appreciate our care partner who is struggling with physical or cognitive limits. We close our ears and hearts to the wisdom they might offer because their problems are too frightening or too difficult for us to face.

When wisdom is buried under fears and concerns, it does not have a chance to surface. In order to be open to learning, you need to "clear the way" by naming your apprehensions, confronting your concerns, and acknowledging your feelings about what infirmity and health mean to you.

CONSIDER YOUR CONCERNS

As a caregiver, feeling anxious about the possibility of your own failing health or disability is a normal response. However, before you can receive the wisdom your care partner might have to offer, you need to be aware of the frailties you worry about for yourself. You will need to take stock of your own deep fears, even those that are unspoken.

As the late Dutch priest Henri Nouwen so aptly said in his book *The Wounded Healer: Ministry in Contemporary Society,* we all bring our own hurts and sadness to any situation in which we find ourselves. When you can reflect upon your feelings, they have the potential to sensitize you to the realities of the one you are caring for.

Unchecked, your worries and anxieties can block intimate caring. They can lead to a sense of "overload" and can interfere with your effective caresharing. In addition, your fear and concerns may subtly spill over to the one you are caring for, making them feel "less than" as a person. And if you stay locked in your own world of concerns, you will miss the lessons your care partner can teach you.

Acknowledged and addressed, your concerns will help you maintain a sense of openness to the pearls of wisdom that the "frail" can offer. With an open mind, you can appreciate the gifts your care partner has to share.

A helpful way to identify and name your concerns is to imagine your own anxieties about aging or becoming ill:

- How do you define being "well" or "frail"?
- What would it mean to you to lose valued capacities, such as cognition, a strong body, vision, or hearing?
- When do you feel that you will be "old"?
- Have some people in your family or close circle of friends had, or now live with, chronic diseases such as Alzheimer's or Parkinson's? Do you dread developing such an illness yourself?
- What scares you most about sharing with those who are frail?

CONSIDER YOUR CARE RECEIVER'S CONCERNS

There is much to be discovered by perceiving the world through the eyes of your care partner. They may feel that people see them only as their "diagnosis" and not as an individual. (And, unfortunately, this may be how they are being treated.) Discouragement may cause them to focus on what they can't do, rather than on what they are still capable of doing. This is especially true for someone who has been a lifetime giver or helper and now finds it especially difficult to ask for and receive assistance.

Struggling and coping with these feelings of dependency are significant. Wendy Lustbader's book *Counting on Kindness: The Dilemmas of Dependency* provides an in-depth discussion of what being vulnerable means for someone with a chronic illness. It illustrates frustrations that develop out of being dependent on another and offers excellent suggestions for dealing with those issues. This book may be a helpful resource for you to share with your care partner, who is wrestling with what disability, chronic illness, or frailty means for them.

SHARE YOUR CONCERNS WITH EACH OTHER

Too many times I have heard care partners confess that they hesitate to talk about their worries because they are trying to protect the other from the heavy load of their apprehensions. Yet I have heard more than one care partner say, "I think my loved one is keeping something from me."

It may also be that either you or your care partner, or both of you, believe it is "wrong" to have negative thoughts, that you should be able to "get over them," so you keep your fears buried inside. Or you may have the nagging suspicion that discussing the worst possibilities might make them a reality. "If I express my worry that my cancer might return, it might actually happen!"

Unfortunately, concerns will bubble up in spite of everyone's best efforts to suppress them. And the hidden thoughts and feelings that go with them can negatively affect the way you treat each other. If you want to maintain openness in your relationship, each of your concerns about being vulnerable needs to be addressed.

There is no doubt that it takes courage to discuss these deeper issues, but overcoming the barriers and getting the conversation going will pay a big dividend in your caresharing relationship. After talking through tough issues, I've known many care partners who've responded to each other with the exclamation, "I had no idea you felt that way!"

When you and your care partner can talk honestly about your concerns, the depth of your connection and your support for each

other will greatly increase. Although your discussion will not ameliorate all the worries and solve all the problems, sharing the load
can make concerns easier to face.

When you are ready to begin this conversation, there are three
things that are especially helpful in this kind of deep sharing:

- It is essential that your talking be gentle and caring, without
  one blaming the other.

- Your conversation needs to take into account the cognitive and
  physical condition of the person receiving care, and it may need
  to be done in little chats. (I want to say a special word here
  about the matter of pain. Carers and cared for alike have taught
  me that unchecked pain gets in the way of sharing. If a person
  is in a great deal of agony because of pain, they truly cannot
  deal with very much beyond that, and their spirits are often
  shattered. Only when there is good pain control can your care
  partner be open to the teaching and learning that can happen
  in caresharing.)

- It can be difficult to reflect on fears and concerns alone. At the
  very least, you may want to write your concerns on a sheet of
  paper (that you can later destroy, if you like) or in a journal.
  This can help you name the unnamable. Talking to a trusted
  nonjudgmental friend, clergy person, or professional third
  party can also aid you in confronting your dread about the
  myriad losses related to chronic illness.

PUTTING YOURSELF
IN THE ROLE OF A LEARNER

If you want to learn from the one you are caring for, the place to
begin is simple: Put yourself in the mind-set of a learner. Keep an
open heart and mind to receive what your care partner may have
to offer. Be receptive to moments of discovery. Whether it is about

the caresharing situation in particular, or a way of understanding life, you can learn a lot if you can "reframe" the situation and look at it from a different perspective. If, for example, you typically think of a wheelchair only as a disadvantage, you might be surprised to hear your care receiver tell you how much they have learned from being at "eye level" with children.

When you become a learner, you are giving your care partner the gift of seeing themselves as a teacher. With so many losses to cope with, the fact that they can teach you can be a meaningful part of keeping their spirit alive. Care receiver and caregiver alike can mentor each other.

The lessons I have learned from those struggling with chronic illness and disability are profound. I offer some of the wisdoms that I've gleaned to help increase your awareness of what you might learn from your care partner.

LEARNING THE VALUE OF APPRECIATION

Those who face infirmity with grace in receiving assistance have taught me much about a deep appreciation of others. I have had the privilege of talking to many caresharing partners, and I have seen, in the most beneficial relationships, an important theme of thankfulness toward each other. The care receiver may express gratefulness for everything the carer does. The caregiver may be appreciative of the opportunity to meet the needs of a person who has cared for him or her in the past. Both may express their gratitude for still having time to be together. And often they experience being thankful as a meaningful part of their spiritual life. This gratefulness can also help get them through the rough times when they are frustrated or angry with each other.

> ✐ What is your care partner teaching you about thankfulness and appreciation?

LEARNING HOW TO BE GRACEFULLY DEPENDENT

Those struggling with chronic illness have taught me how to face dependency and vulnerability. In learning to be gracefully dependent, they embody an important spiritual truth found in many religious traditions, including Christianity, Judaism, and Islam, that there is a normalcy in being dependent. There is an expectation that we are to trust our Creator and surrender our supposed "control" in running the world and our own lives. Our belief systems stress that we are not totally independent, that we are the Creator's creatures and are to live our lives recognizing a Higher Power. In teaching us how to be vulnerable, the "frail" help us understand and accept the core spiritual experience of dependence.

   🖋 What is your care partner teaching you about dependence?

LEARNING THE IMPORTANCE OF TRUST

People who need assistance or care have not chosen the situation they are in. Yet I have seen many who are nonetheless able to rise above it from a spiritual perspective. They have taught me that, when we appreciate that we do not have total "control" in our lives, we have a better understanding of what it means to trust others. Trust becomes more real and more urgent when someone is dealing directly with concerns about "frailty." By necessity, they need to trust others for support and care. Their very acceptance can open your mind and heart to the importance of trust.

   🖋 What is your care partner teaching you about trust?

LEARNING THE VALUE OF LOVE

Perhaps the most elemental wisdom that I have gleaned from those in caresharing partnerships is that, throughout all of the complex difficulties that people face, the basic human need for nurture and affirmation is omnipresent. Our need for love does not evaporate simply because we are of a particular age, or are contending with certain disabilities or illnesses. Even people who cannot acknowledge or respond back need to be told "I love you" in words or by a gentle touch. Even for those who are comatose, the need is present. People who have come out of comas have shared stories about hearing people, especially their loved ones, say, "I love you."

Although affection and regard have different meanings than love, and although they may be sorely tested, they are no less crucial elements in sharing care. I've seen situations where the care receiver cannot respond or reciprocate, so the carer thinks it does not matter whether they are being a kind and loving person. The need to be seen as a person who receives and can give affection does not go away because of limits in cognition or physical ability. Love does matter! Many care partners have told me that mutual love and support is the way they get through their days.

Depending on the frailty of the care receiver, sometimes their expressions of love will be less spontaneous. In the process of working with many care partners, I have seen the multitude of ways love can be shared nonverbally. Care partners who have been together in long-term marriages or partnerships of long standing often teach each other new ways of expressing their devotion. Your expectations of giving and receiving love may need to change, and you may need to give your care partner some cues or make some adaptations to ensure that a caring message comes through, but you and your care partner have the opportunity to teach each other not only new ways of expressing love, but also a deeper appreciation for the value of love.

    ✍ What is your care partner teaching you about affection and love?

LEARNING HOW TO COPE

Over the years I have seen care receivers develop some amazing coping skills and teach their caregivers a great deal about survival.

A social work colleague of mine was working with a gentleman who was very close to death and was experiencing a lot of pain. When she asked him how he handled the pain, he told her, "I feel like I am alive when I feel the pain." The social worker, who was herself struggling with chronic pain from an accident many months before, told me that she had an "aha" moment about her own pain, and it opened up a new way for her to look at how to cope with it.

I've also seen many care partners work together to figure out creative ways of coping with daily care or communication needs. Out of their knowledge from the past, they rig up something that works for their particular concerns. I've seen people with aphasia (loss of ability to speak and understand others), for example, and their carers come up with ways to communicate with flashcards, or use a blinking or hand-squeezing system to indicate yes and no. What makes these methods work is that they are collaborative efforts, with each person contributing to the solution, each teaching the other.

To help care partners start the process of exploring solutions to various issues, I often ask the question, "How have you dealt with difficult times in the past?" As people tell me their stories about past adaptations, we both get a sense of what still might be available to them in coping with their current situation, and what they can do to build on their strengths.

It's important to keep brainstorming and to be open to creative options. I have seen people figure out imaginative approaches to dilemmas and develop solutions to problems that health care professionals had no answers for. I've heard many "wild" ideas that actually work! You might be surprised at your care partner's imagination and their sense of humor. Share a good laugh together. This can go a long way in dealing with heavy burdens. You may not be able to solve every problem, but you can learn much from your care partner in the process. And you can both benefit from knowing that you are walking this long and challenging path of caresharing together. There is comfort in being "alongside" in this journey.

⚲ What is your care partner teaching you about coping?

LEARNING TO LIVE IN THE "NOW"

Care receivers have taught me to appreciate *now*. Sometimes when care receivers are anxious to get tasks done or to get something taken care of quickly, their carers may see this as demanding behavior. Caregivers can rightly become discouraged by the expectations that everything needs to be done *immediately*. There is, however, another way to view this. Those being cared for have taught me that they are acutely aware of having a limited amount of lifetime left. As a result, they see urgency in everything. Time is precious for them, so they have a different perspective on the tempo of caring than their caregiver does.

As a carer, you may feel as if you are juggling many responsibilities at the same time and may resent the clamor for tasks to be done more quickly than is realistic. At the same time, your care partner may feel that their needs are not being met promptly. By recognizing that they have a different perspective on time than you do, you can begin to understand why everything seems to need immediate action in their eyes. Learning what time means for them, acknowledging this view with them, and spending a few extra moments gently reassuring them of your commitment to assist them can sometimes clear the air. In the process, each of you has the potential to learn more about the value of the time you have together.

⚲ What is your care partner teaching you about time and living in the "now"?

LEARNING WHAT REALLY MATTERS

Living with the primacy of a diagnosis or health issue puts other life concerns in perspective. Some issues become less important than they seemed before. I think of an extended family who asked the spouse of a man dying of cancer whether they would be attending a significant family event three months in the future. She told them, "We don't know what will happen *today*, let alone three months from now! Our expectations change daily." This woman and her husband living with cancer were very determined to share with each other the important "daily moments."

Care receivers have chided me about my hectic way of life and have given me the gift of seeing what really matters. They have taught me the value of "being in the moment." This goes against what is often practiced in our busy world of multitasking, where we are always thinking ahead to the next task. But I have learned that if I want to savor time in sharing care, I cannot be worrying about my "to do" list.

Caresharing partners have taught me the value of taking one day, one step at a time. They have also taught me not to "sweat the small stuff." And they have poignantly reminded me that I might be in their situation one day, and they have shown me ways to cope with what life might bring.

As a caresharer, an important part of your role is to take time to be "present" to your care partner. Even though the daily living tasks and doctor's appointments and medical issues may weigh heavily on your mind and the mind of your loved one, this time you share together, often in very intimate tasks, is sacred. You can transform this time into sharing person to person, heart to heart, a time when you are present with them unconditionally, focusing all your attention and awareness on them in that space and that moment, undistracted by the other concerns of the day. You will be blessed by what you learn from your care partner, and they will be blessed by being able to share their wisdom and knowledge with you.

> ✐ What is your care partner teaching you about what really matters?

LEARNING TO SEE BEYOND THE SYMPTOMS

Those with chronic illness have also taught me to see beyond the outside symptoms and problems so I can get a better sense of who they are inside and discover what strengths are present. Any one of us may not feel as old or as frail as our body appears to the world. As an older friend of mine on her ninetieth birthday put it, "I am chronologically ninety in a ninety-five-year-old's body, but in my spirit I feel closer to sixty."

Our eyes may observe someone quite limited in mobility, not able to walk or get around, or we may talk down to a person who may not make sense verbally. Yet as we get to know who they are at this point in their lives, we can realize that there is a special being inside what may seem to be the shell of their former personality.

I remember a nurse who, on visiting a person seated in a wheelchair with tubes protruding from her body, commented, "I saw Mary first, and then I realized all of her problems." She complimented the carers on how well they were taking care of her daily needs, and, indeed, the caregivers had done an excellent job, especially in meeting her hygiene needs. They had tastefully dealt with tubes and all that they led to, and had made sure that this fastidious woman had her makeup neatly on and was dressed stylishly and comfortably. Because these carers built on what was well with the person, the nurse experienced the essence of this elegant older woman, not the picture of a frail person. And because of the nurse's openness, she did not immediately label this person as frail and weak.

When you can look beyond all the signs of aging or illness or deficits, you have a chance to see the essence of the person for whom you are providing care. And it is in that sacred space that you will be able to learn what your care partner has to teach you.

✎ What is your care partner teaching you about seeing the real person inside?

LEARNING TO VALUE LEARNING

As you consider the idea of your care partner as your mentor, you also need to be aware that they might not realize the importance of what they are sharing. Helping them recognize the value of their "educator" role can go a long way in rebalancing the care-sharing relationship. Here are a few suggestions of ways to increase both your awareness and theirs about this valuable learning process:

- If you haven't already done so, you might want to use the reflective questions on page 40 to identify what you have learned so far and share your learnings with your care partner. (You might also want to share your responses with your pastoral counselor or support group, keeping the boundaries of privacy and respect for your care partner in mind.)

- Consider how you might learn more in the future. What might help you be more open to learning from your care partner? What could you do to help them appreciate the value of what they are teaching you?

- If you find it difficult to come up with anything you have learned or might learn from your care partner, consider even the small things. As the old adage rightly suggests, at times it is a challenge to see the forest for the trees. If you can get beyond the barriers to learning, your mind-set about what your care partner can teach you might open up significantly.

- Consider how you could reinforce what your care partner can still do, even if it is a small thing. If you reinforce only their limitations, they can experience a sense of loss of self-worth, resulting in an actual loss of function. But if you can help them feel more "abled" than "disabled," they may feel more empowered to share their gifts and knowledge—if you are open to receiving what they have to offer.

50

- Name and affirm what you hear as wisdom from your care partner. Let them know how valuable their lessons are to you. Intentionally, lift them up as a mentor.

GAINING NEW UNDERSTANDING FROM STORIES

In my practice I have learned a great deal about people by listening to their stories. Dr. Anne E. Streaty Wimberly, in a presentation to the American Society on Aging, used the imagery of tapestries to describe how stories begin to be woven very early in our lives. This is a beautiful image of the sacredness of the unique story each of us possesses. Stories remind us of who we are, what is important about the life we share with others, and what has happened to us during our lifetime. They illustrate the meanings we derive from those events, and how we view and go about living our lives. Our narratives identify who we are and how we relate to our Creator.

The next time your care partner tells a story, listen carefully for what you might learn from their narrative.

STORIES REVEAL UNSPOKEN FEELINGS

Elders struggling with physical and mental concerns have taught me the value of listening to stories, even if those accounts do not make total sense or seem preposterous. Unless there is a legal reason for getting information absolutely correct, such as in filling out a benefits form, you may need to suspend judgment about the "facts" of a particular account. Does it really matter whether something happened on one date or another? Accuracy in the details is not as important as accepting the feelings and the themes behind the account. Don't get so preoccupied about what is "real" that you miss the overarching story and what it can teach you.

One older lady struggling with dementia often recounted that she had been robbed of her candlesticks. I knew that there had been no robbery in the time she said, in the place where she was living. However, I did learn that when she was a young woman, her house had been burglarized. Among the items stolen was a pair of much-cherished family heirloom candlesticks. This experience had upset her terribly, and left her feeling vulnerable. Though her sense of time was off, her feelings about being robbed were still real. And in her current situation of feeling vulnerable in being cared for by others, these suspicions from an earlier time surfaced with a vengeance.

As you listen to your care partner's stories, focus on the feelings and ideas behind the literal tale. Even in a less-than-accurate recounting, there may be a revelation about how they are feeling.

STORIES REVEAL WAYS OF COPING

Stories often paint a picture of how someone has maintained a sense of hope and meaning in the past, and can serve as a reminder about how those same coping skills might help in the present difficulties. I think of an older man who had been a long-haul truck driver. He was having a quiet time of prayer in the hospital with his pastor, prior to the next morning's surgery, and was telling the minister tales about near misses in accidents during his driving career. The day after the surgery, he and his minister were again talking, and the man continued to recount stories about his life. This time, however, the man focused on positive things, telling about his family and the awards he had received for safe driving.

This gentleman's stories were his method of coping with his concerns about the surgery. Before surgery, he was fearful about what could happen during the operation. He had a need to share the tough times he had come through successfully, and they became metaphors for his fears and hopes that he would pull through the operation. Coming out of surgery, he could turn to telling the pastor about the achievements in his life. By reflecting on these stories, the pastor learned not only about this gentleman's thankfulness for a good surgery outcome, but also about the man's way of coping.

There may be times when your care partner tells you a life story that seems, on the surface, unrelated to the present. As you listen, be aware of the underlying message; they may be trying to communicate something that is important to them. This is especially true when they tell the same story over and over again (unless they have truly forgotten how many times they have told it). You can learn much about their ways of coping, as well as how and where they see themselves as valuable. Tuck away these learnings for future times when your care partner might need encouragement—from their own life!

STORIES REVEAL "LIFE WISDOM"

If you listen nonjudgmentally to your care partner's stories, you will not only hear the long and the short of their past, but you will also learn what was and is important in their life. There is much to be learned from the "life wisdom" that can be gleaned from these stories, but you may need to "prime the pump," so to speak, to help someone get started telling their story. You could tell a bit of your own life story, which may prompt them to start reminiscing. Asking very simple questions can also access narratives. The question "Tell me about your life" may be too broad. Usually such a nonspecific query elicits responses such as, "Oh, my life is not so important; I didn't do many interesting things," or "There's nothing special about me."

But if you ask about a *specific* aspect of their life, you are providing a nonthreatening catalyst for them to share their history. Your care partner can then become your teacher and cultural guide. Their story will give a window into their world and a glimpse of their uniqueness.

Once your care partner starts sharing a story, you can learn more by asking focused questions, such as "Tell me about being a teacher in a one-room schoolhouse in the 1940s," or "How has being a nurse changed over the years since you have been in practice?" or "What was it like to live through the Depression?" At other times, open-ended questions, such as "How does your family view illness?" can provide clues to what they are thinking about their current situation.

These accounts may help you understand what has been meaningful to your care partner, and in their shared stories they are leaving a body of wisdom for generations of the future.

- ✐ What are you learning from the stories of the one you are caring for?
- ✐ How have their shared stories brought you closer?
- ✐ How have these stories helped you understand their care needs better?

RECEIVING SPIRITUAL STRENGTH

Over the years, I have met many people who were considered emotionally or physically "frail" but who were very strong in their spiritual lives. They have shared with me their faith stories about how they got over the bumps and bruises of life, as well as the difficult faith questions they have considered in light of their illness. I have often found that these "frail" people have a deep perspective on their spiritual lives. When so many of the trappings of cognition and health are gone, they are able to be in touch with the core spiritual need to depend on a Higher Power beyond human strength and ability. Although it may not seem readily apparent, their inner life of prayer and meditation remains, no matter what their physical and mental limits.

Many years ago I had the wonderful opportunity to be the social worker for a group of elderly nuns. Probably the most meaningful experience for me with this group of religious elders, who were dealing with their own ill health, was that they regularly prayed for my work. One even jokingly said, "When we were teaching and nursing, we had to struggle to find the time to get all of our daily prayers in. Now we have more time to pray, and we are praying for you." I was touched by their concern and felt their support very deeply.

Receiving the gifts of prayer from another is a reciprocal act that emphasizes the value of what your care receiver still has to offer. It is important to be deliberate about discussing this important spiritual role with them. For example, reading favorite verses or passages to someone whose vision has deteriorated would give you an opportunity to ask why a certain passage was important to their life and, in turn, give them a chance to teach you.

Nina, an older woman confined to her bed by severe arthritis, was visited by her minister. She told him that she did not feel like herself much anymore because of all her physical limits. (They were indeed many, and she was not exaggerating the losses she faced.) However, this wise pastor knew that Nina had been a woman for whom praying for others had been an integral part of her life. He said to her, " Nina, you can still pray, and you can start by praying for me."

Nina had had an important role in intercessory prayer for the ministry of that pastor, and as she considered what he said, she agreed to try to renew her prayer ministry. Though she lived in a shell of a body, she once again had a meaningful role for her life. Despite her physical limits, she was reminded that she could make a difference in the lives of those for whom she was praying. The pastor would come by and fill her in on his work from time to time, and she was able to feel a part of a larger community of believers.

Being in the presence of a spiritual person can have an impact on your spiritual journey as well. Consider these questions:

- ✐ What are you learning about spiritual matters from your care partner?
- ✐ How might these wisdoms influence how you relate to your care partner?
- ✐ How might these wisdoms affect your own spiritual life?

The role of a learner may be a welcome role for you, or it may take a little practice and a lot of openness. Seeing the one you are caring for through "new eyes" may be a challenge, but it can also bring some interesting and wonderful surprises. Most of all, learning from someone whom society might consider "frail" or "weak" can bring you both many blessings.

The wisdom of the cared for is profound and sacred. As you open yourself to the dance of learning, hold these thoughts in your heart and mind and actions:

- Honestly face your own concerns about losing strength, mental changes, and aging.

- Take steps to consciously put yourself in the role of learner. Be open to moments of discovery.

- Accept your care partner for who they are at this time, rather than bemoaning what has changed. While you may feel sadness when you compare the person in front of you to an earlier time, it is important not to let that become a barrier to learning from them *as they are today.*

- Be "present" to your care partner in the *now,* without letting other pressures or concerns filter into the moments of being together. This will shift your frame of mind to learning rather than worrying about what needs to be done.

- When you share simple moments of just "being" with your care partner, you give them a time and place to express what echoes deep in their spirit. You may be privileged to learn from their spiritual strength, and it can be a blessing for you both.

• Be open to seeing your care partner in a new light, based on the spiritual stories and wisdoms that they share.

3

FAMILIES SHARING THE CARE
Reinventing the Roles and Rules

FAMILY SYSTEMS

How does your family work? If you are providing care for a family member who is struggling, everyone in the family is affected.

Let's say your aunt is feeling anxious about her sister's (your mother's) health. Her anxiety can become "infectious," causing you and everyone else in the family to feel stressed out. Or perhaps your daughter is mad about the way you are handling things with her father (your husband). Her anger may cause you to feel isolated, and your husband torn between people he loves. As a member of a family, you and your care partner are indelibly part of a larger system with many complex and moving parts. Understanding how family systems work in general, and how your family works in particular, can help you better comprehend and deal with your own situation.

Picture a mobile. When air blows through the mobile, the parts move around. Eventually, though, the mobile comes to rest again, and it remains stable until set in motion by the next wind gust. In a similar fashion, families work toward developing and maintaining a sense of stability even when buffeted by changes and caregiving. The family faces change and things shift a bit, but eventually the system comes back to a resting position.

For our purposes, I define *family* as those who care about each other, whether or not they are related by blood or marriage. Many definitions of family necessarily evolve from legal requirements, but I am using this functional definition purposefully. (I recognize, however, that there are situations, such as applying for benefits, where the legal definition must be followed.)

Families grow and change over the years, but at times they get stuck in patterns or behaviors that are not helpful. And when an illness or a disability upsets the pattern, the whole system can get out of balance, leading to problems. Sometimes caregiving situations can "make or break families." In my practice, I've seen families who have been "blown apart" because of their inability to share and communicate effectively in concert with the needs of the one being cared for. I have also had experience with families who have pulled together, despite great odds, to work together, with the focus on the care receiver. They might not agree with each other, but they put differences aside for the common good.

What's the climate like in your family? Perhaps some are very responsive to the needs of the person receiving care and are rallying to help. There may be others who feel so personally distressed about the situation that they end up needing attention and support themselves. Or still other family members may have a lot of expectations about what should and shouldn't be done and are getting everyone else in the family "riled up." And then there are those who do not seem to care what is happening and are perfectly willing to let others do all the work. Each person's response becomes part of the care-sharing mix. Each position is not inherently good or bad; it *is*, and as such is a part of your family situation.

If your family seems to be going on "tilt," remember the mobile image: Families are always working toward maintaining balance or equilibrium. It *is* possible to reframe a situation so that stability is restored in your family system. There is no exact prescription for balancing everyone's needs, yet if you can understand some of the reasons why people in your family do things the way they do, you'll be better able to understand the situation and make minor (or even major) adjustments as needed.

Having an understanding of how your family works is the first step. There are three primary areas to consider: what role(s) each family member plays, what rules your family lives by, and what secrets your family holds.

FAMILY ROLES

As in a theatrical play, each person in a family system has a role, a function that they take on or that is "assigned" to them. Someone in the family may be the "decision maker," while another may be the "go to" person when it comes to finances, and another may be the pillar of emotional support for the family. Birth order or gender may determine some roles, some are rooted in cultural expectations or the family's religious convictions, and others may stem from personal temperaments or circumstances.

Unlike the roles in a play, however, family roles may overlap and change over time. Roles may have been given out early in life, but they can change—which may lead to discomfort, both for the one whose role shifts and for others who are used to the way things work. I've seen situations where the eldest daughter is expected to suddenly take on the role of primary caretaker for an aging parent, no matter what else might be happening in her life. Or a sibling who has always taken a supporting role suddenly takes on a managerial role, telling everyone what to do, and other members of the family system are not very pleased at the new development!

At other times, family members who have not been involved "step up to the plate" and help out, to everyone's amazement. A son I knew had been willing to let his sister do all of the care for his mom, but he did not realize the incredible pressure it was putting on her. After an intense family discussion about the situation, he started to do the shopping, and he cooked soup for his mom one night per week. While he was there, he visited with her and played cards, and gave his sister some relief.

Roles are "assigned" to family members in various ways, and they each carry emotional and symbolic meaning. Some roles come about because of a marriage, birth, or death. Other roles are functional and are carved out because someone in the family needs help: a mother needs to care for an ill child, a husband needs to care for his ailing wife, a daughter needs to help her mother who becomes disabled. Functional roles also come about when a family member asks for help with a particular matter, such as a legal or financial concern.

Some roles are honorary. For example, a maiden aunt may become the family matriarch when the only other female family member becomes unable to recognize people. Honorary roles can also be assigned to persons who have become "like family." Honorary roles can come out of close and intimate friendships when a friend becomes like a brother or sister. I know many people who feel more closely connected to people from their community, work, or community of faith than to family members. I have often seen local people take on the role of a son or daughter in aiding an elderly person when "blood family" lives at a distance.

Roles are always changing, which means the meaning with which the roles are imbued is changing as well. A big challenge for the family is to let the roles that evolve over time be functional and workable for all. As a caregiver, it is especially important that you consider who has what roles in your family, and how they play out in the caregiving setting.

FUNCTIONAL ROLES

The caregiver role is one that is easily identified. What is not so clear is how that caregiving affects the whole family system. You may have the primary role as caregiver, but there are many functional aspects of the role that can be shared with others. You may need to spell these out clearly to others in the family. Depending on which family members are available and where they live, there may be variations and overlap of these functional roles that include the following tasks:

- legal/financial advisor (the one who is called on for input about wills, use of funds, and other such matters)
- bill payer
- Mr./Ms. Fixit
- "switchboard operator" (the one who keeps everyone on track, making sure they fulfill their designated responsibilities)
- transporter
- medical advisor
- main communicator (the one who keeps the family members in the loop about what is happening when someone is sick, needs support, or has asked for specific help)
- event coordinator
- "fly-away Frank/Fran" (long-distance members of the family)

Seeing that these functional roles are covered is important because this will allow your family to keep a sense of balance when someone needs help. But things can get complicated if there is contention over who plays what role or if there are not enough people to cover all of the functional roles. This can be especially tough if you're the one who has been thrust into the role of primary caregiver and don't feel equipped or able to take on all that the role involves. One thing to keep in mind is that, just because roles developed at one point in family history, people are not forever locked into them. With reflection, and sometimes help from a third party, roles can be renegotiated. (I'll say more about this in the discussions of "Changing Roles," p. 65, and "Shared Roles," p 68.)

Sometimes family roles that are *dysfunctional* need to be addressed as well. A role may have served a purpose for a time, but if it continues when the situation changes, there can be difficulties—especially in caregiving situations. Such roles as "black sheep, "Napoleon," "white knight," family "savior," "shirker," "clown," "martyr," or "favored son or daughter" come to mind. They may have evolved in an attempt to balance communication and tasks within a family. Or they may have developed out of a history of problems, such as mental illness or alcoholism, as a "survival" mode. But if, for example, someone who has held on to the role of "martyr" arrives on the caretaking scene, you may end up needing to care for two people instead of just one. Or if the family "savior" jumps in, insisting that the care receiver try a "miracle" treatment he has read about, you might find yourself in the middle of a conflict. The "black sheep" who left home early in life because of an estrangement may come back to make amends, which is admirable; however, the manner in which this is done may cause difficulties for other family members who are not used to having this person in their immediate network.

In sorting out who will do what to help care for a family member, the place to start is to understand which functional roles people currently have in the family system. I offer here a short exercise that many families have found helpful to get a picture of where things stand:

1. On a piece of paper, draw a circle in the middle.

2. In this circle write the names of the people you consider your "household."

3. Then add a circle around the center and write in the names of people who are part of your extended family or care network. (Don't forget long-distance people. It might be helpful to indicate how near or far various people are from the one needing care.)

4. Where are you in this picture? Are you a "hand-ons" caregiver or caring from afar? Indicate your position with a dot.

5. Name the roles each person plays now or has played in the past. Which family members play functional roles in the caresharing situation you are in now? What are their roles?

HONORARY ROLES

In addition to the functional roles, it is important to consider the honorary roles in your family. Some honorary roles start out biologically but develop over time into much more. They might evolve out of the expectations of your culture or religion. In certain cultures, for example, the honorary roles of matriarch or patriarch are very important. As these matriarchs, patriarchs, grandmothers, great-aunts, grandfathers, great-uncles, godfathers, godmothers, mothers, and fathers age, their roles of the past may become less functional and more a mark of respect.

It is especially important to recognize your care partner's honorary role in the family or in their community. Even if they are suffering from dementia or have mental limits, or are very frail or need constant care, it is vital to find ways to affirm the essence of their honorary role. This can be challenging, and you may need to get creative. If your care partner can no longer do some of the things they used to, you may need to "fill in the blanks" in such a way that they can still retain the honor without having to actually perform the task.

Perhaps your mom has always held the family events at her house, sometimes for as many as forty people. Because of her frail health, she can no longer organize these events. It might be possible for you to pull together such an event with your siblings. You could ask your mom for advice, recipes, or ideas about who to sit with whom. And then at the event she could have a place of honor.

Even though she did not have all of the work to do, she could bask in her long-held role.

I think of a woman named Elsa, who was a matriarch in her church. She took great delight in the ministry of hospitality by organizing all the potlucks. When she was ninety-two and becoming frail, the younger women in the congregation decided to "help" her by taking this task out of her hands because they felt it was becoming "too much for her." But these well-meaning women didn't ask Elsa about her feelings, and she ended up feeling quite depressed about the loss of her ministry. When I talked with her pastor and the people in her support network, they were able to find a way for her to colead the team that planned the potlucks, and her role as matriarch was restored.

To help you understand the honorary roles of your care partner and others in your family system, here are a few questions to consider:

- What are some of the honorary roles held by people in your family network?
- What does it mean for each person who holds an honorary role?
- What roles could be adapted so that people could still comfortably fulfill these positions in the family? In the community?

CHANGING ROLES

Just because a person has played a particular role over time does not mean that they need to stay in that role. Roles are not cast in stone. Families *can* find ways to help people creatively modify cherished roles, either playing a different role or carrying out an old role in a new way. Learning how to do something new can be challenging, but it is possible.

I have witnessed many people in caresharing situations who have learned roles they never thought they could or would need to do. I know of a sixty-year-old woman who became a bill payer because her husband, who was struggling with dementia, was not able to accomplish that task. Even though it was difficult for her to learn how to do this (he had always handled the money), she gained more confidence in her abilities once she started to do it.

Larry also comes to mind. He had never so much as boiled an egg before his wife, Beth, had a stroke that left her unable to cook. He took over the cooking and, much to his surprise, found out that he enjoyed it. I remember visiting them one evening when he proudly served me a piece of pie that he had made all by himself by reading a cookbook.

Some people are positively challenged by learning new roles; for others, adjusting to a new role can be a struggle, emotionally and spiritually. As a caregiver, it is important to recognize what your feelings are as your role(s) changes with the situation. You may be taking on responsibilities that curtail your freedom or a task that requires learning new skills. But at the same time, you may be learning new ways of coping while connecting with your care partner in new ways.

I think of John, a very caring spouse to Martha for fifty years, who became her primary care person as her dementia advanced. One of the basic tasks was bathing, which Martha did not like. In the evening she would often become belligerent and then be too upset to go to sleep. John was also sad about the loss of intimacy in their long-term relationship.

In problem solving with an Alzheimer's support group, he devised a way to bathe his wife in warm water in the evening while playing "big band" music. He would then wrap her in a fluffy robe, and they would dance to the music for twenty minutes. By this time, she was tired and could fall sleep. Because they had always enjoyed dancing, this solution helped him in the functional role of caregiver, and it also gave him and his wife an emotional connection in their roles as spouses.

Some roles don't need to be changed, as much as highlighted. Supporting an elder's honorary role by asking them to tell stories about their life can create new connections with a younger generation. Asking an ailing "Mr./Ms. Fixit" for advice on how to best repair something can support their strengths and self-esteem. Gathering favorite family stories for an event from a person who has been the family historian can help them feel part of family interactions. Although they may not be able to get the story on paper as they might have previously, they nonetheless can contribute to stories for the family legacy.

Understanding how your care partner feels about their changing role is a crucial consideration. Though they might be the "care receiver" now, that is not the only role they have played in life. Cared-for people are not one-dimensional; they are also partners, grandmas, grandpas, church members, friends, or siblings, to name only a few. Even if your care partner is frail or confused, you can elevate these other roles in importance and help keep the essence of those roles alive so they can feel more like "themselves."

Consider which roles need to be adjusted or amplified in your caresharing situation. Go back, for a moment, to the family circles you drew in the "functional roles" exercise above. As you take a look at the roles various family members play, consider these questions:

- Is there any confusion about roles that needs to be clarified?
- Is any adjustment needed in the way roles are distributed or the number of roles each person has?
- Is anyone's role getting in the way of a meaningful life for you or your care partner?
- With what functional roles could you use help?
- Who in the extended family circle might be a good resource for you?

SHARED ROLES

I've seen caresharing situations where one person attempts to take on all the roles, with disastrous results. Not only does it make providing all the care that is needed tough, but it also makes it that much more difficult for them to reach out to others for assistance. And people trying to offer assistance run into a brick wall of resistance.

Before you find yourself in this position—or if you are already there and are feeling overloaded and frustrated—have a family conference! Be sure to include the care receiver, if their strength and mental abilities allow. The relationships and roles of others in their family affect them directly, and too often they get left out of the loop and feel that others are "doing something to them." They need to exert whatever decision-making abilities they can in the situation. You might also look for ways to include important persons in the family network who are not able to be present in person, such as via a conference call. The main thing is to include all the primary people in the care network.

I recommend asking a third party to help you sort things out because, however the roles have evolved, they are powerful. Long-term patterns of learned family roles can be difficult to unravel. A "baby of the family," for example, may have trouble getting their perspective heard. A person who has been doing "everything" may need to be convinced to share their role. A person who considers themselves the "main communicator" may have trouble if they are not "in the know" about every decision being made.

Whatever your family issues are, it is critical for everyone to recognize that, in this caresharing situation, functional roles need to be shared as fairly as possible. Staying "stuck" in old patterns can create major problems. A reasonable goal for a family conference would be to make a list or chart that includes the following questions:

- ✐ What is currently being done, and by whom? (This is especially important if there is someone who is trying to handle all the roles.)
- ✐ What needs to be done in the future?
- ✐ Which roles could be shared?
- ✐ Who will do each task? (Here you need to address delegating responsibility and designating how to share the roles as fairly as possible.)
- ✐ How will information be shared? (If you designate someone as "coordinator," they must understand their role.)

One a word of caution here: If you are the primary caregiver, you should *not* be the person who is in charge of creating and maintaining the "list" that comes out of such a session. That would add still another task to your already-long "to do" list!

As you develop your family "shared roles" list, remember to look at the entire multigenerational family, because all generations are affected when someone in the family needs care. There are many ways to include everyone in sharing the care. Teenage grandchildren, for example, might be able to do yard work or some basic housecleaning for their grandparents. Older family members, even if they cannot actively contribute to day-to-day tasks, might be able to make phone calls. It is especially important to include these elder or more frail members of your family because they may not only be experiencing tensions but may also be watching how other generations care for someone, knowing their turn may be next.

SUPPORTING ROLES

As you reflect on the care needs in your situation, this is also a good time to consider all persons who are "like family" to you, and include them in the caring journey. Intentional caresharing networks of neighbors, coworkers, people from your community of faith, or people who have become "surrogate family" for you can play a very important role in caresharing. One person I know is part of a network of support for her sister that is being coordinated by a neighbor. The neighbor e-mailed a chart to about a dozen friends and coworkers, identifying what needed to be done, inviting people to sign up for which tasks they could cover, and when. Even though they probably won't ever meet each other, they all care about the woman who needs assistance and have formed a network to help her.

These networks can be real lifesavers when there is no "blood" or "marriage" family available to help you, or they might work in concert with your family members, sharing roles to build up the available resource pool. These people who share emotional connections with you can help in many concrete ways, as well as bring new perspectives on the gifts of interdependency.

There are a couple of things to keep in mind with an extended support network. First, the network needs to be organized around your care partner's particular needs. Sometimes people in extended networks start falling all over each other in an effort to be helpful, and not everything they want to do is wanted or needed. It is imperative to have someone in charge of keeping the network informed and working toward the same goals.

Second, it is important that people in the network are responsible for follow-through. If your care partner is depending on someone to be in a certain place at a certain time to do a particular task, you and your care partner both need to be able to rely on that person.

You may also want to consider gathering people together who will make a pact with you and your care partner to become a "committed network of support." In this case, it helps if they get to know each other at some level so they can carry out the needed tasks smoothly. While all of the members of this group may know you and your care partner, they might not know much about each other. As they begin to recognize each other's strengths and availabilities, they can more realistically consider the gifts each person brings and decide together how best to pool their resources to help the person needing care.

One woman I know had a close group of colleagues at work who made a pact to assist her as she went through some lengthy treatments for her illness. Her "blood family" lived far away, so they were not able to help on a daily basis. This group did everything from cleaning the cat's litter box, to transporting the woman to appointments, to shopping and making meals that she could eat. They also provided a great deal of emotional support as she journeyed to her death. She could not believe that the person who had been her boss was helping her with very basic care needs! It was a great blessing to her to be so carefully nurtured.

There's one thing I want to add about a committed care network. Even though these people are not "family," their old family roles can still play an active part. For example, a person who is used to being "in charge" in their family may try to take over or control the network. Or someone who is viewed as the "savior" in their family may volunteer to take on too many tasks. Each person must examine the commitment they have with the cared-for person and ask some pertinent questions.

- ✐ What is the trust level among all involved?
- ✐ Do old "roles" need reworking in the relationships of the network?
- ✐ How will the functional roles in this surrogate family be assigned or divided up?

Knowing about family roles is key to helping care partners and the whole family stay in balance. Balancing the needs of all family members is tricky and takes work. Taking into account your family system and naming family roles can go a long way toward understanding what is transpiring. Making sure that caregiving tasks are reasonably distributed, and making the necessary adjustments and adaptations in roles, can make life smoother for everyone. Being gentle with each other as role changes occur can help bring harmony to all.

FAMILY RULES

Another part of family dynamics includes the rules or the guides by which a family conducts itself. Family rules may be spoken or unspoken, and they develop over a family life cycle. Some rules come from explicit religious teachings, and others develop from norms in society and culture. An individual family might also have very particular rules that they have worked out to deal with certain situations. Family rules tend to rattle around in our heads and our hearts for a lifetime, even when we consciously reject a particular one.

It is important not to label these rules as "bad" or "good," but it is equally important to recognize which rules are helpful in your caresharing situation and which are not. Sometimes long-standing rules can get in the way of sharing care. The rules you learned about parenting or work or being a citizen may come into conflict with the "rules" you feel in your heart about caresharing. You may feel pulled in many directions, which can lead to very difficult decision making. For example, a woman in a valued career may be considered an important citizen under the rule that "work has worth." Yet if she responds to the family rule to "honor your father and mother" and quits that position to care for a parent, the conflict between these two rules can create a huge quandary for her.

Your care partner may also be dealing with family rules. I've seen situations where, even though all the circumstances have changed, the person receiving care is still trying to play by the old rules. This can be hard on both the care receiver and the caregiver, especially if this is a set of rules neither of them values any longer or finds helpful. I've seen families where a daughter is the primary caregiver for her mother or father, but the family cultural rule is that "the oldest son makes the important family decisions." Even though the son has not been involved with the parent's care, the parent wants the son's input about a significant treatment option, rather than the daughter's. This is very stressful for the caregiver daughter because it seems as if what she thinks about the situation doesn't matter.

I've listed below some of the more common family rules that I've heard along the way. After you've had a chance to go over them, you might find it helpful to share this list of rules (and others you think of as you go along) with your care partner. Find out what rules they live by or were taught by their family. You might end up having a very interesting discussion about what is, and is no longer, a helpful rule for your caresharing partnership.

"HONOR YOUR FATHER AND MOTHER"

With roots in societal norms and religious commandments, the rule to "honor your father and mother" is fundamental for many people. Some variation of honoring and respecting parents and/or elders exists in all major religious traditions. Yet this commandment can be tested in myriad ways in a caresharing situation.

If you're facing a situation where you need to turn over some of the care of a parent to someone outside the family, are you still honoring your parent? How do you honor a parent if you are frustrated by their constant demands for help? Where is the honor if you are so exhausted by daily care that you fear becoming abusive toward your parent? I have seen too many carers collapse by attempting to do more than was realistically possible, and usually their break comes because they tried to honor their parent in a way that is overwhelming them. Ultimately, they end up not being able to provide the best care for the very one they wanted to honor.

I have spent much time in counseling sessions, and as a part of scripture study with caregivers, reflecting on this dilemma of how to honor elders. Here is what I suggest to people in the difficult position of trying to figure out how to handle the care of a parent when it is becoming too hard: To *really* honor your parent, you may need to transfer care to people who can give assistance in eight-hour shifts, not twenty-four-hour days. Honoring may be coming to understand that, though you love your parent, you may not be able to give primary care. You may need to entrust that work to another person. "Honoring" may need to be rethought, and you may need to allow others to assist you in that.

"TILL DEATH DO US PART"

Here's another rule that can create a difficult dilemma: the marriage vow, "till death do us part." How does moving your spouse to a treatment center or residence fit into that promise?

One gentleman I knew desperately needed time-out care because his wife's Alzheimer's disease was progressively disabling. He finally consented to have a one-day-a-week respite worker so he could get a break and better face his own life's challenges. The night before the assistant was to arrive for her first visit, he telephoned his sister to ask, "Do you think it's okay if I go out for a short time while the chore worker is here?" Even after having accepted the service, and discussing his concerns with his family, he still felt some guilt about taking time for himself. He was, of course, encouraged to take the time off!

The way in which you work out your response to this dilemma may profoundly affect your ability to continue giving care to your loved one—and being able to receive help from others. Because each situation is unique, you will need to work this through gently for yourself. Only you know how far you can push yourself to do something. But remember this: Even if you utilize assistance from others, in your home or in a nursing home or in another facility, your role as partner still remains. Some care partners have told me that, once they turned over some of the care for their loved one to someone who could respond to the loved one's basic needs, they were able to give more time to basic love and affection.

"OUR FAMILY TAKES CARE OF ITS OWN"

If your family lives by the rule that "our family takes care of its own," you will probably feel uncomfortable when others offer assistance. Like most long-term, ingrained patterns, this one can be hard to break. And when you finally do ask for assistance, or take someone up on an offer of help, you may still feel as if you've done something wrong. Or you might find yourself willing to accept the assistance of another *only* if you can give something back. Even then, you may feel unworthy to receive the gift of their concern for you.

The rule that "we take care of our own" can also pertain to sharing between generations: "My mother cared for me as a baby and child; now it is time for me to care for her in her time of need." Although this mutual respect between generations is laudable, what if the care for your parent is more than you can physically or emotionally manage? This rule can have an enormous impact on whether you ask for assistance, and from whom.

I'll tell you Joe's story. When he was in high school, his mother saved money and made the grocery money stretch so that he could buy a pair of track shoes that he desperately wanted. Later, when she became ill and needed care, he volunteered to do it all, despite some health problems of his own, even though he had siblings who were willing to help out. Joe took over most of the care, but eventually his own situation worsened, and he could no longer do the heavy caregiving needed. When he ended up needing to seek nursing home care for his mom, he felt very guilty about it because his mother had sacrificed so much for him. He had "broken" the rule that was foremost in his mind and heart, and now he was giving up her care to others. Had he asked for help along the way, it might not have come to that.

If the rule about "taking care of our own" is echoing through your consciousness, give yourself permission to test the waters a bit. Try reaching out to someone who has offered help, or who would gladly assist you if you asked. You may be pleasantly surprised at the unlikely candidates who rise to the occasion—and your family's response. You may find that stepping outside the family perimeter not only brings you much-needed assistance, but also opens doors to new relationships that will give you strength in the future.

"WE DO NOT AIR OUR DIRTY LINEN IN PUBLIC"

This rule is a huge hurdle in asking for assistance from others. If you've grown up with the understanding that "we do not air our dirty linen in public," you may be severely hampered in receiving tangible care and help.

This rule of keeping things within the family makes it particularly difficult to evaluate your situation honestly or to get outside help and much-needed information. If the walls around your family are built too high, there may be no way for others to reach in and care. I am reminded of Robin, who was caring for her uncle. She knew that there was a long history of depression in her family that no one talked about. When the physician treating her uncle inquired about any mental health concerns, Robin could not quite bring herself to discuss her family issues with the doctor. This approach backfired when her uncle had a severe bout of depression that affected his physical and mental health.

Perhaps you have a fear that others in your community (especially the faith community) may think less of you if they knew your whole story. In truth, I have to say that I have observed times when families and communities *do* judge carers and question carers' decisions. But there are many who will appreciate your honesty and vulnerability and will genuinely offer to help. They will understand that you are doing the best you can do at this particular time.

While sharing sensitive issues from your family may go against the rule of "not airing dirty linen in public," it is important to weigh this rule against the value of sharing what you know to enhance the total well-being of your care partner. Keep in mind, however, that it is always crucial to treat such information with the greatest respect.

You may remember other family rules from your own background. A frequent and difficult-to-deal-with rule that I often come across is that the eldest daughter (or son) is *supposed* to provide care for the parent(s). Maybe you live a thousand miles away from your parents and have your own children and partner to care for. What do you do then?

The Polish elders in my family followed this rule, and when they became older and needed care, I sometimes had guilt feelings about not being able to be their primary caregiver because I lived so far away. As the eldest daughter, I knew what the "rules" were, yet I also knew that I needed, and we all needed, to give ourselves permission to reconsider the family rules in light of a new situation. What I could provide was financial and telephone support, and frequent visits.

Being in a caresharing relationship changes everything—including the "rules." It is important for you to consider and reconsider which family rules are helpful and which ones no longer apply. Because each of us is human, the guilt of "breaking the rules" may never fully go away. But there are ways to keep guilt under control so it does not negate the possibility of many avenues of caring and relationships. While rules are powerful, they do not have to destroy you emotionally or spiritually. In addition to your personal reflection on the family rules, you may find it helpful to talk with a third party, a social worker, a counselor, a spiritual advisor, or another person who has "been there."

Here are a few reflective questions to stir your thinking:

- What are the major rules you learned in your family?
- How do you feel about these rules now?
- Are there any rules that need to be reconsidered in light of your current circumstances?
- Is asking for help outside of the family circle seen as a strength or a weakness in your family? How do you feel about that now?

FAMILY SECRETS

Most families have secrets, which may or may not be openly discussed. There may be any number of skeletons in the closet: alcoholism, mental illness, out-of-wedlock pregnancy, abuse (physical, mental, or sexual), difficult financial concerns between family members, gender orientation, adoption, or suicide.

Some families choose to share family secrets with just a few "insiders"; others only whisper about the secret among themselves; still others never speak of it. "We don't talk about that" is the motto that often plays out in families with secrets. The proverbial "elephant" is sitting in the middle of the room, but no one mentions it. Tiptoeing around it and never bringing it up, however, affects each family member, and the effects can filter down throughout the family life cycle, even long after an issue such as alcoholism or addiction is resolved.

Ideas about what constitutes a "secret" can also change over time. For example, there used to be closed adoptions, but now birth mom and adoptive mom may communicate before and after the birth. The influence of prominent personalities and celebrities telling personal stories of addiction or mental illness has helped some families become more open about their "secrets." However, secrets, by their very nature, can still cause lots of problems, especially when some members know the secret(s), while others don't have that information. Secrets can create intergenerational stress, such as an older person not wanting to talk about the family's "dirty laundry" even as a younger generation presses them to be open. And secrets can be especially problematic in caregiving situations. The stresses of caregiving have the potential to bring family secrets to the surface, often with a vengeance, and they can blindside you, sometimes when you least expect it.

THE STRESS OF SECRETS

Even if your family secrets are never directly discussed, they are probably still there. Have you ever sensed "something" or suspected a secret that's interfering with caresharing? Consider this scenario, which comes from an actual situation I heard about: You sense a certain tension between your mother and father, who have been married for many years. The caring that your mom is doing for your dad with Parkinson's seems to be taking a greater toll than her actual duties would warrant. Then you discover that your dad had been unfaithful to your mom early in their marriage. They have been coexisting, within reason, all these years. But your dad's caregiving needs have tipped the balance for your mom, and her unresolved issues about his early indiscretions, which she has kept close to her heart all these years, have come back to haunt her and are now affecting the caring.

When secrets affect how care partners relate to each other, as well as to the rest of the family, great sensitivity is needed in addressing them. Letting the "cat out of the bag" has its perils—and its blessings.

I think of an older woman who had kept secret the actual reason for her father's death—suicide. She honestly believed that this was a shameful event in her family, and had kept it secret since she was a child. Her daughter, a genealogy buff, was researching some family history and discovered the truth. When she told her mom what she had learned, her mother was mortified and very upset with her daughter. On the other hand, a gentleman who learned of the suicide of his uncles, and a suicide attempt by his mother, had a better sense of why he had severe depression and suicidal tendencies. This helped him deal with his own feelings of depression

HEALING THE WOUNDS

Newly revealed secrets can cause pain and anger, even a sense of betrayal: "Why didn't you *tell* me?" Even a secret long in the past, or one that has long been out in the open, may leave hurts that need forgiveness. It's a very delicate balance, but sometimes the critical work of bringing secrets to the surface can bring healing to wounded relationships. I'll say much more about this in chapter 6, "Sharing Forgiveness," but I want to raise the possibility here. The work of forgiveness, often with the outside assistance of clergy or a spiritual advisor, can take on special importance in the arena of caresharing. You and your care partner may be able to work through the secrets that need to be dealt with and, in that deep sharing, find new acceptance and understanding that will enrich your spiritual journey of caresharing.

OVERCOMING SECRETS

Sometimes it is possible to overcome family secrets. I've seen situations where a son or a daughter who was abused as a child was required to care for the very person who was the abuser. Even though it was very difficult, I've seen such carers find the inner strength to rise above the family secret. However, there are other instances when the secret is insurmountable and a person may need to walk away from caregiving, in the best interests of the person needing care and for themselves.

A daughter may remember an alcoholic mom, who is now "dry" and living life differently than she did when the daughter was a young, impressionable child. The pain of this mom's behavior, however, is still deeply embedded in the soul of the adult daughter, who is now expected to help out. While outside caregivers may see a delightful older woman, the daughter may not be able to see beyond the hurtful memories.

If you find yourself in a similar situation, you will need to walk your own path in relation to it. Whatever your family secret, your decision about whom to confront, or how to get beyond it, or when to walk away, is yours. No matter what your family secret might be, it is important not to feel judged or to judge others. It is also important not to feel ashamed. Keep in mind that it was probably the intense shame of previous generations that made this a "secret" in the first place!

Although other people may be able to help you sort out the possibilities for decision making, you will need to make your own choices. If you're wrestling with a family secret, the following questions might help you get in touch with the dynamics of your situation:

- Is there a secret that you are aware of that is affecting the caresharing relationship?
- Do you have a sense that there is something "out there" in your family that has been kept from everyone?
- Are there others in the caresharing network who need to be made aware of this secret?
- Taking your situation into account, what are your thoughts about how you might proceed to deal with this secret?

Roles, rules, and secrets are a part of all family dynamics. To keep the dance of caresharing moving, you need to be aware of the interaction of these dynamics within your family system. Naming them is the place to begin. It will not solve all the problems of the caregiving situation, but having an understanding of what is going on under the surface can help you work out what is best for you and your care partner. Remember that each situation is unique. As you reflect on these key points of the chapter, use what seems right for you:

- Family members play many roles over time, and these roles are constantly evolving. Be open to the changing nature of the roles in your family.

- Remember that roles are not good or bad; they just *are*.

- Consider how the roles in your caresharing situation can be shared fairly among all involved in the caring.

- Work toward keeping a sense of equilibrium and balance in your care network. Realize that all network members may have different perspectives on how this balance should be kept.

- Name the family rules that you know of. Although rules are helpful in keeping life running smoothly, knowing where your rules come from, and being open to adapting those that no longer fit, will help you determine what works in your particular caresharing situation.

- Accept that families have secrets that, for better or worse, affect how they operate as a system. Take steps to honestly deal with the secrets when that seems appropriate. Be willing to walk away from situations when necessary, for the sake of the one needing care, or for your own sake.

SHARING "SOUL TO SOUL"

A Special Relationship
with People with Cognitive Limits

FACING DIFFICULT CHALLENGES

Among all the challenges care partners face, coping with memory loss presents some of the most demanding situations. Many care partners have told me that being with someone who has memory deficits on a daily basis is one of the most difficult things they have ever grappled with, and they find it almost impossible to carve out personal moments for themselves.

Much is being written and said these days about dementia, Alzheimer's disease, and other related cognitive disorders. As famous persons, such as Ronald Reagan and Charlton Heston, have spoken publicly about their problems, dementia has gained more publicity. Much research to understand the causes and to develop treatments is being done all over the world. Yet we still do not have all the answers about what the disease process is or how to deal with it. We do know that the term *dementia* covers several illnesses, and that Alzheimer's disease is the best-known one. For our purposes in this book, I will use the term *dementia* to include the many diseases that affect memory and cognition.

If you are caring for someone with dementia twenty-four hours a day, you know some of the difficulties. They may continually repeat the same question or follow you every place you go. Or they may not cooperate with basic daily care tasks, such as bathing and eating. It may seem that the most commonly expressed feeling between the two of you is anger. It's easy to become overwhelmed. The daily frustrations can be so all-encompassing that time for real sharing between you and your care partner is limited and often stress-filled.

I would pose this question: Is it possible that people with dementia present models of living for us all? Many with dementia have a wonderful capacity to live in the moment. They epitomize the value of living in the *now*, as it may be all they understand. Think about it: Those of us with a wider range of cognitive abilities can easily get distracted into musing about the past or worrying about the future. Our care partner's ability to live in the *now* may have much to teach us. However, it takes a suspension of our usual mind-set if we are to connect with them "soul to soul," and be present for them.

Care partners have taught me that love, care, intimacy, and hope are possible even in the face of cognitive decline. And they have developed some imaginative ways for improving interactions, which I will share in this chapter, along with ways to understand a person with mental limits and how to reduce your own stress as a carer.

UNDERSTANDING THE STAGES OF DEMENTIA

Many misconceptions about memory loss exist and, in turn, these have resulted in much fear. For starters, it is important to recognize the difference between *normal* forgetfulness and dementia. One eighty-year-old woman said to her daughter that, at her age, it was really difficult to remember "everything I know"! And in many ways this is true. Getting forgetful is something we all face to some degree as we age. And when we are under severe stress or experience a shock, such as a loved one's death or a massive societal tragedy, we may experience exaggerated, but temporary, symptoms of memory loss.

Although this kind of forgetting is normal, dementia is *not* a normal part of the aging process. It is true that, as we get older, our chances of developing dementia increase, but many people get anxious at the first sign of memory loss. Then they worry themselves into being more forgetful.

It is important to be realistic about the scope of the problem. For example, someone may become worried that they can't balance a checkbook. But maybe they've *never* been able to do that! On the other hand, if someone who rarely makes an error with numbers is suddenly unable to balance their checkbook, there is some cause for concern. Changes do come on subtly, and it may only be in retrospect that you or your care partner realizes the scope of the problem.

If you are noticing a number of changes in the way someone goes about their normal routines or connects with others, there is reason for you to pay serious attention. Having a general understanding of the stages that occur with dementia is helpful. However, it is important to keep in mind that everyone is unique, so your experience with this illness may differ. Any stage can last any length of time, and there is no "average" time for how long particular symptoms or concerns may last. Keep in mind that cognitive changes are always in flux. People do not stay in one static place as their illness progresses.

EARLY STAGES

Early-stage dementia is tricky. You may recognize that something is wrong with your loved one but not be able to pinpoint its origins. At the same time, your loved one may be trying to cover up their memory loss or limitations. You might notice that they have trouble finding the right word or that they use the wrong word: "I can't find my ... my ... you know ..." Or they may struggle to retrieve a word, saying, "It's just on the tip my tongue!" This can be very frustrating for them, which in turn can be upsetting to you. Here are some of the symptoms you might begin to notice:

- *Memory loss.* This is the most noticeable early change. Unlike normal forgetfulness, these memory problems occur more frequently and become more severe over time.

- *Personality changes.* You may notice observable personality changes that are affecting your relationship long before a diagnosis is determined. I've seen marriages experience big upheavals, even dissolution, before a diagnosis of dementia is even made. You may notice that your loved one is becoming more withdrawn or easily gets upset over things that, in the past, would not have affected them. They may show less interest in things that they once enjoyed and take less initiative in independently doing things. The closeness they've shared with you in the past may be missing. Long-term partners tell me that these early signs are most unsettling.

- *Automatic speech.* You may notice changes in speech patterns, such as a prevalence of "automatic speech." This might be a common phrase used over and over again, such as "yes, yes." Or you might hear more formulaic patterns of socially appropriate polite talk. Even after someone's language is seriously failing, they can make small talk by using routine phrases such as, "Thank you for coming," or "So what else is new with you?"

- *Diminished understanding.* People with early-stage dementia can read, but they may not grasp the meaning of what they're reading. They may see a sign that says, "Do not enter construction area," but not understand it. (STOP would be a clearer message for them.) Or they may appear to be enjoying a newspaper, magazine, or book but be comprehending very little.

- *Difficulty with routines.* Another sign of early-stage dementia may be that normal, routine activities are becoming more difficult. For example, it may take someone all day to mow the lawn, when normally it would take two hours. Or someone may struggle to remember all the ingredients for a recipe, or they may not have the concentration that it takes to create a meal and serve it in proper sequence.

- *Poor judgment.* Judgment may also begin to fail. People with early-stage dementia might be easily persuaded to buy something they don't need or to make unwise financial decisions. Unfortunately, that may make them more vulnerable to unscrupulous persons.

EARLY DIAGNOSIS

If some or all of these issues concern you or a loved one, it's time to talk to medical providers about what you are observing. It is critical to obtain a good diagnosis, even though, to the frustration of many, the diagnosis may not be exact. However, there is much positive research at this time, which is increasing the number of Alzheimer's cases diagnosed with greater accuracy. You might want to check out www.pbs.org/theforgetting to get a better picture of some of the more recent research, along with some helpful tools for dealing with diagnosis and treatment. (The documentary *The Forgetting* was filmed in 2004, and this site includes a retrospective discussion on what research has uncovered in the intervening years. If you want to hear the panel's discussion, click "Watch the Program" and then choose "Watch the Follow-Up Show.")

Testing can ensure two things. If the causes behind the symptoms are reversible—for example, if the symptoms are being caused by depression and malnutrition—there is treatment available. If the concerns are not reversible, it is crucial to know this as early as possible because some symptoms can be held at bay with medication. And as research goes forward, we continue to learn that there is more hope for future treatment.

I've seen many people so worried about dementia that they do not express their fears to their loved ones or their physicians. Just hearing the word *Alzheimer's* scares people, especially if they have family members who have had the disease. Some go into denial that such a process is going on for them; others self-diagnose and don't seek the diagnostic procedures that could help clarify their situation. Both approaches are fraught with potential problems.

Although it may be difficult to encourage someone you care about to go through the testing process, it is well worth the effort. Getting a realistic perspective on what you are both facing can alleviate some needless worrying. An honest picture of the illness and its effects could make your lives less stressful, and an early start on treatment could help reduce or delay the symptoms. And it will reassure you that you are doing all that you can in your particular situation.

You might approach this need for assessment by telling your care partner that you need a physical and it might be a good idea for them to get one at the same time. Another idea might be to mention that you have been doing some reading about a particular illness and the progress they have made with medication. You might gently suggest that they might want to be evaluated to see whether this might work for them. Stressing the positive aspects of reaching out for assistance is a valuable approach.

EARLY RESPONSES

People in the earlier phases of the illness may be acutely aware of such changes and losses. They may be struggling with grief, which may be expressed as anger toward those closest to them—including, or even especially, you. You can empathize and gently talk with them about their losses. It is important for you to listen and be open to what they are saying. It may be very difficult to hear what your care partner is sharing, but be wary of offering platitudes like "Everything is going to be all right." People facing these losses need to hear that you understand that this is a tough time for them. It is all right to be gently realistic and to let your care partner know that you do not have all the answers. Your care partner needs assurance that you will walk this journey with them, no matter how difficult, and that you will continue to love them.

On the practical side of things, it is important for you to create ways of protecting them if they are vulnerable. If they are showing poor judgment, you may need to be more vigilant about phone or mail solicitations, or more involved in financial decisions. If they are communicating by giving "pat responses" to someone in a social situation, you may need to step in graciously so they can maintain some dignity. All of this requires a delicate balance, and you and your loved one may find it helpful to locate a support group tailored to the particular needs of those in the early stages of dementia. Perhaps you could attend sessions together. Many care receivers have told me they found great relief in sharing their concerns in such groups because they do not "have to pretend" to be doing better than they are. They also may learn new ways of coping that had not been part of their repertoire in the past. Most of these groups stress that people do as much as they can in using the strengths that they still possess. At the same time, they advise people to reach out to others and form bonds of interdependency when there are activities and decision making that need to be shared with others.

Many times I see a lot of energy being expended on the person with an Alzheimer's diagnosis, but dementia also affects everyone around them. And I've seen carers often put the needs of their loved one ahead of their own, even to the point of neglecting self-care. As a care partner, you will need assistance, encouragement, and prayer support just as much as the one you are caring for. The strongest advice I can give is that you need to care for yourself if you want to "be there" for your loved one. This is true even in the early days of the illness process.

Once your loved one has been diagnosed, you will need some time to reflect on what is happening—for them and for you. You may be sad about the changes you are seeing and scared about what the future will bring. You may be wondering how on earth you're going to handle it all. Acknowledging your feelings and concerns, and setting up ways to take care of yourself mentally, physically, and spiritually, are especially important in this early stage so that, as the disease progresses, you will have supports in place for your well-being.

In particular, you might find it very helpful to talk with others who have the same concerns and share some of the same challenges. Support groups can help you deal with transitions, grief, and losses; cope with your feelings; and adjust to difficult changes. You will also be with people who can celebrate the small accomplishments and joys. This kind of mutual give-and-take among people who are living your experience can be an invaluable support for you as a carer.

MIDDLE STAGES

As the process of dementia unfolds, you will need to adjust your responses to your loved one. Understanding what is happening can help you deal with the practical realities you and your care partner face. Middle-stage symptoms might include the following:

- *Early-stage symptoms worsen.* Your care partner may have more difficulty in finding words and increased trouble keeping on a topic. You may notice that they have more difficulty understanding complex directions and tasks. They may forget recent events and increasingly comprehend less of what they are reading. They may begin to experience delusions (seeing things that aren't there), become obsessive, or have anxious thoughts, and they may withdraw more and more. And, perhaps most alarming, they may get lost, even in familiar places.

- *More obvious behavioral changes appear.* You may begin to see outbursts of anger or anxiety. They may become very suspicious of you. (People with dementia often direct these feelings toward those who are closest to them.) Problems with movement may start to appear, and they may not be steady on their feet. They may have disturbed sleeping patterns, which in turn can affect your sleep patterns. They may need assistance with personal care and other activities of daily living. Confusion about time worsens. As one gerontologist, Anne Basting, has expressed it, "Time slips." More and more, you may need to supervise your care partner to ensure their safety.

LATE STAGES

Late-stage dementia has its own challenges, and as a carer you may be observing many changes. Some of these include:

- *Incoherent verbalizations.* Sometimes only a core word or two is understandable.

- *Repetitive vocal and physical behaviors.*

- *Severely limited ability to understand what is being said.*

- *Increasing dependence.* In the late stages, walking, independent eating, and other skills may be lost, making your care partner more and more dependent on you.

- *Nonrecognition.* Perhaps one of the hardest times of this disease is when the person you are caring for no longer recognizes themselves, or you. Carers often describe the time of nonrecognition as a breaking point in the relationship.

- *Physical deterioration.* Swallowing problems may occur, and there may be concerns with bowel and bladder incontinence.

You may have to watch your care partner's behaviors to learn what their particular needs are; for example, when they are tired or hungry or need to use the bathroom. Through trial and error, you can learn the ebb and flow of their behaviors and, by being observant in a proactive way, you may reduce your care partner's feelings of stress. And for you as a carer, the reward is not having to be worried all the time.

- *Swearing.* Some forms of dementia cause a person to respond by swearing, which you might find personally embarrassing, especially if your care partner never talked in that manner before they were ill. It is important to remember that it is the *disease* that causes the outbursts, and that your loved one is probably not swearing on purpose.

- *Need for hospice care.* In the last stage of dementia, your care partner may require hospice care as they—and you—begin to prepare for their death. You may have to face some tough questions about how much extraordinary treatment to provide and when to say, "Enough is enough."

As you are trying to take in all the information that doctors, social workers, friends, and family may be giving you about dementia, there is one important thing you need to keep in mind: *Dementia is different for each person.* Cognitive difficulties show up in different ways, and each person struggling with dementia has their own unique path as the disease progresses.

Perhaps you've known someone who had dementia and are thinking, "I know what I'm in for." Or perhaps you've heard or read stories about people with dementia and assume that your situation will be the same. It is critical that you understand that *when you've seen one person with dementia, you have seen ONE person with dementia.* And you've seen them in a particular *phase* of dementia.

Their situation and how they respond to it is fluid, and so it will be with your loved one.

Dorothy Seman, a practitioner who specializes in working with persons with Alzheimer's disease, remarked at a National Alzheimer's Conference that it is "more important to know what person the disease has, than what disease the person has." Wise words indeed when you are exploring the unique concerns of care-sharing with someone who has dementia.

As a carer, you can use the questions below to help you get a handle on where you and your loved one are in the course of the disease process. You might also want to revisit this list again in the future.

- What are the particular signs and symptoms of the illness that my loved one is dealing with?
- How might I best respond to these?
- How is the dementia affecting my care partner today, emotionally and spiritually?
- What are my feelings as I watch my loved one change?
- How can I best take care of my needs in all this?

BUILDING EFFECTIVE COMMUNICATION

I am well aware that the list of dementia symptoms and stages can be daunting, if not downright terrifying. Yet I also know that understanding what is happening at each stage is a useful way to begin to understand how your communication with your care partner can take different forms as the dementia progresses.

In order to maximize your ability to understand and respond, the first thing I recommend is to *suspend your usual beliefs about communication*. Throughout our lives, we use communication to engage in social interactions, get our wishes met, convey information, and keep us connected to others. But because of the memory loss in all the stages of dementia, the usual means of communication no longer apply. People with dementia repeatedly ask the same questions, not remembering that they just asked, or that you've already answered. They may have trouble following a conversation, which can worsen if they have hearing problems or there is too much extraneous noise. As the illness progresses, many forget that they have a memory loss. (However, keep in mind that even persons with severe dementia can have moments of lucidity where they are frightfully aware of their situation.)

Although communication may well be one of the most difficult issues you have to deal with, keeping lines of communication open between you and your care partner is at the heart of maintaining a satisfying relationship. There is no one "best" approach. What works for one person may not work for another. What works at one time may not work at another. However, there are some general guidelines you can follow for communicating effectively with someone who has dementia.

VALIDATE THEIR FEELINGS

People with dementia have taught me to be flexible and patient, and to listen for feelings, not necessarily facts. I cannot be in a hurry with my own agenda, but need to respectfully try to enter their world. Although their feelings may not be an accurate response to what is happening, and their worldview may be "off" in some ways, whatever they are sensing is real for them in that moment.

Validating feelings is key to helping your care partner be all that they are able to be. By listening beneath the words and responding to the underlying feelings, you will be letting them know that you really hear them. At times, you may need to put their feelings into words for them. To do this, you need to enter their reality.

I think of the daughter who was visiting with her mother in a nursing home. The daughter became concerned because her mother was so anxious about the "gorilla" that entered her room at night. Although the daughter was sure that this was not happening, she made a point of being in her mother's room around sundown, when the "gorilla" reportedly came in. As she sat in the twilight, another resident, also struggling with dementia, entered the room and began going through her mother's possessions. The man had dark hair, dark clothing, and a dark beard. From the perspective of her mother's diminished eyesight and in the long shadows, the daughter saw what her mother had seen and understood her mother's perception. But to get there, the daughter first had to look at things from her mom's perspective.

You can learn a good deal by observing and trying to understand how your care partner sees the world. You probably will have to suspend your sense of reality to perceive what they perceive in order to be reassuring. This can be very difficult, but it is well worth the effort. You might consider asking yourself:

- What clues do I have about how my loved one sees the world?
- What do I know about their past that might be affecting their feelings today?
- Are there vision or hearing limitations that are affecting their perceptions? How might I help them with these?

VALIDATE THEIR STORIES

No matter what your care partner's cognitive abilities or limits are, their life narrative is still paramount. Their story tells who they are and, even if they repeat it often, or not quite accurately, it is important for you to validate each story *as it is told*. They may tell their story in snippets or in a long chronology at one time, and the facts may be way off, but the feelings are often an accurate reflection of their perceptions.

Perhaps you've heard the same story repeated so many times that, even though you remind yourself that they've forgotten how often they have told it, you're not sure you can listen *one more time.* Here are several considerations that you might find helpful:

- Each time the story is repeated, see what you can learn about how your care partner is faring that day.

- Each time you listen, remember that you are demonstrating how much you respect and care for them.

- Think of their story as a window of time that you have to make a connection and to be present to the storyteller. The quality of the moment you can share together during a story can be a gift.

You might want to check out Naomi Feil's helpful ideas in *The Validation Breakthrough.* She offers specific ways to "step into the shoes" and "see through the eyes" of a disoriented person. By utilizing these tips to empathize with the feelings behind the story, you will be respectfully listening to and accepting their worldview.

Another reason that personal stories are so important is that communication with someone who has a cognitive impairment is often dependent on knowing about past experiences and relationships. If the person you are caring for is not someone you know well or have known long, their stories can help you get to know their history and hobbies, likes and dislikes. Taking these into account will go a long way toward helping you connect with them. And you may be surprised by how much they remember. Persons with memory loss often retain their long-term memory even though they can't recall what just happened.

One creative way you can learn or share a person's history is to make what occupational therapist Carly Hellen calls a "LifeStory" book. It can include anything of significance for your care partner: their home, pictures of family, pictures of people in military uniforms, a favorite place they've been, awards they have received, their church, a pet, or whatever else might have been important to them. (You probably don't want to put original photos in the book. Color copiers are inexpensive now, so you can make prints. Cover them with plastic sleeves to provide a durable book that can stand up to thumbing through.) You and your care partner can talk together about the contents, or they might enjoy looking through their "LifeStory" book by themselves. Consider sharing this book with other family members as part of the family history.

There are also many commercial products, such as the "remembering kits" offered by Bi-Folkal (www.bifolkal.org), that can help you encourage your care partner to tell life stories. Public libraries or the Alzheimer's Association often have these available for checkout. Bi-Folkal kits contain pictures, music, "props," and questions to help people tell their stories. By getting this material together ahead of time, you can have it available to share with your loved one when you wish, and when you feel it would be a good time.

When your care partner tells you a story, consider:

- What does my loved one's story tell me?
- What practical things can I do to honor that story?
- Are there resources that I could use to make the story come alive for my loved one?

COMMUNICATE NONVERBALLY

It has been my experience that people with dementia often have finely honed nonverbal skills, at least up until the later stages of the illness. Even if they are no longer using words, a person with dementia communicates, and you can benefit from reading their clues carefully. Watch for their body language, tone of voice, gestures, eye contact, and facial expressions. The trick is, of course, to determine what their nonverbal clues mean. As you spend time with your care partner, these will become clearer. For example, when they are very tired, do they start to fidget in their chair more than usual? Do they push their plate away when they are no longer hungry? Being tuned in to these kinds of cues will help you communicate more effectively with your care partner.

Nonverbal communication is a two-way street. *Your* nonverbal communication is a powerful tool as well. Because your care partner can understand the nonverbal long after they have forgotten language, even the simplest gestures can be a source of communication. If your care partner is having trouble understanding complex thoughts in a sentence, you can use nonverbal cues, along with shorter concepts, to communicate an idea. For example, instead of telling them that it is time to wash their face, you might say, "Let's wash your face," and then take a washcloth to your face and make the motions of washing it. Your nonverbal cue will help them mirror your activity.

The importance of touch cannot be overemphasized. It is a crucial part of relationships throughout life and becomes even more important when words are gone. Touch connects you in a very physical way with your care partner and signifies your love and concern. It can communicate that you are present with them, here and now. It can comfort them when they are feeling anxious.

Often when I have been in conversation with a person with dementia and their family, I find that people start talking around the person with the dementia. While I try to steer the conversation back to the person so that they are part of the conversation, not the object of the conversation, I will take their hand or gently touch their shoulder to let them know I am there for them.

A word of caution about touch: If your care partner feels that you are rough in your touch, or coercing them in some way through that touch, this can be upsetting to them. You will need to pay attention to their responses and adjust your actions accordingly.

BE CONGRUENT

The "golden rule" of communicating with people with dementia is that what you say and what you do need to fit together. Thomas Kitwood, in his wonderful book *Dementia Reconsidered: The Person Comes First*, calls this "congruent care." Essentially, this means that fact and feeling messages match. If, for example, you tell your care partner, "I love you," but you sound angry as you say it, they will receive the message of anger. If you are speaking calming words but sounding stressed, the stress is what they will perceive. If you are trying to calm your care partner but are tugging at them to get moving, they'll pick up on your anxiety (and probably resent that you are treating them like a child). In all your communications, it is important that your actions mirror your words. Being congruent will help you stay connected.

LAUGH

Sharing simple things can be a source of mutual pleasure for you and your care partner, and perhaps the most basic pleasure is a good laugh. Some carers have told me that the only way they survive some long days is to laugh at some of the funny things in their situation. Some care receivers tell me that, in the early stages of their illness, they have effectively used humor to ease the tension that friends might feel around them. Although some subtle humor may be lost as the illness progresses, obviously funny things can still be shared. Humor can go a long way toward strengthening communication and helping with daily coping. Even something as simple as sharing a funny picture and making up a story about it, or enjoying children who do this, can introduce a bit of humor into the day. Some care partners watch videos of humorous programs together, such as reruns of *I Love Lucy*, to enjoy a good laugh. Wherever you can, create a bit of humor. As comedian Victor Borge once said, "Laughter is the shortest distance between two people."

Developing your own ways to connect with your care partner can be challenging but rewarding at the same time. As you explore ways of communicating that connect you, ultimately the most important communication is to convey to your care partner, in words and in actions, that they are loved. This will encourage their feelings of self-worth, and in that process, raise their spirits. Keeping the spirit alive—both yours and your care partner's—is probably the single most vital thing you can do in the caresharing dance with someone with dementia.

KEEPING THE SPIRIT ALIVE

Those struggling with dementia frequently ask, "What am I good for now?" If your care partner is feeling worthless or discouraged, you face a challenge to find ways to keep a sense of their spirit alive.

I vividly remember Amalia, a woman in a late-middle stage of dementia who could not always connect words together. She had her own language that took a bit of deciphering to understand. (I like the term that filmmaker Doris Chase, in *Glass Curtain*, uses for such language: "duets of disconnected memories.") Amalia had once been prominent in her community and had lived an outgoing social life. Although she was now frequently disoriented and would become lost, when she was given tea in a china teacup in the context of a social event, she was transformed into a most gracious hostess and social person. Her conversations were garbled, but her impeccable social graces still shone through. Putting her in a familiar role brought out the best in her, and she seemed to derive joy from the experience.

As a carer, there are four key things in particular that you can do to help keep your care partner's spirit alive: See the whole person, affirm their value, build on what they can still do, and meet their needs at their level.

SEE THE WHOLE PERSON

When a person has some cognitive impairment, it is important to remember that *this is only one facet of their identity.* They are still a retired worker, wife, partner, member of a faith community, friend. They still experience strong emotions and feelings, even if they are not always sure of the realities of their life or cannot verbally express their feelings. They may, in fact, be even more "tuned in" to the nonverbal cues of others and their environment. People with dementia are whole people, not victims who have lost their mental abilities.

I've seen too many situations where a person diagnosed with dementia is immediately dismissed as "less than." A poignant story I heard at an aging conference brought this point home very clearly. A gentleman diagnosed with early-stage dementia told the audience about his experience at a dinner with friends. They were enjoying a delightful meal and conversation when he mentioned that his doctor had just diagnosed him with Alzheimer's disease. After a few moments of stunned silence, the conversation started again. This time, the dinner companions included his wife in their discussions, but not him. They did not mention Alzheimer's at all.

Did this gentleman suddenly change from being one person to being another, just by divulging his diagnosis? Obviously not, yet he was treated as if he were invisible, no longer a whole person, and he was shut out of that previously pleasant evening.

This is something that you will need to be extra vigilant about to ensure that your loved one does not get locked out of interactions simply because of their diagnosis. As you learn alternative ways of interacting, you can gently share this idea of seeing the whole person with the people in your care partner's circle of friends and acquaintances.

AFFIRM YOUR CARE PARTNER'S VALUE

Ethicist Stephen Post, in his book *The Moral Challenge of Alzheimer Disease,* labels our society a "hypercognitive culture," where mental abilities are so valued that we ignore persons with memory loss. If you want to interact effectively with your care partner, you will need a different perspective. You will need to affirm their value beyond cognitive abilities. (This is equally true for those who have development disabilities or brain damage; they, too, still have much to offer.)

One of the most affirming things you can do is to talk *with,* share *with,* not *do to* a person with cognition deficits. It is important to persistently, lovingly, do what you can to enhance your care partner's sense of "personhood." Treat them as the adult they still are. Although adaptations may need to be made and things simplified as their cognitive abilities change, you need to guard against treating them like a child. They are an adult struggling with the loss of some of their faculties.

Call them by the name they choose. Encourage them to speak for themselves in whatever way they can. Remember to consciously include them in discussions when friends visit. And when you ask them something, wait for a response. Too often there is a tendency to talk around a person with mental limits or to talk too rapidly for them to comprehend. Then the person becomes invisible.

I like the perspective that Virginia Bell and David Troxel offer in *A Dignified Life: The Best Friends Approach to Alzheimer's Care* (www.bestfriendsapproach.com). They recommend connecting with your care partner as you might with a best friend. By employing the basic elements found in any good friendship—respect, empathy, support, trust, humor—you can help your care partner feel safe and valued. You will be adding to their quality of life and reinforcing their sense of self-worth. Consider what qualities of friendship you have had with your care partner in the past that you can build on at this point in their illness process.

BUILD ON WHAT YOUR CARE PARTNER CAN STILL DO

Another way to keep your care partner's spirit alive is to build on what they can still do. It may take some creativity on your part, and you may need to take the initiative to set up things to do, but encouraging the things they can do will help them—and you—stay connected, and it will shore up their sense of self-worth.

As their dementia progresses, you will need to "fill in the blanks" more to compensate for their lost skills. You want them to have a failure-free experience. One wife, referring to her artist husband, put it this way: "He used to do creative things; now he does created things." When her husband, who had been an accomplished painter, could no longer organize the steps needed to paint independently, she put out the paint and prepared the canvas for him so he was again able to paint.

The adage "Use it or lose it" is true. If you do not encourage your care partner to do the things they can, their abilities will atrophy, and they will lose a key part of their identity. If, for example, your care partner used to sing a lot but has grown quieter, when you do hear them singing, you might say, "You have a beautiful voice. I love hearing you sing." Or if they have been active members in their faith community, you might look for ways to help them continue to participate.

A pastor told the story of a woman who had been a reader for Sunday worship. As her dementia progressed, she still read beautifully but was not always sure where to begin and end the day's lesson. Her congregation developed a "buddy system" for her so that when it was her turn to read, a friend would accompany her to the lectern, point to the passage's beginning, and stand next to her as she read. Then the friend would point out the ending, and they would walk from the lectern together. The congregation had found a way to creatively build on her ability as an accomplished lector. Encouraging her to share in this familiar ritual connected her meaningfully with the worship service and with the people of her faith community.

Keep encouraging your care partner to engage in meaningful activities. It doesn't have to be something big; look for small ways. Your care partner still has a need to feel that they can contribute in some way. Explore what options there are in your community for them to become involved in helping or supporting a cause. I know, for example, of a church-sponsored adult day center that stuffs envelopes for fund-raisers, and it gives participants an opportunity to feel that they can do something of value for someone.

In whatever ways you can, encourage your care partner to share and to contribute as much as they can for as long as they are able, as long as it does not increase their frustration or create a safety hazard. As you find your way along this path, be sensitive to clues they give you about what they like and don't like, and adapt to their deficits so they can have success.

MEET YOUR CARE PARTNER'S NEEDS AT THEIR LEVEL

To keep the spirit alive, it is important to know where your care partner is in the progression of the illness. How is it for *them?* At any particular time, they may be showing symptoms of more than one stage of dementia, or they may be having a "good" day, when they are functioning fairly well. Some days, you may need to make sure your care partner's glasses are on, their hearing aid is in place, and they are in a spot where they can see you. Or you may need to assist them in remembering meaningful things.

Because of these shifting differences, you need to try to meet their needs at their level *as they are that day.* You need to pitch your conversation to their level of understanding *at that time.* Although this may be difficult at times, by doing this you can build on what is still whole in them.

Many carers tell me that there is a lot of trial and error in finding the right balance between offering help and promoting independence, so I encourage you to keep practicing this delicate balancing act. The benefits are worth the effort. By meeting your care partner at their level, you will be maximizing your connection and helping them—and yourself—come to terms with the changes in both of your lives.

DEALING WITH DIFFICULT BEHAVIORS

Make no mistake: Coping with dementia is very difficult. Dementia can cause people to act in unpredictable, sometimes unsafe, ways, and such behaviors can frustrate—or scare—you and force you to face even bigger concerns. How can you keep your care partner safe without taking away too much independence and autonomy? Is it possible to affirm who they are and still take care of your own needs as a caregiver? Here are several approaches that I've found helpful.

WHAT'S GOING ON HERE?

You may continually need to remind yourself that the person you are caring for is *not* acting out on purpose to make your life miserable. Changes in their behavior have many causes, including physical discomfort, pain, infection, overstimulation (usually from an environment that is too busy or too loud), unfamiliar surroundings or an inability to recognize home, complicated tasks or having difficulty with activities, and frustrating interactions. These all may significantly affect your care partner.

Each time behavioral issues become troublesome, try to identify the specific challenges and consider alternate solutions. Try to keep levelheaded. I know that it is easy to feel overwhelmed at times, and that it can be hard to stop and pinpoint the specific causes, but if you can keep a calm attitude and matter-of-factly try to identify the source of the particular behavior at hand, you can bring comfort to both you and your care partner, and take steps to keep the behavior from raging out of control.

THE ABC APPROACH

One successful method of dealing with difficult behaviors is the "ABC approach," used extensively at the University of Washington in their Alzheimer's research. The approach has three key components:

1. *Antecedent.* First, determine what was going on just before you observed the behavior. What seemed to trigger it? Did the environment or you somehow contribute to the behavior? Was it too noisy or were you rushed when the incident happened?

2. *Behavior.* Once you've identified what triggered the behavior, try to identify what actually happened. What specific behavior did you see? For example, rather than observing that your care partner was angry, it is more helpful to recognize that they shook their fists or hit the table. Then you have a specific way of acting that you can watch for.

3. *Consequences.* Then look at the response to the behavior. How did you or others react? Did you get angry yourself? Did you move your care partner away from the situation? Identify specifically what you did and how effective it was. A word of caution: At times, negative behaviors are reinforced when people receive added attention that they did not receive when things were on an even keel.

When you have examined all these factors, you will be better able to consider ways to resolve or deal with the difficult behavior.

POTENTIAL SOLUTIONS

When you are trying to figure out potential solutions to a particularly problematic behavior, ask yourself the following questions. Your thoughtful consideration will not only help you deal with the behavior in the moment, but will also help you design preventive approaches to head off the behavior in the future:

- What might my care partner need?
- What can I do to change the environment to reduce the behavior?
- Most important, what can I do to change how I am reacting?

However you approach a difficult behavior, you still need to be affirming of your care partner. At the same time, you also need to be honest about your own frustrations so you can deal with them and not let your frustrations spill over into communications with your care partner. There is a delicate balance here. If you can, and if your care partner is in a safe situation and not in immediate danger of falling or hurting you or someone else, take a deep breath and move out of the situation mentally for a moment. Try not to get agitated yourself; this will only exacerbate the situation.

CONNECTING SOUL TO SOUL

Despite all the debilitating changes that accompany the progression of dementia, there is one truth that you can hang on to: No matter how extensive your care partner's memory loss is, no matter how difficult their behavior becomes, the core of the person is still there; the spiritual remains. And you can build many connections on this spiritual base. The spiritual is one facet of a person's life that does not totally depend on cognitive abilities. You can access your care partner's soul when other avenues seem blocked.

Even when people do not understand things on a cognitive level, I am convinced that they comprehend in their heart, and it is in the heart and soul that most of us experience the spiritual throughout our lives. I believe that connecting soul to soul is the root of sharing between care partners when one of them has a memory loss. When you can access the soul, and not worry so much about the mental limitations, a whole world opens up.

This image of connecting soul to soul was presented to me many years ago when I heard someone ask a resident assistant in a nursing home, "Isn't it difficult to work with people who have severe memory loss?" She answered, "No, I just communicate soul to soul."

Shortly after I heard this, I was with a woman who was valiantly trying to share an idea with me. Her advanced dementia made it impossible for her to get all her words out. She was frustrated, and I gently reassured her by telling her about connecting soul to soul. She tenderly stroked my face and responded, "I like that ... I really like that."

This idea of a soul-to-soul link continues to resonate for me as the most powerful approach in connecting with those with dementia. Donald McKim's excellent book of essays, *God Never Forgets: Faith, Hope, and Alzheimer's Disease*, makes the important point that God never forgets us, even when we might not remember important facts. God remembers even when a person forgets who they are or who the people in their care network are. The community around them may not know how best to talk with them, yet God stays with them. When other people stop interacting with them, the Presence of Love is constant. Even with their limitations, people with dementia are always much loved by God. Through love and relationships, the sense of being cared for and the connection "soul to soul" happens.

A chaplain in an assisted-living center shared an illustration that captures this truth. Ruby, a former missionary, entered the dining room in her church-related center wearing an odd mix of clothing. As often happened, this garish ensemble elicited loud negative comments from her peers. Understandably upset by these remarks, she left in tears. A chaplain who visited with her later that day gently encouraged Ruby to ask the staff for assistance in dressing . Ruby agreed that maybe she was beginning to need that help.

Then Ruby sadly asked the chaplain, "Will I eventually forget even my name?" The minister honestly responded, "You might … but I will not forget your name, and more importantly, God will not forget your name."

You may need to emphasize this reassurance over and over for the person you are caring for, and for other people in the network of care. There are many things you can do to share the spiritual together, even into the latter stages of dementia. Since long-term memory remains well into cognitive decline, your care partner can still access liturgies and rituals, prayers, and music that they learned early in life. I've listed some ideas below for keeping this soul-to-soul connection alive, but I also urge you to be open to holy moments that can emerge spontaneously. The simplicity of your care partner's faith may lead you to a new understanding of your own spiritual truths.

LITURGIES AND RITUALS

Although mental ability may be needed to understand the commandments and tenets of religions, it does not take full cognition or speech to experience liturgies and rituals. Your care partner may welcome hearing or participating in liturgies and rituals that they learned as a younger person. It is best to use the versions and the language that they are familiar with. You may also need to simplify more complex rituals. Remember, even if your care partner's response is slightly unusual, the rituals still have meaning for them.

I think of a woman named Nicole, whose pastor brought her the sacrament of Communion. He spoke the traditional words over the bread and wine and gave her the wafer. When he handed her the small Communion cup, she held it delicately in her hand like a glass of fine wine. She asked, "Is this wine?" He responded,

"Well, yes, Nicole, it is," to which she answered, "Well, here's to you and to me."

Although her response to the Eucharist was unorthodox, from the pastor's liturgical tradition, he did not try to correct her. He later made the comment, "Maybe Nicole understood the Communion of all believers better than my parishioners on Sunday mornings!" At a deeper level, the pastor understood Nicole's connection to the sacred, and he was leaving it to the Spirit to make whatever adjustments needed to be made.

PRAYERS

The ability to pray is something that remains with people even in the advanced stages of dementia, and their prayers often get to the heart of the matter quite quickly. You may need to pray aloud to help rekindle their memories. Or you may need to encourage them by doing whatever they are familiar with to create an ambience for prayer, such as folding your hands, bowing your head, or kneeling, so they will mirror your behavior. Using familiar prayers from their tradition, such as the Lord's Prayer in the Christian tradition, can be a good place to start. A meditation chant that they might have used in the past can be comforting to a person who has practiced an Eastern religious tradition. The Shema (the foundational prayer in Judaism proclaiming faith in one God) might be significant for someone of Jewish faith. Blessings over a meal or table grace are also easy prayers to share.

Over and over again, I have been amazed by the fervency of the prayers shared by persons with dementia, as were my friend Linda's. In her women's prayer group, Linda's prayers for the world and social concerns were as strong as they had ever been. Despite the fact that her dementia was encroaching into other areas of her life, her prayer life was still very real and alive, and gave her a good deal of comfort.

SYMBOLS

When memory and words fail, symbols become very important. A Christian might welcome a Bible or a cross, or, if they are Catholic, a rosary. A Native American might respond to eagle feathers. Someone from an Islamic tradition may be comforted by having a Qur'an or Misbaha (prayer beads) brought to them. A Jewish person may respond to having a *kippah* placed on their head or a tallit (prayer shawl) draped around their shoulders. Consider which cues you could bring in to help create a sacred space for sharing the spiritual. If you are not familiar with your care partner's faith traditions, you may need to find out what has meaning for them. Or you may need to experiment with symbols familiar to both you and your loved one to see which ones they respond to.

OLD SONGS AND HYMNS

Old songs and hymns can get through when words and other means of communication fail, and they provide an important connection to the spiritual. I have observed almost totally nonverbal people share a favorite hymn or song. Anne was one such person. Her dementia had progressed to the point where it had left her only humming and making unintelligible sounds. One day, by accident, I was singing the old Sunday school song "Heavenly Sunshine" as I visited with her. Her eyes lit up, and she began to sing the song with me. I cannot say for certain that it connected to her soul, but I firmly know that the music connected us in sacred space.

If you don't already know, find out which hymns and gospel songs are well known in your care partner's tradition and, if you can, which songs were their favorites. (Be sure to locate the old forms of these hymns, as newer versions may have changed the words.) These favorite hymns—sung, played live, or listened to on a recording by the bedside—may become especially meaningful as the person's condition deteriorates. I've seen many times how familiar music has been very comforting to those who were in the dying process.

FAMILIAR TEACHINGS

One wife found another way to share the spiritual with her husband, who had been a teacher in their church's adult Sunday school classes. She encouraged him to "teach" her Sunday school lessons that were still deep in his early memory. He found a sense of meaning and purpose in something he had always enjoyed, and together they reflected on biblical passages. This sharing kept a strong connection between them. Though the discussions were not as cognitively satisfying as they might once have been, they were still very important for both partners.

Again, learning about your care partner's spiritual teachings may take a little research on your part, if you have not grown up in the same religious tradition. You may need to consult a rabbi or imam or priest from your care partner's tradition for ideas on what might be most meaningful to them. A Jewish person might welcome hearing a recitation of the Shema; a Muslim, *al-Fatihah;* a Christian, Psalm 23 or John 3:16.

THE FAITH COMMUNITY

Helping your faith community understand what is happening with your care partner can go a long way toward their acceptance of your care partner in formalized worship. Keep in mind, however, that there is a delicate balance between informing the congregation of any special concerns and maintaining respect for your care partner as they were and are. You will want to be careful to avoid revealing any confidential medical information. You will also need to be careful to convey that you are sharing information so your care partner can remain an active participant in the community of faith, not that they are in some ways weak or "less than" others.

I think of Edith, who came to church with her carer. As a long-time member of her church, she was much loved as a teacher in the community and as a Sunday school teacher, by young and old alike.

Even though she would often mix up parts of the service, there was a general feeling of acceptance of her limits among her congregation, and she appeared comfortable in these familiar surroundings.

One day after church, she greeted me and asked, "Are you still working at the Lutheran Home?" I answered, "Yes, I am." Then she responded, "God bless your ministry!" Only a moment later she was standing at the church door, clearly confused about what she was supposed to do next. That blessing, offered in a rare moment of lucidity, strengthened me. It is always good to be open to such grace-filled moments and celebrate them when they occur. They can provide a lot of encouragement when things are not going well.

In my years of practice, I have found that the creative arts offer a broad avenue of soul-to-soul connection that is closely linked to the spiritual. Even for people who don't think of themselves as creative or artistic, the arts convey a life force so powerful that many have written about creativity as being an expression of God in us. New research shows the connection between the arts and improving the brain's function. (See the National Center for Creative Aging, www.creativeaging.org, for more information.) Even in people who have limited language or expression, there is still something that responds to the beauty and joy of the arts. The arts can greatly enhance the communication and relationship between you and your care partner, and enable you to share in meaningful ways despite their cognitive limits. Here are a few ideas you might want to consider to help you and your care partner share this special spiritual connection.

MUSIC
Music can be an important link in sharing between care partners because it can get through when other forms of communication fail. Because music stimulates the most basic part of the brain—the

brain stem—people who have difficulty processing language can still appreciate and respond to music, especially if it is familiar music from their past. As neurologist Oliver Sacks has written, "It is the inner life of music which can still make contact with their inner lives which can awaken the hidden, seemingly extinguished soul."

Music not only has the power to stir memories and stimulate movement, but it can also bring emotions you thought dormant to the surface. However, it is important to recognize that no one "music prescription" fits all. Just as you have musical preferences, so, too, does your care partner. The music that may be soothing for you may be far from relaxing to them. Classical music may be your favorite, but they may like the "big band" sound. If you need to, ask around to find out what your care partner likes. Or try playing music that was popular in their teens or twenties. Whether your care partner responds with smiles or tears, moving to the music or simply tapping their foot, the moment will open a door for you to experience a sacred connection with them.

Another facet of music that you might not ordinarily think of is writing music together. This can be a powerful way to interact. In my community, Judith-Kate Friedman and her colleague at Songwriting Works are doing excellent work with people with dementia (www.songwritingworks.org). Their process, which they liken to "musical mural painting," invites people to collaborate on the story and music that goes into a song. It helps people who are cognitively impaired connect with others in a group, connect with their memories, and stay in touch with their personhood. The depth of the music created by this project is amazing and reveals the spiritual dimension of the participants' lives. Even if you don't consider yourself a songwriter, you could still adapt Friedman's ideas for one-to-one sharing by using a familiar tune and collaborating with your care partner to add lyrics based on their memories.

ART AND PICTURES

Exploring art and pictures is another way to touch a deeper spiritual core. I know of a memory-loss group in a Canadian care center, which calls themselves the "circle of friends," that fashioned a banner depicting hands in a circle. I was fascinated when I later visited a similar group in a California facility, and they had developed a poster decorated with hands as well. What a wonderful image of those who, despite their dementia, were sharing hands, heart, and art!

Creating art can be a wonderful way for you to share some spirit-filled time with your care partner. Even as memories fade, the capacity for imagination still exists. You might encourage your care partner to paint or draw. They might depict something they have in their own mind, and you might need to suspend your judgment about what it is, but you will still be able to connect with their inner spirit and they will be able to connect with the inventive part of themselves. If your care partner has previously been a competent artist, they might still be able to create a delightful picture.

If your care partner is able, consider taking them to an art museum where you could enjoy the color and the paintings together. Alternatively, looking at art books or simple pictures together is another way to connect through the pleasure of the visual arts. Colorful photos of familiar things, or pictures from magazines, can make emotional memory come alive.

If your care partner is experiencing the later stages of dementia, they may only nod or smile. But if the one you are caring for is in the earlier stages, they may be able to make up a story about the picture. In her breakthrough work, Anne Basting, director of the Center on Age and Community, has used pictures that tell a story to enable those with dementia to develop whole scenarios. (See www.timeslips.org for examples of the humorous pictures that have been used as discussion starters for writing skits.)

POETRY

Using poetry is another avenue for creative communication that encourages the spiritual. The rhythm and rhyme of words can be pleasing to share, and even people in the late stages of dementia can still remember lines they memorized early in school. If your care partner grew up in a Jewish or Christian tradition, the psalms are especially good as poetry and can bring a rich spiritual dimension to your sharing. Or you might want to develop a poem around a spiritual theme, such as being thankful or praising the Creator for a beautiful day.

When I write group poetry with people with dementia, we pick a topic and talk about it, using pictures and props to get some discussion flowing. Then each person shares an image for the poem we're going to create. In one group, where summer was the general topic for the poem, the participants offered the following images: "Hot hot it's too dang hot ... running through the dewy grass in the morning ... ice cream holidays." We then fashioned these images into a group poem that we shared together and later posted for family and staff to see. Wonderful word pictures came alive for these people who had severe memory deficits. And their spirits were touched as well.

If poetry reading or writing is something you might want to try with your care partner, check out the nonprofit organization Alzheimer's Poetry Project (www.alzpoetry.com) for further ideas. Here's just a taste of the possibilities, posted on their website:

> The people we serve are often in late stages of Alzheimer's and have a hard time holding a conversation or, in some cases, even speaking. When you see and hear them respond to the poems by saying words and lines along with the poet, it can be quite moving. When you hear them laugh at a funny poem, or see their tears start to flow when hearing a poignant poem, the effectiveness of reading these old

poems the patients learned as children is apparent. Often a mother in late stage Alzheimer's will not recognize family members. For a daughter to read poems to her mother and have the mother respond emotionally can offer the daughter a connection she needs and craves.

Connecting soul to soul is possible and will go a long way toward affirming the one you are caring for. With a little imagination and a lot of patience, both of you can still be in a meaningful relationship, despite, and maybe even because of, the dementia. Connecting in this way enables the dance of caresharing to continue.

As you strive to have the most meaningful relationship you can with your loved one, keep these ideas in mind:

- Learn as much as you can about where your loved one is in the disease process so you can understand and communicate in supportive ways.

- Use nonverbal communication to get through when words do not.

- Keep your "fact and feelings" messages congruent.

- Validate your care partner's stories and feelings, even if they are not totally "realistic."

- Affirm your care partner's abilities and build on what they can still do.

- Remember that behaviors, though difficult, are challenges that can be worked through.

- Utilize the creative arts to connect you and your loved one in new ways.

- Connect soul to soul, remembering that you and your loved one are precious children of God.

5

SHARING GRIEF

Coping with the "Large" and the "Little" Losses

THE PRESENCE OF GRIEF

Grief and loss—and the resulting sadness—are constant companions in caregiving. Even if they are not spoken about, these feelings are present. Our society tends to think of grief only as it relates to death, dying, and bereavement. And while it is true that many care partners face these "large" losses in the future, there are many "little" losses in the present that can create large concerns.

Knowing how grief and sadness affect everyone in the care-sharing setting will not only help assuage the intensity of grief but will also go a long way toward helping everyone cope. Be aware of *all* the losses involved and don't be afraid to speak about them. It is also important to remember that grief is a normal response to any kind of loss, at any age.

My hope, in this chapter, is to give you some helpful insights and tools to use as you navigate the losses that disability and aging can bring. As you read, you may find that some of your feelings mirror those of the people in the examples presented, while others do not. Keep in mind along the way that your experience is uniquely your own. Each of us deals with loss and grief in our own way.

FACING TRANSITIONS

Transitions and losses of many kinds are part and parcel of our middle and later years. Going from full-time work to retiree status, downsizing from a large house to a small apartment, or watching children move to other cities are just a few common examples.

As a caregiver, you are also likely to be facing transitions in your priorities, your daily living routines, and your emotions. One of the things I often suggest to caregivers, and I offer this to you as well, is to sit for a few moments with these three questions to clarify exactly what it is you are facing.

To whom are the changes happening? The first and most obvious answer is that your care partner is the one experiencing changes. Yet the changes that are happening to them are affecting you as well. For example, if your care partner has suffered a paralyzing stroke, you may feel the stress of a change in lifestyle as intensely as, or sometimes more than, they do.

How are the changes affecting you or your care partner? Although it is natural to look ahead and think about what may happen, to ask "What if?" and "How will I ...?," take some time to focus on what is happening now. What are the day-to-day changes—in functioning, in emotions, in spirits, in physical changes? Be sure to consider the changes that both you and your care partner are experiencing.

How have you or your care partner dealt with change in the past? Under the stress of a caresharing situation, it is easy to forget that you and your care partner have used your strengths in the past to "get through" difficult situations. It is good to remind yourselves that these strengths have gotten you to where you are now. Are any of these ways that you could employ to get through this time? Talking with others—especially in a caregiver support group or in one-to-one counseling or with a spiritual advisor—and reflecting on what you have done in the past may help you find strength to deal with the present situation.

The transitions of change and loss can be bumpy. You or your care partner may have times of feeling really "up," when you experience something good. Then there may be "down times" of sadness, times of trying to find out the meaning (the why) of what you are going through. And there also may be times when one or the other of you gets "stuck" in one place for a while.

There is no "rule" about the transitions of grief, nor is there any precise way to experience grief. Most people go through some "normal" grief stages, including shock and denial, emerging awareness and intense emotion, and then a reengagement in life or some resolution to the losses. The important thing to know is that there is no particular way that you and your care partner *should* do this, and that you will bounce back and forth in your feelings. As you walk the grief road, you will likely encounter griefs from the past and anticipate future griefs, but the journey of facing losses starts with where you and your care partner are right *now*.

FACING LOSSES

When someone dies, we all understand and respond to this "big loss." We recognize it as an important event, and we have proscribed rituals that help us deal with the grief. We sit shivah, we go to a wake, we attend a memorial or funeral. We are used to sharing the grief of death with those who are hurting—whether it's with casseroles or hugs or flowers—and we do what we can to help.

But when a person is aging or dealing with chronic illness, there are many transitions and "little losses" that often go unrecognized or unnamed. Because there are no rituals for these times, many people don't know how to respond to these sadnesses in a helpful way. Even those who are attempting to offer support may say or do something that has just the opposite effect. Many people have recounted how comments offered by someone trying to comfort them felt hurtful. (If this happens in your situation, try to understand that the person is not being deliberately mean; rather, their response likely comes out of not knowing what to say.)

In a caresharing scenario, what might seem like a "little loss" to an outside observer may be a very big loss for the person who is experiencing it. One of the loving things you can do for your care partner is to honor and recognize that each loss is uniquely theirs. "Little losses" can have a cumulative effect, and the person you are caring for is suffering the emotional and spiritual consequences. Each loss is real and painful for them, no matter how "small" it might seem in the face of other, more serious concerns.

Take a look at the following examples of some of the more common losses that people who are aging, ill, or disabled experience. Which of these apply to your caresharing situation? What would you add to this list?

LOSS OF PETS

One example of what some might consider a "little loss" that I see often is the loss of a pet. Many people do not realize the deep sharing in pet-to-person connections. If your care partner has had to give up a beloved cat or dog—say, because their new assisted-living complex prohibits pets, or because they have moved in with you and there is no room for a pet—it can be a big blow. One of the most caring things you can do is understand the significance of this pet in their lives. Ask them who gave them the pet. What was the funniest thing their pet ever did? What were some of the things they liked to do with their pet? Listen carefully as they share with you. Be aware as well that their grief about the loss of their pet can be a mirror of their grief about loved ones who have died, or about their own failing health or aging, or even grief about their own dying.

✐ Consider making a memorial book or album with your care partner to celebrate the life of their pet. You could look at it together from time to time and share some "pet stories."

LOSS OF HOME

Moving from a home of fifty years is a lot harder than some people believe. Giving up the "stuff" of life can be overwhelming. Things such as books, dishes, and pictures hold memories, and telling their stories while sorting through a lifetime of objects can take a long time and be extremely draining—physically and emotionally.

If your care partner is facing the loss of a home, you will need to give them time to gently and quietly process each memento of life, especially if it is the family home in which they raised their children (perhaps including you!) or a home in which they've built a life. The overpowering sadness is very difficult to process, and the experience of moving is a powerful emotional and spiritual transition.

If the home has many memories for you as well, you are likely dealing with your own struggles with grief. You might find it helpful to have a person to journey with you, such as a spiritual advisor or another counselor, to help you sort out your own feelings. Having a third party who will listen to the full range of your emotions can also help you balance the level of grief you decide to share with your care partner. At the same time, don't close off avenues for reciprocal sharing. Times of laughter and tears over shared "house memories" can be very treasured and healing.

You may also need to remind younger family members who have a sense of "let's get on with it" about the meaning and importance of this "stuff." There is a tendency to "get this stuff packed up." But this sorting through the mementos of a lifetime can be turned into a time of intergenerational learning and sharing that will help the entire family make this transition, as stories are shared and physical things are divided up among those who might enjoy them.

✍ Consider planning a time when you and your loved one can say "good-bye" to a well-loved home before moving. Some people perform a "good-bye ritual" that is something similar to a "house blessing" that people do when they move into a new place. They go through the home room by room, sharing the memories of that space, and then say a prayer or sing a hymn. Something of this nature might be a very helpful way for you and your care partner to process your grief.

LOSS OF ABILITIES

As a carer, you probably know more than anyone else what your care receiver's physical losses are. Things they used to do easily may be very difficult, or even impossible, now. Be sensitive to how *they* are experiencing this loss. Are they angry? Frustrated? Ready to face the challenge? Discouraged?

You can help by "hearing them out." Listen to what they are feeling about their day-to-day routines, whether it concerns feeding or bathing or hygiene, mental lapses, or physical weakness. As a care partner, you might want to share with them how sad you feel about their declining health. And you may be able to find ways to adapt situations so that they are not so daunting.

One woman who had suffered a stroke, which left her somewhat unable to speak clearly and unsure of who people were in her life, took a picture of all the important people in her life and labeled each with their name to help her remember. As she needed to, she could point to these pictures to let people know which person she was talking about.

Let your care partner know that you want to hear what is hard for them and how they are feeling about it. That way you can share the grief and explore new ways together of compensating for the losses.

🔏 Consider bringing home some adaptive devices, such as a special chair to put in the shower to make bathing safer and more comfortable, which will help your care partner cope with their losses. If at all possible, give them choices about which model might work best for them.

LOSS OF FRIENDS

One of the things I often see as a person ages and their health fails is that their friends are aging and failing at the same time. At the very point when they need good friends, sickness makes these friends unavailable. In addition, as people reach their older years, the death of friends also becomes a fact of life and, one by one, they see their support systems diminishing. Ties to friends can also be severed by distance. As their health declines, friends move to be closer to family or they move into nursing homes or assisted-living facilities.

Loss of friends also happens when a person's cognitive abilities begin to fail. Someone who was once an active partner in a bridge group, for example, may now be treated as a fifth wheel among old friends. Or your care partner may be embarrassed to be around old friends, not wanting others to see their "failings." Or friends who feel uncomfortable around someone with memory loss may gradually begin to show up less often.

You can help to some degree by inviting people in to visit, but a wider range of social contact may just not be possible. Though you can never replace your care partner's old friends, you can listen and understand what their friends meant to them, and what they still need from you and others as a friend. You may also need to gently coach long-term friends on how to best communicate with your care partner.

There's one more thing: In all the attention on your care partner's loss of participation and interaction, don't forget your own losses. Perhaps you've had to limit your social interactions because you need to be home for your care partner. Maybe you feel as if you've lost your "best friend." You may be missing a conversation partner at dinner, times of intimacy, and easy companionship with them. How are you feeling about your own loss of friends and, perhaps, your partner as you once knew them?

Too often care partners feel a need to "protect" each other from these difficult feelings, and then you both lose valuable opportunities for communication. The more you can share with each other, the less alone each of you will be.

- Consider the possibility of making whatever arrangements might be needed (such as a wheelchair and transport service, if necessary) to take your care partner to a place where their friends gather, even if it is just for a short visit. For example, arranging for a special visit to their church might be very much appreciated. By going the "extra mile" to help your care partner reconnect, you will be letting them know that you recognize how important their friends are and how difficult it is for them not to see their friends as often as they would like.

LOSS OF FREEDOM

If you or your care partner has always been a person who drove places and made spontaneous decisions, the loss of freedom just to "do" something at the time you think about it can be very hard on you. In dealing with illness or disability, you might have to make alternative arrangements for getting somewhere, or enlist someone to go with you on an outing to assist you and your care partner. It takes advance notice and planning to do these things. Giving up this freedom is difficult and not to be underestimated. It takes much adaptation on everyone's part to make it work. It is important for you to recognize how this loss of freedom has affected both you and your care partner.

- Consider which activities you and your care partner really like to do and make special dates to go out to something you both enjoy once a month. Take into account all the advance planning that you need to make sure the outing goes smoothly.

LOSS OF HOPES AND DREAMS

You and your care partner might have made plans for the future or been looking forward to retirement, maybe traveling and spending time with grandchildren. Perhaps you and your partner dreamed of growing old together, but in your middle years, one of you has been diagnosed with inoperable cancer. Loss of hopes and dreams for the future can be as much a cause for grief for you as for your partner, and these losses may be especially painful because a good deal of your time and thinking, and often money, have been tied up in those dreams.

I think of one gentleman who was on a trip to Europe by himself, using the itinerary he had developed with his wife years earlier. He told people he met that he was doing it as a memorial for his wife. When she was first diagnosed and could have traveled, he had been too busy working to take the time for this trip.

I'm not suggesting that you and your care partner dash off on a trip to Europe before it's too late. There may be ways to live a piece of your dream now, even if it is not quite how you pictured it. I know one elderly woman who had always wanted to see where her family came from in the Netherlands before she died. Her daughter found an inland waterway cruise that allowed for her mother to be in her wheelchair and still see the countryside and small towns. You might be able to adapt your plans in some way, even if it takes some creative thinking to work out the alternatives. Enlist others in your care network to help you with your plans. Even if leaving the house is not feasible, you might host an "armchair travelogue" in your home by renting a movie or inviting people to bring movies of their trips.

> ✐ Consider whether there is a part of your hopes and dreams that you could adapt and do now or enjoy in some way now.

Even if neither you nor your care partner uses the term *grief,* it is nonetheless omnipresent in the life losses of aging and disability. Sometimes these "ordinary" griefs are not clearly visible, which means they may go unacknowledged. Yet when these losses occur, everyone in the care system can be affected. Some may experience stress. Others may be sad or depressed. Still others (both caregivers and care receivers) may be angry. Arguments may ensue about what is "more" or "less" important. Everyone is different, and there is no one way that people approach these changes.

Of paramount importance is that you and your care partner "be with" each other emotionally and spiritually as much as possible. At the close of this chapter, I'll offer some specific suggestions that might help you walk this journey together and be open to allowing others to accompany you.

DIMENSIONS OF GRIEF

Grief is multifaceted. The way that you or your care partner reacts to a loss might depend on when it happens, or your age, or how many other losses precede it. Grief can vary in intensity, according to how you are feeling physically and emotionally. It can surface before, during, or after a loss. And it can have many layers left over from previous grief experiences. Each of these variables needs to be considered when you are dealing with the losses in a caresharing scenario.

ANTICIPATORY GRIEF

A common aspect of grieving is not about what someone has *already* lost, but what they *expect* to lose. Anticipatory grieving arises from future losses your care partner expects, and it can surface in many areas.

Your care partner, for example, may be having trouble keeping up with work around the house, and they know that they will soon need to leave their beloved home. Long before moving day arrives, they may start mourning the upcoming loss. Each painful disposition of a possession or memento of meaning may be a catalyst for another round of grieving. Actually, the giving away of treasured things can be a double-edged sword. If a person gives a book, for example, to someone they know will enjoy it, this gift-giving may make them happy, knowing that the book will continue to be valuable to someone. But if the reason they are giving up the book is that the print is too small and they cannot read it, this may be very sad indeed.

Or perhaps your care partner is scheduled for an upcoming surgery where they expect to lose a body part, such as a breast because of cancer or a foot because of diabetes. Or, if they are going though chemotherapy, they may dread losing their hair. Some women and men deeply mourn this loss long before it actually happens.

If you are caring for someone who has Alzheimer's, you and your care partner may experience pre-loss grieving about the massive changes that will inevitably come and the resulting loss of relationship ahead, as memory loss becomes more and more acute. Some have called living with Alzheimer's a "funeral with no ending." As each of you tries to cope with the present, you are already grieving the next effects of the illness.

Similarly, if you are caring for someone who is inch by inch losing their physical abilities due to extreme old age or illness, either or both of you may experience times of being overwhelmed by anticipatory grief. I have heard this gradual failing called "the dwindles," and each noticeable loss can cause sadness for the present as well as grief for what is yet to come.

An especially difficult anticipatory grief comes when you know you are losing a care partner to a terminal illness. Either or both of you may have periods when you are flooded with a sense of loss about what is to come. It is important to recognize that, because each person deals with grief in their own way, your way of grieving and your care partner's way of grieving may look totally different. One of you may be weepy, while the other is more reserved, but that does not mean that the reserved one is not grieving. As Elisabeth Kübler-Ross explained in her groundbreaking work about death and dying, people tend to die "in character." In other words, people die in much the same way as they live. For example, if a person has always been introspective and kept their own counsel, they may not display or disclose the "expected" signs of grief. Others in the family may feel as if the one who is dying is not realistically facing up to their situation. In truth, both the family and the person dying are grieving; the one who is dying is simply experiencing grief in character with who they are.

I had a clear example of this in my own life with my father-in-law, who, when he was told he did not have much time to live, made appointments with his accountant and lawyer and set up all the paperwork for his wife's benefit. Then he went to the basement and labeled all his tools. He was not a person who would communicate with us about his dying, even though we wanted to talk through our loss and grief at losing him. He had been a stoic person in life, so indeed he died "in character." Though this was difficult for those involved in his care in his last days, his way of anticipatory grieving was to take care of his business to ease life for his family after his death. And it did give us some comfort in the days that followed.

The methods of helping and coping with anticipatory grief are much the same as dealing with "normal" grief, which I'll say more about later, but I want to point out a few ideas here that could be especially helpful for you and your care partner in dealing with anticipatory grieving.

- Plan a farewell celebration for a much-loved house before you start packing. If possible, invite people who have memories associated with that house to join you. Include time for your care partner, guests, and yourself to describe your most memorable events in the house.

- Go shopping with your care partner for an assistive device, such as a walker or wheelchair, before they need it. Help them get used to it, even to view it as a reassuring friend.

- Go wig or hat shopping with your care partner if they are going to lose their hair. Talk about what their hair means to them, and what part of themselves they feel they will be losing with their hair. One of my friends asked for her care network to lend her their favorite "chapeaus" when she started her treatments.

- Make a "LifeStory" book (see chapter 4, page 96) with a person who is grieving the expected loss of their memory. You could work on this with your partner, making it a shared endeavor as you anticipate what's to come.

- Help a person who is terminally ill write a "loving letter" or an "ethical will" for their loved ones (see chapter 7, page 216).

INCOMPLETE GRIEF

One grief can set off a chain of grieving. Oftentimes a person dealing with current grief is reminded of griefs they have experienced in the past. And if the past grief is unresolved, their reactions may be especially strong.

At times, people have had to suppress their grief in the face of more pressing concerns. For example, wartime refugees fleeing the site of a battle may have no time to mourn the loss of family or friends killed in the conflict. In order for them to survive at the time, they had to repress any signs of grief. Or they may have experienced multiple losses that occurred over and over, with no time to take a deep breath and grieve in between.

Sometimes a death in someone's past is so sudden or violent, such as a car accident or a murder or a suicide, that many unresolved grief feelings can bubble up as they face their own impending decline or death. This can be complicated even further if their relationship with the deceased person was ambivalent (hostile or dependent, for example), or if the deceased person's body was never found.

Any of these past griefs can have a huge impact on your care-sharing situation. Incomplete grief cannot stay underground forever, and it often surfaces as a person faces the losses and griefs of illness or disability. If your care partner experienced a deep loss earlier in life without the opportunity to grieve at the time, you may see signs of long-postponed grief, especially as new griefs act as triggers. Perhaps their loss was too overwhelming when it happened, such as during a pandemic flu epidemic or even a national catastrophe, such as 9/11 or Hurricane Katrina. Or your care partner may have grown up hearing the injunction, "Big boys don't cry," or never been given permission to grieve. Now in their later years, and as they face other losses, the loss that they had to push inside so they could and "get on with life" comes back to haunt them. People with dementia may be especially at risk because their long-term memory stays intact, even after their short-term memory diminishes.

As a care partner, you can help by "bearing witness" to these untold or unrecognized stories of loss and grief that your care partner might not have been able to process earlier. Whether their grief emerges as sadness, excessive anger, or guilt, be especially sensitive in your listening. Keep in mind that these feelings may have been buried for a long time.

GRIEF OVERLOAD

Grief overload happens when several losses occur at the same time, or multiple losses accumulate over a longer period. These kinds of overloads can be overwhelming and can create concerns in later years. You might see this if you are caring for someone with a long-term chronic illness or someone who is declining as they age. As the physical or mental losses pile up, your care partner may have fewer and fewer reserves to deal with the grief. As the losses accumulate, all their emotional and spiritual reserves are depleted, and they may have trouble coping because the mental and physical changes are overwhelming. Equally, you may find yourself feeling grief overload because the caregiving situation is all-consuming. Both of you may be having trouble finding replacements or alternatives for what you are losing.

Grief overload is common and can deeply affect both you and your care partner. You need to be constantly aware of this. In particular, be aware of "anniversary reactions." Your care partner may feel especially sad around the time of a birthday, wedding anniversary, or the anniversary of a death. I remember the time my mom had a terrible fight with a vacuum cleaner salesman one year after my father's death. As she was telling me about her experience, we remembered what the date was and understood that the real issue was her understandable anger at my dad for leaving her life so soon.

Keeping a calendar so you remember as your care partner faces certain dates can be very helpful. One lady I know laid out a special tea for her caregiver and got out pictures of her deceased husband. As she told the story of his life, she grieved and remembered, and shared the day with her care partner. Recognize that *talking* about an anniversary does not bring the grief on. The one you are caring for does remember those special days and times in their life, and they will appreciate when you take the time to remember as well. If the person they are grieving was an important person in your life as well, this is an opportunity for each of you to support the other as you share your sadness on this special date.

"On Time," "Off Time," and "Out of Sync" Grief

A woman who loses her husband after sixty years of marriage may say, "We had a good life," and she and people in her network perceive her husband's death as "on time." It doesn't make the grief easier, but there may be more supports available from peers who have also had the same experience.

On the other hand, the grief felt by a thirty-five-year-old with multiple sclerosis who needs full-time caregiving at home may be seen as "out of sync." This is very young for a person to need heavy physical care, and there may be few friends or relatives who understand this.

Grief also may appear "off time" when a person experiences grief long after the event. Mrs. M. had been very involved in her role as a pastor's wife when she was younger. Now, severely debilitated by dementia, she often made little sense of her world as she lived out her last days in a nursing home. However, when she would go to the nursing home chapel, the cross and other symbols in the chapel reminded her of her life with her minister husband. Grief would wash over her in waves. Though time was not in sync with the event, she experienced that grief as strongly as she did when he died some ten years before.

If you are caring for someone with memory impairments, you may also see grief that is "out of sync." For example, a person with dementia may seem to go back and forth in their understanding that a person has died. "Is my sister dead?" was the question asked by the younger sister of a 102-year-old for days after her death. If your care partner is constantly asking about someone who has died, they can benefit from your kind and frequent reminders. But regardless of the time elapsed, *never assume that someone with memory loss does not feel grief.* It is very real.

DISENFRANCHISED GRIEF

Disenfranchised grief is a phenomenon that has been talked about more openly in recent years. Sometimes called "silent or hidden grief," it relates to "unspeakable" losses that aren't publicly acknowledged or mourned, or aren't grieved because of social or emotional constraints. Some examples include grief over the death of a person with whom someone had an affair, the death of a gay or lesbian partner that was not acknowledged, a suicide that was not talked about, or a miscarriage, abortion, adoption, or infertility that was kept as a silent loss for years. A returning veteran may suffer from post-traumatic stress syndrome that no one mentions. An older adult may be haunted by a loss of innocence due to incest or rape. There are also disenfranchised griefs that relate to global issues, such as when people have fled their country of origin because of religious or political persecution and can't talk about the deaths they've witnessed, even the murder of persons dear to them.

Disenfranchised grief can also affect people who experience grief that others don't acknowledge. Sometimes I run into this in situations where people believe that those with developmental disabilities or dementia, because of the cognitive decline, do not understand or feel grief. This is *not* true, and when those around them believe this, it disenfranchises their grief even more. They never have a chance to grieve because they are not recognized as a griever.

If your care partner has not been able to speak about and share their grief about something they went through, this may become an important element that affects everyone in the caresharing situation, especially as your care partner gets closer to the end of their life. Given the familial and societal pressures at the time of their loss, or the amount of shame or fear or misunderstanding in the experience, your care partner may only now be beginning to discuss what that experience meant to them.

If think of Mrs. C. She and I were filling out eligibility forms for her application for state assistance, and one of the questions was whether she or anyone else in her family was pregnant at that time. This seemingly innocent question of an eighty-year-old led to much weeping. When I asked Mrs. C about it, for an hour she told me the story of how she could never get pregnant, and about her husband's unfaithfulness. A simple question on a form set off a very poignant reaction in this woman who had never talked about this grief before.

If your care partner is dealing with disenfranchised grief, I urge you to be as aware as possible of their past experience and as sensitive as possible in inviting them to share their experience and their feelings with you. It is important for you to not react with such great shock to the previously unnamed grief that they shut off any discussion of it. You will need to walk gently with them and recognize that this pain has been there for a lifetime, with nowhere to go. Validating their feelings and loss in a nonjudgmental way will go a long way toward helping them cope with it. You might help them turn to their spiritual or religious beliefs to deal with such grief. Talking with a counselor or spiritual advisor might also assist them in dealing with any forgiveness issues that may arise and can help "normalize" a situation that has been hidden for a long time.

Because of the unnamed nature of the loss and grief, many people who suffer from disenfranchised grief have probably dealt with it only between themselves and their God.

Your role may be to help your care partner not only tell their story but also share it with others. Giving grief a voice enables people to heal and, in whatever ways they can tell you about their experience, their disclosure will help you and others respond in more helpful ways. Keep in mind, however, that it is especially important to respect their decision about what they want, or don't want, to share. You may only get bits and pieces of the whole story, and you do need to honor their choice about what they disclose.

COMPLICATED GRIEF

Another dimension in the grief and loss picture is that of complicated grief, or "traumatic grief," as it is sometimes called. Essentially, this is grief that won't go away. Long-lasting sadness and other symptoms affect a person so intensely that they are not able to resume life in their ordinary way. They feel totally devastated by the death of a significant person in their lives and are overwhelmed by a great sense of meaninglessness and a great longing for the person who has died. They are, literally, stuck in the grief process. There is little lessening of the outward signs of grief, and their depression persistently hangs on. People who have witnessed violent and untimely deaths, or who feel guilty about not doing enough for someone or not being able to save someone, or people who have experienced multiple losses are at high risk for complicated grief.

Complicated grief can create its own issues for you and your care partner. The biggest problem in caresharing might be that your partner cannot live out the daily tasks of life in a reasonable way. They may have such a sense of hopelessness about today or the future that it is difficult to deal with the tasks of daily life or talk about today's issues. In addition, complicated grief will put them at greater risk for medical and mental health concerns.

If your care partner is experiencing complicated grief, you will need to walk this path with them carefully. You may find it beneficial to consult with a counselor not only for your own support, but also to help your partner deal with this significant and life-impairing grief.

REKINDLED GRIEF

If your care partner is older and facing the griefs and losses of aging, their griefs from a long-ago event may resurface, such as memories of an untimely death in their family, especially of a child or young adult. Even though they may have come to some acceptance or resolution of the event in the past, their failing health and increasing losses may trigger another round of grief for these difficult circumstances of the past. I have known older adults, for example, who in their very late years remourn the death of their young husband or a fiancé in wartime.

Margo was one of those women. She lived a full life into her eighties, when she became disabled and went to live with her sister, Jean, who had cognitive impairments but was physically healthy. They compensated for each other by Margo becoming the "brains" of their partnership and Jean becoming the body. As Margo's losses, due to her physical disabilities, increased, so did her need to recount the death of her fiancé, Joe, some sixty years earlier in World War II. She reaffirmed that she had never given up loving him, and it was very important for her to talk about this with her family.

I have also known people with dementia or a developmental disability who, because their sense of time was mixed up, relived an incident as if it had *just* happened when, in fact, it happened years before. This can occur when something in the present reminds them of some past trauma, and their original grief gets rekindled. I remember seeing this in a woman who was mugged long ago but now felt that her caregivers were attacking her.

Rekindled grief reactions can be extremely disconcerting for family members (and you) who may not know about the original trauma. You never know when an old grief may be rekindled. So be extra sensitive if something in your care sets off a grief memory about something in your care partner's past.

CHRONIC GRIEF

If your care partner seems to be frozen in an emotion, such as anger or guilt or denial, over a situation that caused them grief in the past, their grief can become chronic and their reactions exaggerated. I've seen this many times when a person's negligence (either real or perceived) may have caused the death. An example of this might be a child dying in a bathtub when a person went to answer the door. Elders have told me that you never get over something like that.

When a person's health is declining, guilt over something that happened in the past can resurface in vivid ways. You may see "unexplained" reactions, such as the grandfather who became very angry with his grandchildren over a minor skirmish. He was still grieving his wife's death two years before because they had been having severe marital difficulties at the time, and he was still feeling guilty.

Obsessive guilt can lead to strong grief reactions. Often I have heard this expressed in statements such as, "I should have done … I might have done more," even about events that had occurred decades earlier. This is not uncommon when a caregiving situation has stretched over many years and a person has had a long time to ruminate over the situation. Unresolved guilt and chronic grief can create problems for your care partner's quality of life and for your ability to share an emotional connection with them. Although there can be limits to how much you can do to alleviate chronic grief, the fact that you can name it is of value.

When losses from the past surface in the caresharing setting, or your care partner is dealing with multiple losses, they may not have the ability to cope with all these losses at the same time. Their grief may come in waves, and you need to recognize that the "unexpected" can be "normal" when it comes to grieving. Some griefs are readily apparent, and some are deep in the heart. Both your care partner's expressions and your emotional responses to the many possible dimensions of grief can be unpredictable—and that's okay. The most important thing is to understand that these feelings exist and be open to each other's grieving process.

GRIEF RESPONSES

Grief is a *normal* response to loss of any kind, and it can affect you and your care partner emotionally, physically, and spiritually. In reality, all these responses are closely intertwined, but it is helpful to look at each one separately. As you are living with loss, you may find it tough to articulate how one response to grief is affecting you over another, but separating them out may help you find ways to deal with them.

PHYSICAL EFFECTS

Grief can affect people physically in many different ways, such as stomach distress, tightness in the throat, tenseness, headaches, and changes in appetite. Grief can also put people at risk for increased illness, which, added to a chronic illness or advancing years, can pose a double jeopardy to care partners. I've seen too many times when these effects are ignored or written off as part of an illness process, so it is important for you and your care partner to both acknowledge and attend to your physical responses to grief and loss.

EMOTIONAL EFFECTS

Emotional effects of dealing with grief and loss are varied but may include depression, loss of hope, feelings of helplessness, fear and anxiety about the future, or crying that seems to come out of nowhere. You may notice these grief responses in your care partner, and you may be experiencing them as well. As a carer, not only may you be dealing with issues related to the loss of your care partner as you knew them in the past, but you may also be in transition situations yourself, perhaps with your own health problems or with financial concerns. This adds to the complexity of the whole situation. Some caregivers have told me that they feel "disconnected," "strange," or "out of it." Understanding that these are normal responses to grief may help lessen your sense of being overwhelmed.

Struggling with emotional responses can be especially difficult for those have been stoic in their responses to life in general, and you or your care partner may need to adjust your attitude about sharing your feelings. And if any of your emotional struggles are making it impossible to live out your life, they may be symptoms of something serious. Again, this is a situation where you might want to seek third-party assistance to talk through your feelings.

SPIRITUAL EFFECTS

Intertwined among the physical and emotional dimensions of grief are the spiritual ramifications. Some people have a sense of losing their faith. Others may deeply question the faith that has always sustained them because the God or Higher Power in whom they have always believed seems not to "be there" for them. Even though these issues are difficult to consider, it is especially important to pay attention to the spiritual effects of loss and grief on your care partner's spiritual life because this is the very basic level where they make sense out of their life. If these foundations are challenged, the spiritual grief may be too deep for words.

There can also be many positive spiritual effects of grief, such as increased prayer and scripture reading, a renewed sense of the sacredness of life, and more interest in talking about the Divine and the afterlife. Paying attention to what you can do to support your care partner's spiritual needs is an important aspect of sharing care in grief, and I'll say more about this in a few pages.

Grief is a process that people experience in many different ways. Granger Westberg's classic, gentle, and helpful book *Good Grief* may be a useful resource for you in understanding the grief process. He sensitively outlines some of the normal reactions that people experience in grieving.

As you pay careful attention to your and your care partner's responses to loss and signs of grief, remind yourself, as many times as you need to, that there is no one process or correct progression for grief. Not only is each person unique, but different grief responses may surface at different times. The best thing you can do is be present to what you and your care partner need at that moment to cope with grief. Allow plenty of time and space, and remember that it may take a lot of energy, time, and patience with yourself and others—even with God or a Higher Power—to cope with grief and loss. Be patient with the process when you are grappling with spiritual questions and concerns.

COPING WITH GRIEF

Have you ever felt that you needed to "walk on eggshells" around someone who was grieving? Or maybe you've been hesitant to encourage your care partner to share their innermost concerns because you're a bit fearful of your own reaction, or you're not quite sure how to "handle" their strong feelings. Being present or "with" another is a wonderful gift, but it can be difficult to do. Some emotions are very raw and tender. You do need to walk gently with your care partner and realize that what they share about their grief will bring you together in a very sacred space and time.

Over my years of practice, I've seen many different ways that people deal with grief, and I've collected here some of the practices that I have seen help people. Although sadness and grief may be omnipresent in caresharing, there are things you can do to help yourself and your care partner cope.

NAME THE SADNESS

Too often I've seen that the immediate reaction to someone feeling sadness and grief is to offer comfort. A very wise counselor I know cautions, "Don't immediately jump in to dry the tears. Don't give the tissue … let the person reach for it." In other words, don't shut off a person from sharing what is very important to them. Naming the sadness and the losses is the first step toward coping.

Contrary to what many believe, talking about losses does not make a situation worse. It may well be that both you and your care partner (consciously or unconsciously) are looking for the acknowledgment that someone "gets it." Naming the sadness will help you recognize and face the grief before it becomes so overwhelming that it makes functioning difficult.

I want to add a special word here to you, as a caregiver. In situations of loss, it is imperative to name the grief and loss that *you* are feeling as well. If you only suffer silently while you take care of your partner, any platitudes you might offer to them will ring hollow. Many caregivers I have known often express a wish that there were someone in their family, circle of friends, congregation, or care network that they could be honest with and share the difficult feelings of grief. While I certainly suggest that you share what is appropriate with your care partner, I also urge you to look for support, either in a friend or counselor, with whom you can share your toughest feelings and questions, "no holds barred."

GIVE PERMISSION TO GRIEVE

Be sure to give your care partner (and yourself) permission to grieve each loss. This includes giving your partner a chance to clarify why this is an important loss, and what it meant in the past (if an old grief has resurfaced) or in their present reality. Don't feel as if you have to have all the answers. Don't worry so much about saying something "wrong" that you don't say anything at all. Let go of trying to come up with "solutions." There is no "solution" to grief, only resolution over time. Grief resolution will be uniquely defined by you and your loved one, but generally it means that you are able to live out your life in as normal a way as possible, with as much quality of life as possible.

If you're at the point where your care partner is coming to terms with losing their life, they may need your permission to "let go" of all the things and people around them. Your permission to fully grieve their losses may be one of the greatest gifts you can give them, even though it may be a very difficult experience for you.

Remember: Though you will be losing the person as you have known them, they are losing everything. As you share this grief with your care partner, it might be especially important for you to have someone—other than your care partner—to support you in your grief, someone with whom you can share your deep sadness so you can be available to help your loved one let go.

GIVE IT TIME

When you are dealing with losses, working through grief and transitions always takes time. This is especially true as someone copes with chronic illness, changes in mental ability, or getting used to a body that does not work the way that it used to. If your care partner is aging, it may take even longer to process grief because there may be more losses to face at the very time they have fewer physical, emotional, and spiritual reserves to help them cope.

While, on the one hand, you should be concerned if your care partner is not functioning because of a long, drawn-out grief process, on the other hand, you need to remember that they need to grieve at their own rate. You cannot do the grief work for another, but you can stand by them. This kind of support is invaluable as your care partner navigates their grief journey.

As part of that grief journey, your care partner may need to tell many stories, sometimes over and over again. They need time to explain their situation of loss, whether it is the loss of a limb due to amputation or the loss of functioning due to a stroke. It can take great patience and incredible love to listen to a story you've heard many times before. It has been said that, shortly after a loss, people may tell a five-hour version of the story. As time goes on, they may tell a five-minute story about what happened. But the compressed version does not mean that the loss is any less meaningful.

Don't put your care partner or yourself on a timetable. Grief takes time to process. Be gentle and patient with yourself and the person you care for.

ENCOURAGE DAY-TO-DAY FUNCTIONING

While reaction to loss will gradually decline in intensity as your care receiver and you are able to process your emotions, in the "storm" of grief, you may need to help or encourage your care partner to maintain day-to-day functioning. If you see daily functioning declining or not returning, you may need outside assistance. I remember one woman who went to bed on the death of her husband. She did not get up except to eat and go to the bathroom, and basically gave up on her own life. This is an extreme reaction for sure, but people may struggle to get through the day as they deal with losses and changes. Good day-to-day functioning, being able to go through situations in some kind of a logical manner, is a key factor in healing.

LISTEN

As obvious as this may sound, taking time to listen is critical. In the daily needs of caresharing, time out for listening often gets shortchanged. Allow time—even to carve out time, if necessary— for personal sharing, time when your care partner can tell their stories and know that you are trying to understand. Your listening will let them know that they do not have to face their struggles with loss, grief, sadness, and pain alone. If you are fearful of not knowing what to say, I have found that people really do just want you to listen; they do not need you to have answers. Sometimes, in sharing something with a supportive person, they can work out their own answers. And sometimes it is best to say nothing except that you care and that you will be with them through this difficult journey.

LISTEN BENEATH THE WORDS

When you are listening to your care partner's words and expressions of grief, it is important to hear not only the words but also the underlying feelings. For example, if you hear a barrage of angry accusations or complaints from the one you are caring for, ask yourself: "What is really happening here? Is this anger about what just happened, or might it be connected in some way with their grief and loss?"

Be especially aware of nonverbal communication. Even though our society tends to be "word-bound," people do not need words to communicate what they are feeling. Don't be quick to try to fill in all the empty spaces. Silence is important. It gives you and your care partner time to respect the depth of their feeling and absorb the many layers and associations of their grief.

If you are in a situation where your care partner is using language that seems strangely out of place for the grief they are expressing, you may need to respond to their "symbolic language." Their words may relate to their experiences over a lifetime or to their work. A pilot, for example, may talk about going on a flight as he tries to verbalize his thoughts about his own impending death. It is important not to mistake such verbalizations for confusion, but to be open to what your care partner is attempting to express. What they are saying may include glimpses of another world, or the way they view this world. A good reference on this subject is Maggie Callanan and Patricia Kelley's book *Final Gifts: Understanding the Special Awareness, Needs, and Communications of the Dying*.

HELP RESOLVE UNFINISHED BUSINESS

At times in the long caring process, your care partner may request that something be done before they can let go and die. This "unfinished business" may involve old conflicts or resentments, guilt, or anger, or it may be something as straightforward as making sure that things are taken care of. One woman asked for a gravestone to be placed on her mother's grave before she could let go and die peacefully. Years before, she had promised her mother that she would do this, and it weighed heavily on her mind and heart until it was done. Then she was able to quietly die. I think, too, of my 102-year-old aunt. She needed constant, gentle reassurance that her sister would be cared for before she breathed her last breaths.

This kind of closure is crucial, and you need to take your care partner's concerns and requests seriously. Sometimes the things that need to be taken care of are emotional resolutions. In order to be at peace, they may need your help to express held-back feelings, to ask for forgiveness, or to offer forgiveness. (In fact, forgiveness is such an important issue that I've devoted the entire next chapter to it.)

As a caregiver, you may also have some unfinished business with the person who is dying. Try to work out any unresolved issues—such as asking for their forgiveness or offering your forgiveness for an old hurt—so the unfinished business will not get in the way of being open to your care partner. This is also an important part of taking care of yourself in the situation you are in.

TAKE CARE OF YOURSELF

Although I've emphasized self-care several times already, I can't stress enough how important it is, especially when you are dealing with issues of loss and grief. You need to be honest with yourself, and others, about how you are feeling. Remember, as a caregiver your nonverbal expressions are coming through even when you are valiantly holding your emotions in check. Your care receiver will likely perceive the nonverbal expression of your grief negatively, and you may end up adding to their stress rather than helping to ease it.

The reality is that you need to care for your physical, mental, and spiritual needs in order to care for another. The old sayings that you cannot get "water out of a dry well" or "blood from a stone" ring true. If you are feeling emotionally exhausted and physically depleted, you will be of no help to your care partner.

Taking care of yourself is not selfish; it is imperative. I would even say that the standards for self-care apply doubly because of the extra stress of grief in caresharing: Get enough sleep, exercise, eat healthfully, and socialize with friends. Be gentle with yourself as you walk with grief—hopefully, with others by your side. Try to carve out time for spiritual comfort and nurture as you deal with the loss and grief issues in the dance of caresharing.

Although loss and grief are almost always present in caring, they can be shared, and you and your care partner can grow emotionally and spiritually as you navigate the grief process together. If either of you tries to hide feelings, perhaps to "protect" the other, you will miss out on a very special intimacy. Walking alongside someone who is going through difficult losses, transitions, and grief is treading on sacred ground.

Protecting each other from the pain does not work anyway. What really matters is joining each other on this journey. As a caregiver, you are not responsible for the "answers," but you can help offer comfort with the questions. Asking for assistance and counseling as needed can be a valuable part of understanding grief and a process of growth for everyone involved. Many people I know who resisted the help of others have told me, in retrospect, that they wish they had reached out sooner. Use the resources available to you and your care partner, and be open to the movement of the Spirit as you walk gently together.

SPIRITUAL DIMENSIONS OF GRIEF

In times of loss and grief, spiritual questions often arise. If you and your care partner share a similar religious background, some of the questions that they are asking may be questions you have as well. Together, you may be able to share thoughts and come to a place of insight. Or you may want to invite someone with a greater understanding of the issues to talk with you—especially if you are not familiar with your care partner's faith teachings. I've identified here some of the spiritual issues that typically arise, as well as some resources that might be available to help you and your care partner with the spiritual dimensions of grief.

RECONCILING QUESTIONS OF SUFFERING

Not only does each of us deal with loss and grief in our own way, but each of is also influenced by the culture around us, the way in which we have been raised, our religious background, and our spiritual beliefs. Yet even the most ingrained lessons can be called into question in the face of suffering. One of the questions I hear most often, across cultural and religious boundaries, has to do with religious teachings about suffering: Where is God in my suffering? What purpose is there in this suffering? Why is God allowing (or making) this happen? Although these spiritual questions can create anguish, they are part and parcel of the spiritual journey of sharing care.

Because the role of suffering looms large in the face of grief, and because the subsequent questions are so fundamental to the very meaning of existence, it is crucial that you and your care partner not shy away from these spiritual questions. Reflecting on what your faith tradition teaches, as well as the tradition of your care partner, is a useful place to start. There are many different perspectives on suffering. Some Christians view suffering as something to be endured, with relief coming when they get to heaven. Other Christians believe that they suffer because they are being tested or because it is "God's will." Others take comfort that the God of Love is always with them, no matter what the circumstances. Others struggle because they believed that, if they lived a good life, they would not face suffering and are asking themselves, "What have I done wrong? Why is God punishing me or my loved one?" Buddhists believe that, while pain is inevitable, suffering is "optional," that it comes from "grasping," from wanting reality to be other than it is. They advocate for control over suffering with an end goal of tolerance. People of Jewish faith may wrestle with the concepts of a benevolent God and the meaning of suffering.

These are just a few examples, and your struggles with grief may call into question some of your own beliefs. The beliefs that served you or your care partner well in the past may be hard to reconcile under the current circumstances, and that's okay. At times, adapting your values and beliefs, or "reframing" them, can be helpful. You may need to come to an acceptance, for example, that even though your care partner has lived a "good life," suffering is their companion now. Or you may need to reconcile that, even though God might seem very distant, your belief that God has been and is always with you will sustain you. You might also find that you need to revitalize beliefs that helped you make sense of your life in the past. Or perhaps you will come to understand a belief that you had rejected earlier in a new way now.

As you and your care partner cope with the grief of suffering, and the suffering of grief, it is important to sort out what has value and strength for you now.

SEARCHING FOR MEANING AND PURPOSE

Developing a sense of meaning about what is happening for you and your care partner is key to holding off despair. I remember an about-to-retire gentleman and his wife who, in the days prior to his final day of work, were in the midst of planning for long-term travel. They bought a new camper to take an extended trip, but a month before his retirement date, he suffered a major stroke. They never did make the trip, and until they were able to sell it, the camper sat in their driveway as a constant reminder of lost plans and dreams. The challenge for them was to find meaning in the life they still had together, even though it was not what they had pictured. Together they talked to a counselor who was able to help them name the grief and to move on to a new phase in their lives.

Many care receivers have told me that they feel like "damaged goods," and they wonder why a Higher Power would allow them to live as less than "whole." This issue can become especially acute in long-term rehabilitation, chronic illness and losses, extreme frailty, or dementia. I've heard people who suffered a stroke, for example, wonder why God would do this to them. Others may question why they are still around while other "better persons" have died ahead of them.

These questions are normal and very tough to wrestle with, but you do not need to be afraid to consider them, even to question or be angry with God or a Higher Power as you try to cope. As you wrestle with your spiritual questions, it is important to recognize that your story about meaning and suffering is not only your story but also the story of others. Maybe you can relate to the biblical story of Job. Here was one man, burdened with many afflictions, suffering unthinkable pains and plagues, and people were questioning him and his faith. Yet, some "stuck it out with him," even in his darkest hours.

You may have your moments when you feel like Job. These are the times when you need to remember those who are sticking by you, without judgment, during your spiritual search. Seek out those with whom you can share your questions and from whom you can draw spiritual nurture and support.

FINDING COMFORT IN PRAYER, MEDITATION, AND RITUALS

Some carers have told me that they could not make it through a day without prayer and/or meditation. As you and your care partner face the daily losses—as well as past losses that may surface and future losses you may anticipate—it can be very helpful to reflect on what is happening by adopting an open and receiving stance.

Whether you call on God or a Higher Power, whether you pray or meditate, whether you pour out your heart or sit quietly to receive comfort, your prayers and meditations will go a long way toward helping you find an inner source of peace.

Sacred or religious rituals can also be very comforting. The familiar and well-known rituals of your faith can provide reassurance and strength in the midst of a sea of changes. Rituals offer ways for you and your care partner to share your experience of grief with each other, and they also open ways for others in the care network to share with you. I'll say much more about rituals in the next two chapters on "Sharing Forgiveness" and "Sharing Hope," but I do want to suggest that you take a look at Kathy Black and Heather Murray Elkins's wonderful book *Wising Up: Ritual Resources for Women of Faith in Their Journey of Aging,* which offers ways to develop rituals for a variety of circumstances. I was intrigued by the story of one woman who developed a ritual for a pre-death memorial when she became aware that her cancer was advancing and that death would be coming quickly.

As you look for ways to encourage or help your care partner participate in the spiritual practices that have meaning for them, also remember to share with your care partner what their prayers and rituals mean to you on a spiritual level.

FINDING COMFORT IN A COMMUNITY OF FAITH

If your care partner has been a longtime member of a faith community, the familiar blessings and prayers and the nurture of faithful spiritual friends can bring comfort beyond measure. It may be very beneficial to see what arrangements you can make either to bring members of this faith community to your care partner or to bring your care partner to this community.

As supportive as communities of faith can be, however, I've also seen times when spiritual networks struggle with how to offer nurture and support to caregivers and care receivers who are dealing with the griefs and losses of a chronic illness, aging, or disability. Although religious institutions are practiced at offering rituals and consolation to the bereaved after a death, "living" grief presents some more immediate dilemmas. Part of this has to do with how a person might receive an offer of assistance. Some who are dealing with loss in private may tell others in public, "I'm fine, just fine," and effectively keep available help and support at bay.

It may be important for you, as a caregiver, to help educate people about what your needs are, and what your care partner needs. (This would be a good time to review the suggestions in chapter 1 on "Asking for Help," page 9). Discuss with your care partner what they want others to know about their diminishing abilities or frailties before you disclose private information. There is a sensitive balance to be struck in knowing what is appropriate to share and when to honor boundaries.

FINDING COMFORT IN HOSPICE CARE

If your care partner is reaching the end of life, the gift of hospice care can be an enormous spiritual comfort and support to you both as you face the final loss. As your partner gradually goes through a progression of letting go and moving on, you have an opportunity to share in this profound process and grow emotionally and spiritually.

Some people put off getting hospice involved in care because they don't want to "give up" on their loved one. Please do not wait too long to access this very helpful benefit! I have seen over and over again how much hospice can facilitate a better quality of life at the end of life. By providing the key aspect of pain management, hospice enables you and your care partner to share quality time, unencumbered by chronic pain. Spiritual care is an important part of the hospice philosophy, with emphasis on the spiritual even mandated in the Medicare law. As a caregiver, you will be a key part of the holistic care provided, and you will receive emotional and spiritual support right along with your loved one.

Among the many other things that I might say on the subject of grief at the close of this chapter, there is one statement in particular that I want to leave you with: *In coping with all the grief, transitions, and losses that accompany caresharing, it is imperative to keep realistic hope alive.* The losses may be overwhelming, and the coping is difficult, but there is always room for—and great need for—hope. I'll explore this vital subject in the last chapter of the book, but for now, I offer these wonderful words credited to Václav Havel, playwright and first president of the Czech Republic: "Hope is not about believing that you can change things. Hope is about believing that what you do makes a difference." Here are some of the key points from this chapter that can help you make a difference in dealing with the grief and loss issues of caresharing:

- Remember that reactions to grief are unique to each person. Be open to dealing with your care partner's response in individualized ways.

- Name the transitions and losses you and your care partner are experiencing so that you can face them together, supporting each other as emotionally and spiritually as possible. Be sure to include the "little" and the "big" losses.

- Try to be sensitive to all the ways that losses are affecting you and your care partner so you can make adaptations when needed.

- Understand that grief has many dimensions, and be aware of how grief from the past and anticipatory grief, as well as other forms of grief, are affecting your situation. Don't hesitate to seek assistance to deal with these.

- Do not be afraid to examine what suffering means to you and your care partner.

- Use your strengths to cope with grief and be especially aware of the spiritual strengths that are there for you. Consider educating those in your spiritual network who might be helpful if they knew what to do.

6

SHARING FORGIVENESS

A Key Spiritual Journey in Caresharing

THE IMPORTANCE OF FORGIVENESS

Forgiveness is a basic need for all of us. Because we are human, we can make hurtful mistakes. We may say or do things that bring pain and suffering to others emotionally, spiritually, mentally, or physically. And others may injure us. By the time we are older or struggling with chronic illness, or caring for someone who is, we may have a huge room in our hearts filled with accumulated hurts and frustrations.

The issue of forgiveness is not often spoken of in terms of a major health issue in caresharing. Although it has been long discussed in religious and counseling circles as crucial to spiritual well-being, forgiveness is now recognized as pivotal to physical health as well. At Stanford University's Forgiveness Project, they have been studying this concept for some years. The John Templeton Foundation and the Fetzer Institute have also funded major initiatives to look at the whole arena of forgiveness.

Researchers are finding mounting evidence that forgiveness holds many restorative benefits that include lowering blood pressure and heart rate, reducing stress, reducing chronic pain, and decreasing the risk of substance and alcohol abuse, among others. Conversely, nursing anger and resentments and not dealing with them has been shown to have negative effects on health.

Stanford's approach has been an educational one, in which persons are taught a process that includes guided imagery and homework practice where they learn how to forgive. (Even though most of us have been told all of our lives that we need to forgive, exactly *how* to do that remains a trial-and-error process.) The Stanford team has found that forgiveness is a behavior that not only can be learned but can also prevent other problems from occurring. Although results are just beginning to emerge from such research, there is much to consider in the way we understand the importance of forgiveness in the caresharing setting. When someone is ill or disabled or dying, the situation can be an especially strong catalyst for forgiveness issues to surface.

THE PAST GETS "STIRRED UP"

In a caresharing situation, the hurts of the past may resurface or take on a new significance. Past wrongs may be stirred up in the intimate contact that comes with personal physical care. For example, if your care partner was abused by someone in the past, the intimacies of receiving care may bring those old wounds to mind. Alternatively, if you are caring for a parent who has abused you in the past, a renewed awareness of that old hurt and anger can bubble up, and you may feel bent over by the heavy load of collected injustices. Or, if you and your care partner have an unresolved marital issue from early in your marriage, this may haunt you in the caregiving situation.

END-OF-LIFE ISSUES BECOME CLEARER

If you are caring for someone who is facing a terminal diagnosis or imminent death, they may have a pressing sense of making amends before it is too late. This is a critical time of heightened awareness of hurts and wrongs. Many seriously examine whom they need to ask forgiveness from, and who they want to offer forgiveness to. They may realize how much they need to do, or should have done in the past, on forgiveness work. Because they are aware of how little time is left to sort things out and become reconciled, their need to work on unfinished business may be increasingly urgent.

At this critical time, chances to mend fences and build bridges by forgiving or asking for forgiveness abound. The alcoholic father, who feels he failed his son as a young man, may want to say "I'm sorry" and reconcile with his son before his death. The mother who had ostracized her son-in-law for being from another religious tradition may, in her later days, want to make peace with him and thank him for treating her daughter well. At the end of life, things that once seemed important in a personal argument or a business dispute or a family feud may not matter in the way that they did when people were younger.

NOT FORGIVING DEPLETES ENERGY AND WELL-BEING

Asking for, or granting, forgiveness can be restoring and empowering, but being unable to work through forgiveness issues is a big hurdle to well-being. When we hold on to hurts over time, they fester and have a negative effect on our emotional and spiritual health. And, as researchers are discovering, buried hurts also impact our physical health. In severe cases, holding on to hurt, anger, and frustration can impair a person so much that they are nonfunctional. As a colleague reminded me, "Holding on to a grudge and refusing to forgive is like taking poison and expecting the other person to die." Allowing past hurts to fester can create a vicious cycle of relationship problems and self-destruction.

Perhaps the person you are caring for verbally rehearses, over and over again, the wrongs that have been perpetrated against them but never takes a step toward reconciling with those who have done wrong or have been wronged. This kind of stubborn "unforgiveness" can eat at them in many unhealthy ways. Clinging to negative emotions can unbalance the mind-emotion-body connection; holding on to anger and hurts can actually make people sicker. Although working on forgiveness can be a very complicated process, it takes even more energy and effort to hang on to resentments.

In caresharing, because of the intimacies of caring for and about each other, there are many opportunities for forgiving and being forgiven. And because inner and outer health is very much connected to emotional and spiritual strengths, forgiveness is an integral part of a healthy lifestyle for care partners. The ability to forgive is an essential foundation not only for a caresharing partnership but also for healthy aging and for peace-filled dying.

THE NATURE OF FORGIVENESS

As a child, if you got into a fight with a playmate, or broke something that didn't belong to you, or lied about something, you were probably told to say, "I'm sorry." Given that this is what most of us learn about forgiveness as we grow up, it is not surprising that many of us have the common misconception that apologizing is the same as asking for forgiveness. That may be an important *part* of the process, but it is only a part. Asking for forgiveness is much more than saying "I'm sorry."

Before you or your care partner embarks on the journey of forgiveness, it might be helpful to reflect on the full nature of forgiveness. Here are some fundamental concepts to consider:

- Forgiveness is a *choice* you can make to release the beliefs, feelings, and actions that negatively affect you. Forgiveness does not happen without your conscious decision to forgive or to ask for forgiveness. Before you can begin the process of working on forgiveness, you will need to make the choice to let go of anger and hurt.

- Forgiveness is an *individual act*. No one else can do it for you. Although prayer and the gifts of others who listen to you and show empathy can help you sort out your options, ultimately, you alone make the decision to move along in the process.

- Forgiveness is *not condoning what another did, or excusing, or forgetting*. Although the adage "Forgive and forget" suggests otherwise, forgiving does not mean forgetting the wrongs and situations that have caused pain. Past wrongs may have caused deep wounds that, with time, heal over, yet scars may remain. What forgiveness does so is to help you move on with other aspects of your life—or, in the caresharing setting, perhaps with the process of dying.

- Forgiveness is a *multilayered process*. There is much that can be learned at each step in the process, and the process does take time. Rushing into forgiveness because you feel pressured by others is not really forgiveness. Being forgiven in this manner is not helpful, either. I want to add a word of caution here. Be careful not to give in to fake or compulsory forgiveness if people in your faith community, your 12-step program, or even your family are pressuring you to forgive when you are not ready to do so. There are situations of abuse, for example, or a crime, or some other very difficult thing that has transpired in which forgiveness may not be possible. Working toward acceptance of the situation may be a more realistic goal.

- Forgiveness requires *respect*. When you decide to enter a process of asking for forgiveness, or forgiving another, you need to start with being respectful of the other person. Although it is true that really awful things do happen between people, the person who has hurt you is still a person worthy of dignity. They have their personal issues, struggles, and hurts, as do you.

There may be times when you feel that you are justified in treating a person as less than worthy, but for real forgiveness to occur, a sense of humility, together with regard for the other, is crucial. If you think of situations where you have been in need of forgiveness and remember how you felt at the time, it may help you to have more empathy and understanding for the person who has wronged you. How you approach them may be constrained somewhat by their illness or cognitive limits, so you will need to ascertain what the other person can truly understand, and respect those limits.

- Forgiveness requires *honesty*. It is important to be truthful with yourself, as well as with the other person, about the depth of the hurt and the depth of your forgiveness. If you take a superficial approach to the forgiveness process, you might struggle in the long term with not having fully worked through the process to make the forgiveness truly meaningful.

- Forgiveness is *not the same as reconciling*. Reconciling may come after forgiving, after a series of many steps, but it is not always achieved. Yet that does not diminish the gift of forgiveness. (I'll say more about reconciliation in just a bit.)

THE BARRIERS TO FORGIVENESS

Forgiveness is a complex process that calls for coping skills, problem solving, and learning from past experiences, both positive and negative. So it is not surprising that many barriers may stand in the way of asking for forgiveness or giving forgiveness. Over the years of working with caresharing partners, I've encountered many who want to forgive (or be forgiven) but just don't think it's possible anymore. Alternately, I've seen others who feel that they were "right," so why should *they* ask for forgiveness! Either way, the resentments still linger, the pain still hurts, and the need for forgiveness still exists.

Maybe some of these barriers to forgiveness will sound familiar to you.

"It's Too Late"

Perhaps the one you are caring for has told you about an experience in the past that still hurts. They may have expressed a wish that things could be different now, yet they fear that too much time has passed to approach the other and ask for forgiveness. Or perhaps you have a forgiveness issue with your care partner, but, given their failing health or cognitive abilities, you are thinking it's too late—they're too frail or confused or in too much pain to deal with this.

If there is one thing I emphasize in the caresharing setting, it is that *it is never too late!* I have learned this important lesson from families I have worked with over the years, and from my personal experience. The healing that needs to occur is indeed possible. Even when someone feels as if the original hurt or conflict was too long ago, or if there's been too much else that has accumulated on top of it over the years, people *can* still change and grow. Exploring complicated hurts and frustrations and forgiving can happen at many times in the life cycle, but the vulnerability of illness or disability can temper some of the most entrenched hurts and angers. This may open a window for forgiveness that didn't exist before.

"It's Just Not Worth the Effort"

Perhaps you've heard your care partner say something like this: "They're not going to change anyway, so I'm not even going to try to say, 'I'm sorry.' It's just not worth the effort." This stance assumes that relationship healing is not possible before even attempting to look at who and what needs forgiving. For some, this belief comes out of years of failed attempts and a certain life weariness at this point.

But I also think it is important to recognize that this protest (and the next one as well, "It's no big deal") might also be a cover for a variety of underlying feelings. Some may be afraid of punishment if they ask for forgiveness. Some may feel too ashamed to approach someone they have wronged. Others may fear rejection and would rather not take the risk.

It is true that we always take a risk in asking for or offering forgiveness, and we may not achieve our desired outcome. But it is also true that we are changed by the process of seeking and granting forgiveness, even if we don't always gain our hoped-for end result. There is value in the process of forgiveness in and of itself.

"It's No Big Deal"

Perhaps your care partner has mentioned an issue with someone that's bothering them but has shrugged it off, saying, "It's no big deal." Denying the seriousness of a festering issue, or being unwilling to admit that an unresolved issue creates other concerns, is a little like leaving a wound untreated and expecting it to heal. Maybe someone in your care partner's family keeps promising to visit but never seems to show up. Or perhaps someone whom your care partner used to consider a "close friend" now manages to find any number of excuses not to call or come by. Or the issue might be between you and your care receiver. I've seen instances where a carer unwittingly acts or speaks negatively toward their care partner, but the partner never mentions it. Instead, the unspoken tension is suspended uneasily between them.

It has been my experience that, if there are needs for forgiveness—even things that are "no big deal"—that are not dealt with, they pop up somewhere else. Taking one step forward in the forgiving process, by acknowledging directly what has transpired, can move the relationship down the path of forgiveness.

"BUT I WAS *RIGHT!*"

Sometimes people feel justified in what they did and do not see the need to ask for forgiveness, even if another person took offense or was hurt by it. Or some may fiercely cling to the notion that they were the "innocent" victim in a situation, rather than a perpetrator, and fiercely hold on to their hurt. But in caresharing, these self-protesting and self-protecting stances are counterproductive.

If, for example, you feel that your care partner has done something against you in a situation where you had the right perspective, this kind of self-righteousness may keep you from fully interacting with your care partner. Hanging on to being "correct" will fester in your heart and keep you from connecting with your care partner. You will be limiting the depth of your relationship because the unspoken protest will be hanging between you.

"I DON'T DESERVE TO BE FORGIVEN"

In the caresharing situation, past issues can weigh heavily between care partners. Perhaps you have a concern related to your care partner that has affected you for a long time, yet you have never brought it up before. The stress of their chronic illness or their limited life may bring you to the point where you need to carefully examine this.

Or perhaps your care partner has a family situation where they feel so bad about something they've done that they don't believe they deserve to ask for pardon. I see this with people who have thrown a family member out of the house, or have abused drugs or alcohol, or have been in trouble with the law. At this point in their lives, they may have done considerable inner work, become sober, or made restitution, but they may still want to work out issues with partners, parents, or siblings. Yet, at the same time, they may feel that what they have done is unforgivable. This can be very difficult to work through, but I hold to the same premise that I emphasized above: *It's never too late!* This may be a time when a counselor or spiritual advisor can be especially helpful in clearing the way for forgiveness to happen.

"HE CAN'T UNDERSTAND WHAT I'M SAYING ANYWAY, SO WHY SHOULD I BOTHER?"

The whole issue of forgiveness can get even more complicated if one of the parties does not have the mental capacity to understand. What do you do, for example, if you are caring for a parent with dementia whom you would like to offer forgiveness for past abuses? Or from whom you would like to receive forgiveness? Yet you know that their limited cognitive abilities would prevent them from any meaningful comprehension and exchange.

It does not take full cognitive ability to say "I'm sorry" to another, or to understand it at some level. Although we can never be sure what gets through in dementia, my stance is this: If there is a need to say "I'm sorry," say it! And know that there may come a time when your loved one with dementia will say it to you. Listen and accept their statement, however they phrase it. At some level, however basic, there can be a sense of healing.

If you feel that you will never be able to ask for forgiveness from or grant it to your care partner, there is a suggestion that I often make in counseling that I offer to you as well: Sit across from an empty chair that symbolizes your care partner, and tell the chair (substituting for the person) how you feel and what you need to say in forgiving or asking for forgiveness. You might be surprised at the sense of release and the feeling of relief you can achieve from such a simple exercise.

These barriers to forgiveness, and others you might identify, may be tough to consider. They require you and your care partner to be honest with yourselves and about your situation. But there are steps you can take to help you and your care partner, and the potential for physical, emotional, and spiritual healing is well worth the effort.

RELATIONSHIP MATTERS

Forgiveness has past, present, and future implications. In the intensity of a caresharing situation, memories of difficult *past* events can take on a new dimension of pain. Old hurts and angers that may have been silent for years may flare up with a vengeance. The *present* course of an illness or healing may, in turn, be affected by how you or your care receiver hangs on to and perceives these past hurts. Sadly, I've seen situations where old emotional injuries have caused people to treat their care partners in negative ways. And, ultimately, past unresolved issues can be passed on to *future* generations through these attitudes and actions.

In truth, one of the important aspects of forgiveness is that it usually doesn't happen in isolation. As individuals, we may be able to pray to our Creator for forgiveness, we may be able to forgive ourselves, knowing that God forgives us, and even if someone is not able to forgive us, we may be able to forgive them and move on. However, most of the forgiveness needed in the caresharing setting is in a relationship.

FAMILY FORGIVENESS

Because our family relationships are the most long-standing and the most intense, often the greatest needs to forgive and be forgiven occur in families. Family struggles and a lifetime sense of injustices can build up and be passed on from generation to generation. In the emotional overload of the caresharing setting, long-suppressed issues, family secrets, and "unfinished business" are more likely to surface and are often at the heart of the need to work on forgiveness.

As you work with your care partner, pay attention to the family issues and names that seem to be arising. They might identify someone within the family from whom they want to ask forgiveness, such as an estranged brother who hasn't been in touch for years because of an old feud or a misunderstanding. Or there may be someone in the family, such as a child who "abandoned" them at an early age, to whom they want to offer forgiveness.

If your care partner is a family member, it is also important for you to pay attention to your own family forgiveness needs. For example, if you are doing hands-on caring for an aunt who has always favored other nieces and nephews in the past but who are not part of the caring now, you may feel mad about the unfairness of the situation you're in. If you can forgive them, you can give yourself the gift of letting go of the anger, resentment, and frustration so you are better able to be present to the one who needs your care.

CARE PARTNER FORGIVENESS

Caregiving situations can catch us off guard. You might have been living your life and, all of a sudden, there was a crisis, and you were expected and needed to step in as a caregiver. Or the need for care may have evolved slowly, and your role as a caregiver somehow seemed to evolve right along with it. Either way, you might find yourself in a position of caring for someone with whom you have had a past conflict, or for someone who has hurt you deeply in the past. In order to move ahead, you need to find a way to forgive them or your deep resentment could compromise the actual giving of care.

This need for forgiveness may be especially critical if the one you are caring for is a spouse or life partner. Over long-term relationships, issues arise. This is to be expected, and it is normal. You and your long-term partner have experienced a good deal together over the years, but maybe you have been carrying a silent hurt or anger.

I think of a woman named Susan. She was a very competent executive, and she had been married to her husband, Edward, for more than forty years when he was diagnosed with Parkinson's disease. Susan gave up her role in her successful small business to take care of him, because she felt that was what a good wife would do in that situation. But in taking over the carer role, she had to do much examination of the marital relationship. Edward had been physically and emotionally abusive when he drank, and they had never spoken of this to anyone. Before she could feel comfortable in the skin of a caregiver, she talked to her counselor and did a lot of inner work on forgiving him.

I've also seen situations where a carer is assisting someone whom they had significantly hurt at one time. A "black sheep" or "wayward child," for example, may be back in a care receiver's life out of necessity. Sometimes these carers do too much to try to gain absolution for what they previously did. If you are caring for someone whom you have hurt in some way, you will need to ask their forgiveness before you can be an effective caregiver.

Unresolved hurts and wrongs can have very negative effects on how care partners treat each other, but forgiveness can remove some of the barriers that get in the way of healthy caresharing. I've seen forgiveness connect people in surprising ways. The deepening and promoting of personal relationships may, in fact, be the prime reason why the work of forgiveness is so important to the health and well-being of you and your care partner.

If you are identifying with any of these situations as you read, I want to insert this word of encouragement: Just as there are many possibilities in relationships for hurting, so too are there many opportunities for forgiving and, ultimately, reconciling with each other. There is *always* the possibility of making peace with the past; there is *always* the potential for growth and change emotionally and spiritually. Later, I'll offer some specific ways you might embark on this journey of forgiveness, for yourself, for something between you and your care partner, or for your care partner.

DAILY MATTERS

Because we are human, we are in need of forgiveness—sometimes on a daily basis. Forgiveness for issues from the past happens over an extended period, and may include a variety of people, but the issues of today are right in front of us. When there is something that needs forgiveness in the day-to-day process of caresharing, we have an immediate opportunity to say "I'm sorry," and do what we can to right the situation.

FORGIVING YOUR CARE PARTNER
FOR THE DIFFICULTIES OF CAREGIVING

Caresharing creates hardships. That is a reality, and you may be having a wide range of feelings in response to this. You may be angry at the changes that the illness has brought, especially if the one you are caring for is a soul mate and confidante who used to support you through bad times and is now causing you the most difficult time you have had to face. And you have to face it alone. You may be missing the person who is no longer there for you emotionally. Or you may be missing their practical support. Perhaps your care partner used to be the handyman and provider, but now you have to "do everything." Or they may have been the one who kept the house running smoothly, and now they need you to make three meals a day.

You may need to forgive your care partner for totally upending your life. At a time when you may have been planning to take life easy in retirement, at a time when the heavy load of responsibilities for children and debt has been lessened, you may find yourself doing some of the most challenging work of your life. This is work that you are the least prepared for, with no financial compensation. You may also be feeling a sense of a loss because your own freedom has been curtailed by the demands of caresharing, and other people may not recognize these losses—so you're angry with them, or disappointed in them, as well! This series of losses can be painful in so many ways, and you might be feeling these changes pretty intensely. These are normal and understandable feelings.

If you keep these feelings locked up, they can come back to haunt you. You need to find a way to honestly acknowledge how you are feeling and find a place in your heart to forgive the person you are caring for so you can go on. Even if their illness is a direct result of not taking care of their own health over the years, it does no good to hang on to your anger about the past. What *is* is now, in the moment, and needs to be dealt with on that basis.

FORGIVING YOUR CARE PARTNER
FOR HURTFUL BEHAVIOR CAUSED BY THE ILLNESS

If your care partner is dealing with dementia, or is in great pain, or is simply worn down by the relentlessness of treatment and isolation, they may say or do things that are very unkind to you as their carer. Recognize that it is often the *illness* that is causing this behavior. It is often the illness "talking." Your care partner's abusive words are not something they would normally say if their social graces were still intact, and their behavior may stem from a loss of the control they once had.

It is easier to forgive them if you remember that it is the *illness* that has changed the behavior and, indeed, changed the very person they used to be. However, that is not to say that you won't be hurt or angered by their behavior or remarks. The gift of forgiveness is that it can help you get beyond the hurtful actions or words. You will be freeing yourself from the potential to hurt back or withhold care and forgiveness opens ways for compassion to keep flowing.

FORGIVING YOURSELF FOR NOT DOING "ENOUGH"

In the intensity of caresharing, it is easy to feel pulled apart inside by all that is happening. I've seen many carers set expectations for themselves that are not realistic, and in the process, set themselves up to fail and end up feeling terrible about not meeting their own expectations. They may even end up feeling as if they have failed the person they care about.

It is okay not to be perfect in your caregiving role! The first person you may need to forgive is yourself. Maybe you've been frustrated and said some angry things in the heat of the moment—and then felt bad about being angry. Maybe the one you are caring for has been a loving partner, parent, or friend throughout life, but in the course of their dementia has said something really nasty to you. Though you know in your head and heart that they are struggling with something they may have no control over, it is easy to snap back in kind.

You may blame yourself for not being a better care partner, or feel a great sense of guilt about not doing a good job in this role that was thrust upon you. You feel even worse if others, especially other family members or friends, have little understanding of how hard it is to be a carer and seem to be critical of the job you're doing.

If the relationship with your care partner was stressed prior to the caregiving situation, you might feel even worse about your sins of omission or commission. Past unfinished business in your relationship can add strain to the current daily care. Perhaps you are dealing with some guilt held over from the past. It's easy to see, in retrospect, what you "might have done" or "could have done" or "should have done." In working through past issues with a pastoral or spiritual counselor, or even through time itself, things become clearer. You need to find a way to forgive yourself for things you've done or not done so you can move on to what today's needs are.

Equally, you need to be forgiving about what you "should" be doing today. It is important to recognize your limits and to forgive yourself for what you can't do. Someone once said, "Even Superman is Clark Kent most of the time." You cannot be all things to all people. You need to realistically consider what is "good enough" for your caregiving situation. That does not mean you care any less, only that you are more realistic in your expectations.

There may also come a time, in working through the problems confronting you in the caresharing situation, when you need to make a decision that you cannot be a primary caregiver for someone. Others may be pressuring you, saying that they think you "should." However, I've seen many times where someone's decision not to take on full-time caring is the best for all concerned. Only you can know the path you have walked with your care partner. Only you can make the decisions that you need to make.

ASKING YOUR CARE PARTNER FOR FORGIVENESS

There may be times in the caresharing process when "forgiving yourself" for your actions (or lack of action) is not enough. Situations may arise in the day-to-day give-and-take of caregiving when you need to ask your care partner for their forgiveness. While you have taken on the role of a caregiver, you also have other things going on in your life, such as a job, or children, or financial stresses. These things can add to your anger and frustration, and you may find yourself "dumping" your feelings on your care partner. Your concerns are real, and things indeed may be "awful" for you, but you may later regret that you burdened your partner with your problems when they might have been having a terribly bad day as a result of chronic pain or a treatment. How small your complaints must have seemed to them at the moment!

When you apologize to your care partner for being so insensitive, you may be surprised. I've had people tell me that they were glad to hear about my problems because it took their mind off their own! Whatever the result of your apology, you will have communicated your understanding of how difficult things are for your care partner and kept the channels of communication open between the two of you.

In any caresharing setting, there is a lot of room for mistakes. Some are "legitimate"; that is, they come out of not knowing what to do or how to handle a situation. Some are understandable, when everyone is stretched to the limit of trying to handle pain or loss or restrictions or frustrations. Some days, you may need to recognize that your heart is not in the caring, or even the relationship. And there may be times when you need to look at the situation and acknowledge that you did not do the right thing.

If you find that you are angrily responding to situations and feeling misunderstood, if your friends are reflecting to you that you seem to be carrying around a big chip on your shoulder, or if your friends start avoiding you because you are so resentful or angry, take these concerns seriously. None of us is perfect. However, there is work to be done. When you can identify the problem and ask for, or offer, forgiveness, you will be able to keep your focus on the issues that matter most.

WHERE TO START

In the dance of caresharing, there are many tricky steps in the forgiveness process, and how forgiveness is helped or hindered can affect the delicate balance in caring. Yet there is no complete blueprint for how to go about this. There is no cookbook that applies to all situations or persons. Even though our religious traditions teach us that we are to forgive, we often have not been taught how to apply this seemingly abstract concept to our daily lives.

The Chinese Taoist philosopher Lao-tzu once said, "The journey of a thousand miles begins with one step." In the forgiveness process, taking that first step is crucial.

DO NOT WAIT

If there is one thing that I have learned in working with people who are ill or aging, it is never to wait until someone is on their deathbed to do the work of forgiveness. While there is always the chance at the end of life to make amends, if you wait, you may never get that opportunity. If you need to say "I'm sorry" to your care partner, do it now! If you have not seriously considered what might be done to ameliorate the situation, think about it carefully, now. Do not put it off. If your care receiver has expressed a need to forgive or be forgiven, do what you can to facilitate the process.

MAKE THE FIRST MOVE

If there is an issue between you and your care partner, you may need to make the first move. Waiting for them to initiate the process is a prescription for failure. If it is in your heart to forgive them for hurting you, you need to make the approach. And if you are the one who has hurt them, all the more reason for you to take the first step.

Keep in mind, however, that you cannot force someone to forgive you. You can only candidly acknowledge the wrong that you have done and humbly ask for forgiveness. As you and your care partner gently look at the issues between you, there may be other avenues you need to explore, such as how you or they will make emotional, spiritual, or even financial restitution for what has been done. But the process can begin only when someone makes the first move. By taking the initiative, you can gently help begin the journey.

LOOK FOR CATALYSTS

Because the issue of hurts and forgiveness can be so delicate, it can be difficult to suddenly open a conversation on this topic. Oftentimes, it is helpful to pick up on "catalysts" from other conversations or events to help introduce the process.

I remember a time when I was reading Kathleen Fischer's book *Winter Grace: Spirituality for the Later Years* while visiting with my mother, with whom I had had a conflicted relationship over the years. I fell asleep while reading the chapter on the "healing of memories." My mother picked up the book while I was sleeping and began to read. Fischer's concept of the "healing of memories" served as a catalyst for us. We were able to discuss and work on some very hurtful things that had occurred between us, and ask for and receive forgiveness. As is true for many people, the perspective of time had finally enabled us to walk this forgiveness path. My mother and I came to an understanding of what had transpired between us, and then moved forward in a changed relationship. Although there were still difficulties, a measure of healing had taken place, and I was grateful.

Another catalyst for a forgiveness discussion can emerge out of the stories that your care partner tells about their life. They might reminisce about significant events and, as part of the process, do some reflecting and reexamining of their life. They may express some regret about something they did, or a wish that they had done something differently. If they say—even in a passing comment—that they wish they could change the way things were left in a situation, or talk to someone they felt they have wronged, this is the time to respond and explore with them the possibility of pursuing this.

As stories are told, issues between you and your care partner may also arise. These narratives can take on a new significance and urgency in light of their declining health or impending death, and I have often seen these life reflections become catalysts for family members to work on forgiveness.

Sometimes situations happening in the "outside world" become catalysts for discussions of forgiveness. Any major catastrophe, for example, may lead you and your care partner to a broader examination of what really matters in life. This certainly happened after 9/11, and it happens when there are major torna-does, floods, or hurricanes that wipe out whole communities. In the face of a disaster, it's natural to immediately want to tell the people you care about, "I love you." Part and parcel of this response can be the impulse to make amends before it is too late. As you and your care partner discuss any world events or disasters, either of you may realize anew the need to say "I'm sorry" to those you have wronged.

Other catalysts for forgiveness discussions can arise out of family and networks of friends. The unexpected death of a well-loved friend, for example, might make your care partner more aware of their own vulnerabilities and intensify their wish to seek out the people with whom they need to make amends.

ASK REFLECTIVE QUESTIONS

Sometimes the best path to a forgiveness discussion is the most direct. If your care partner has told you they are concerned about past hurts or wrongs, you might want to use some gentle reflective questions to help them consider whom they need to forgive, or request forgiveness from. As a carer, you might also find that taking some time with these questions can clarify your own thinking about the issues.

- Is there someone who has hurt or angered you whom you would like to forgive? Think of times when have you for-given someone else. What happened as a result?
- Is there someone you have hurt or angered from whom you need to seek forgiveness? Remember the times in the past when people have forgiven you. What did that feel like?
- Are there lessons from these experiences that you could use now?
- What are some of the steps you could take to initiate this forgiveness?

Remember, even small steps in moving through the process of forgiveness are important. The sense of healing can be a powerful goal and gift.

KEEP A JOURNAL

Keeping a journal is another helpful tool in the forgiveness journey. Putting thoughts and feelings into written form is a good way to sort out what the real issues are so that they can be explored frankly. If, for example, your care partner is having trouble talking to you directly about a painful issue from their past, you might suggest that they write down a description of their experience and make note of their thoughts and feelings about it. Whether or not they choose to share those deep hurts with another will be up to them, so remind them that they don't have to show their writing to anyone if they don't want to. They can always destroy the papers, if they choose. You can affirm to them that, by putting their issue into writing, they will at least have acknowledged their concerns to themselves, which is an excellent first step toward dealing with a difficult issue and exploring what and who needs forgiveness.

As a carer, you might also find the journal process a helpful way to sort out your thoughts and feelings, so you can be clear when forgiveness needs surface. If you are working with a counselor or spiritual advisor, your journal can become a tool for discussion and processing where you are in the forgiveness journey.

SEEK OUT SUPPORT

Sometimes it can be very helpful to talk through forgiveness issues with a trusted advisor, counselor, clergyperson, or spiritual director before approaching the person whom you are seeking forgiveness from or offering forgiveness to. A neutral "third party" can gently reflect back to you what they understand the main issues to be and help you sort out the options in your situation. If your care partner has limitations, a support person can also help you consider what is appropriate to say directly to your partner and what things you might want to channel in other ways. Being extra sensitive to your care partner's limitations is especially critical when there are forgiveness issues between the two of you.

A third party can be helpful to your care partner as well. If they have expressed a need or concern about forgiveness issues with someone in the family, they may feel more comfortable talking to a "neutral" person rather than to you as their caregiver.

For both you and your care partner, it is important to seek out someone with whom you can be honest and lay out all the issues. Having such a person beside you in the work of forgiveness can be invaluable in sorting out the complex layers of old angers and hurts that make forgiveness difficult.

CHECK AVAILABLE RESOURCES

Much has been said and written on the subject of forgiveness, and I readily admit that I do not have the final word on what works. This is a tough area, and we all need all the help we can get! However, I can recommend some excellent resources, and I hope you will peruse what fits for you and your caresharing situation.

Families and Forgiveness: Healing Wounds in the Intergenerational Family. This insightful book by Terry Hargrave identifies four "stations of forgiveness":

- *Having insight.* What were the factors that were responsible for the hurts and frustrations that caused the pain?

- *Understanding.* What might have been occurring for the offender at the time that caused them to be so hurtful? What might I have done if I were in the same situation?

- *Exonerating.* What needs to be said to clear the air? To make amends? To honestly deal with what has happened? To prevent building on, or passing on, the negative feelings? To address any guilt or shame?

- *Restoring relationships.* What can be done to restore the trust in the relationship so things can be different in the future? How can there be mutuality and reciprocity again?

Forgiving Your Family: A Journey to Healing. Using a similar approach, Kathleen Fischer lays out three fundamental elements in the work of forgiveness within families:

- *Dealing with emotions.* Facing the negative energy that keeps the hurts alive.

- *Changing perspective on the person who inflicted pain.* Seeing the person through a "new lens"—not as totally "bad," but as a person grappling with their own life struggles. (I would add to that seeing the other person as a person of value, despite what they have done; this is key.)

- *Opening to the possibility of reconciliation.* Unlocking your heart and mind to the challenge of restoring relationships beyond forgiveness.

I highly recommend this book. It is an excellent tool for a family who wants to spend some dedicated time working on the forgiveness process in earnest, and it also has very helpful reflections and prayers to ponder. It could also be used in a class on forgiveness for caregivers in a community of faith.

Forgive for Good: A Proven Prescription for Health and Happiness. Frederic Luskin, who directs the Stanford Forgiveness Project in California, approaches the concept of forgiveness from the standpoint of the forgiver. His research has shown that people who forgive seem to have less anger, be less stressed, and be less depressed than those who hang on to old wrongs. The research has also shown that people with high blood pressure have been able to lower it significantly by learning to forgive. These are certainly important findings to consider in looking at forgiveness issues in caresharing, and the nine steps Luskin suggests for letting go of resentments and old hurts can be very useful for the one who has been wronged.

www.loveandforgive.org. Recently, I discovered this website devoted to love and forgiveness. Developed and maintained by the Fetzer Institute, it is called the Campaign for Love and Forgiveness. The site offers some very helpful interactive exercises for dealing with forgiveness, especially an online ritual of forgiveness called "Letting Go."

Twelve-step programs. The twelve steps of the anonymous groups have given us a model for a forgiveness process. As people work through the twelve steps, they create an inventory of their lives and make a list of people they have harmed. Then, with support and guidance from a sponsor or third party, they approach the people they have wronged and ask for forgiveness, make amends, and restore what has been damaged as much as possible. This series of actions takes the work of forgiveness seriously.

Whether you or your care partner is at the beginning of the forgiveness journey or somewhere along the way, it is important to remember that, even if you cannot complete the work of forgiveness, there is still value in going through the process. The exploration and action steps can be healing no matter where you are along the forgiveness continuum. And remember as well that, though forgiveness starts individually—very likely with you making the first move—it has broader implications. You may be dealing with past issues, but forgiveness is ultimately meaningful work not only for fuller relationships today but also for the future. Even when you take the smallest step in acknowledging honestly who has been harmed and where forgiveness is needed, you may break negative cycles for future generations to come.

SPIRITUAL DIMENSIONS OF FORGIVENESS

Our spiritual and religious beliefs are the underpinnings for the way we understand forgiveness, and most of the world's religions teach and encourage the practice of forgiveness. The Hebrew Bible, for example, is full of stories of God's people who managed to do all manner of terrible things and yet were forgiven by a God of mercy. Christianity is based on the idea of divine love, that Jesus died to offer humankind the chance for forgiveness. Christians believe that we are forgiven not because we are deserving of it or because of things we've done, but because of God's grace. Islam also teaches that forgiving each other, and the mercy and forgiveness of Allah, are paramount. And in Buddhism, forgiveness is seen as an act of letting go of hurt feelings and extending goodwill to those who have hurt us.

If you are working with your care partner on issues of forgiveness, it is important to understand their religious beliefs about forgiveness. For example, many Christians I know count on the promise that God forgives, over and over again: "I am a forgiven child of God. I do my best, but I have made, and do make, mistakes. If God can forgive me, how can I do less than to forgive myself and others? I can trust in that forgiveness to allow me to get through this day and all others."

Religious traditions also offer some practical supports for the work of forgiveness, especially in the areas of rituals and prayers.

RITUALS OF FORGIVENESS

Many of us benefit from structured observances to forgive and be forgiven, and our various religious traditions have rich rituals to help us do that.

In the Jewish tradition, Yom Kippur, or the Day of Atonement, is the holiest day of the year. It is a day for people to reflect on and deal with the sins of the past year. Since the day of Yom Kippur itself is set aside as a day to ask forgiveness from God, Jews must atone for their wrongs against other people, and seek reconciliation, during the ten days in between Rosh Hashanah, the Jewish spiritual new year, and Yom Kippur. The time in between these two holy days is known as the Ten Days of Awe.

In Christianity, the ritual of Eucharist, or Holy Communion, is a reminder of the sacrifice that Jesus made for the forgiveness of all. The reflective seasons of Advent and Lent, and the private and collective confession and absolution in many Christian traditions, are also key observances. These can be very meaningful rituals for an individual's forgiveness journey, giving them the inner strength to do the work of forgiveness in their own lives.

In the Islamic tradition, the month of Ramadan is called the Month of Forgiveness, and the practice of daily prayer and fasting is also a time of seeking forgiveness from the Creator.

If your care partner cannot get to the religious observance of their choice because of health limitations, you may need to be proactive about asking other people to help make that possible. For example, you could request that a clergyperson visit your care partner and offer the rituals and prayers that are important to them. If the one you are caring for is dying, it is especially crucial to make arrangements for them to participate in the rituals or ceremonies of forgiveness that are significant for them.

As part of your own self-care as a carer, observing forgiveness rituals that are part of your tradition can help you have a clear mind and heart to better focus on the caresharing relationship. If you need to, ask someone to stay with your care partner so you can attend services.

You might also consider developing your own personal rituals and rites of forgiveness. At times, I have encouraged people to write a letter to the person they want to forgive, or to the person from whom they need to ask forgiveness. The goal is to record all the issues *for themselves* as specifically as possible, expressing their real feelings about the incident or event that led to the hurt. They can then choose to send the letter, burn it and scatter the ashes, bury it, or tear it up. It is a way of letting go, which is a key part of the healing process of forgiveness. You or your care partner might find this personal ceremony very meaningful. If your care partner is not able to write, you might offer to be a scribe for them, to put their words in writing (assuring them of complete confidentiality, of course). This kind of letter-writing ritual might also be healing for other family members or people involved in the caresharing situation.

Whether your forgiveness ritual is part of your religious tradition or a simple ritual you have created, there is a transformation that happens because of the action you have taken. Very often, these tangible symbols and ceremonial acts can change your feelings, help you in your healing, and aid you in moving forward.

PRAYERS FOR FORGIVENESS

Prayer can be a very meaningful part of the work of forgiving and being forgiven. Prayer is important on many levels, and for many people it offers strength and support throughout life. When it comes to forgiveness issues, many people pray by name for those who have wronged them, or for those whom they have wronged. Others make their personal petitions first, asking God to forgive them, before they ask forgiveness of another. Many find that dealing with the difficult issues of forgiveness in prayer first helps them do the difficult work of forgiving and being forgiven. The formalized prayers of various religions can provide helpful templates for your forgiveness prayers.

The Lord's Prayer in the Christian tradition, for example, includes the line, "Forgive us our trespasses as we forgive those who trespass against us." I know many people who repeat this line over and over to help them center on forgiveness.

Another helpful forgiveness prayer is the Prayer of St. Francis, which in AA is referred to as the "Eleventh Step Prayer": "Lord, make me a channel of thy peace; that where there is hatred, I may bring love; that where there is wrong, I may bring the spirit of forgiveness."

Praying the Psalms can be beneficial as well. Psalm 51 is an example of the cries of the psalmist for cleansing and pardon: "Have mercy on me, O God, according to your steadfast love; according to your abundant mercy blot out my transgressions" (v. 1).

Psalm 103 is a reminder that God is a forgiving God: "[God] is merciful and gracious, slow to anger and abounding in steadfast love … [The Divine] does not deal with us according to our sins, nor repay us according to our iniquities. For as the heavens are high above the earth, so great is [God's] steadfast love toward those who fear [God]; as far as the east is from the west, so far [the Divine Presence] removes our transgressions from us" (v. 10–12).

Prayer can be very effective for those who believe in its power. The specific wording or style of prayer is less important than the practice and intention of prayer. Prayer not only offers a connection with a Source of Love and Power beyond human limits, but the familiar words and routines also provide a comforting place to start the process of forgiveness, especially when you are under stress.

RECONCILIATION

If your *only* goal in forgiving is reconciliation, you are missing the bigger picture. If that statement startles you, consider the nature of reconciliation. *Reconciliation* means to rehabilitate a relationship, and both parties need to respond to the idea of working things out before reconciliation can happen. Both need to be doing their own healing work, and this takes a sense of reciprocity and a mutual commitment.

Although reconciliation may be something you wish for, or helping your care partner reconcile with their family may be high on the priority list, in reality, there are times when reconciliation is just not possible. If, for example, someone does not accept your apology, the forgiveness is one-sided and there is no reconciliation. Remember that reconciliation will not take you or your care partner back to living your lives the way you did before an offense occurred. You have already been affected by the incident and have been changed by it. This is not good or bad; it just *is*.

Marcia Ford, in her reflective book *The Sacred Art of Forgiveness: Forgiving Ourselves and Others through God's Grace* (SkyLight Paths), offers three suggestions regarding reconciliation. First, the choice to approach reconciliation with another is a personal choice. No one can pressure you into it. Second, just because you have thought about starting reconciliation, you have no obligation to follow through on it later if it does not seem like the correct choice. And, most important, you do not have the final say about what the outcome will be. You cannot force reconciliation on someone else, nor can they require you to reconcile with them.

These are helpful considerations for the caresharing setting. If you do not achieve the resolution you want, it is not useful to beat yourself up about it. I think of a situation where a daughter approached me about her mom. The mother had been living alone but had recently taken a turn for the worse. The daughter was very concerned about her mom, yet as we talked, it was clear that a lifetime of hurts had accumulated between them. Each time the daughter had attempted to talk with her mom about their relationship, her mother had rebuffed her. The daughter told me that she wanted to do what was best for her mom, that she would financially support a good option that would help her mother's living situation, but she also said, quite candidly, that she could not do hands-on care for her mom: "I have been in therapy for years to get my own life together. I love and forgive my mom, but I cannot care for her." This daughter eventually made a choice to care about her mom by finding and paying for good-quality care. The hurts were too great to overcome to make any further reconciliation possible.

If this situation sounds familiar to you, or you are feeling like a failure in trying to reconcile with someone who needs care, I'll repeat this important statement for emphasis: *Reconciliation is not always possible.* You may have done, and may be doing, the best you can with the abilities and opportunities you have. Sometimes, in fact, there are situations where you might have very good reasons *not* to reconcile. There may be times, for example, when it is not safe to reconcile. If you have been the victim of a crime or have been abused by someone close, and suffered the irreparable breaking of trust that often goes along with that, you may not be able to reconcile, nor may it be the best course.

I've also seen families who never get to the restoration of relationships, even though the care partner has made some serious attempts. There is just too much hurt for the reconciliation to happen. But, again, remember that any work on the forgiveness process can be helpful.

Think of it this way: Forgiving does not automatically *equal* reconciling, nor does forgiving *require* reconciling. Forgiveness is a valuable process in and of itself. Even working through the earlier stages of the forgiving process can help you and your care partner live more fully. And by doing your own work of forgiveness, you can keep hurts and anger from undermining your energy and compassion in the dance of caresharing. It is *always* beneficial to do the work of forgiveness, even if you are the only one who receives the healing benefit.

No matter how it is configured, forgiveness is an ongoing process. No person has only *one* event in a lifetime where forgiveness or forgiving is required. Making mistakes and hurting another is part of the human condition. And forgiving those mistakes and hurts does not happen overnight, nor does it happen easily. Forgiveness involves many steps and requires a true willingness to face the concerns and to move forward.

The road to forgiving, or accepting forgiveness, is uneven, with many twists and turns along the way. It is not a direct path from one place to the next. And you need to remember that forgiving does not always restore a relationship. Yet the process of forgiveness is a healing experience that is a vital part of making peace within, strengthening relationships with others, and making peace with God.

Many years ago I saw the play *The Old Settler* by John Henry Raymond. The main characters are two sisters with long-standing, unresolved issues between them. Although these hurts had kept them physically and mentally apart for several years, at another level they were strongly tied together by the negative energy that it took for each of them *not* to face up to these issues. As the play progresses, one sister is given an opportunity to change her life and experience happiness in a new relationship. The other sister has great difficulty allowing this, because of the past hurts, and their emotional connection deteriorates further. In the course of the play, the sisters discuss the delicate and painful issues that hang heavily between them with great honesty, and, eventually, they forgive each other and reconcile.

For me, this play is a poignant reminder of the importance of forgiveness in families across time. There is a wonderful sense of grace in the forgiveness journey. Although it may be difficult to do, working on forgiveness issues can create healing both for the person who has been hurt and for the person who has done wrong. Being able to request forgiveness, and to offer forgiveness, is an important part of caresharing work that opens the way for the dance of caresharing to go on, unencumbered by the baggage of past issues.

As you consider the forgiveness issues that you and your care partner face, I'll leave you with a few reminders of some important considerations about the forgiveness journey:

- Forgiveness has implications for your mental, physical, and spiritual health.

- When barriers get in the way of asking for or granting forgiveness, you can ask for third-party help.

- Forgiveness is a process, and it takes time. Be gentle with the person you love and with yourself. You may need to see things through a new lens.

- Issues that arise in caresharing can be catalysts for forgiving and being forgiven.

- Each person and relationship is unique, and you and your care partner will each make your own way in dealing with hurts, resentments, and anger.

- Use familiar religious rituals of forgiveness, or develop rituals of your own, to help you and your care partner with the forgiveness process.

- Reconciliation is not always the final answer, but the process of forgiveness, at any step, has value.

- As you are able to accept God's forgiveness for your limits, so, too, can you forgive others. This is grace. You do not walk the path of forgiving alone.

SHARING HOPE

An Active Process One Step at a Time

THE IMPORTANCE OF HOPE
IN CARESHARING

"Don't worry. Everything will be all right." When you hear the word *hope,* does this unrealistic platitude come to mind? This cliché is not real hope but simply an attempt to help people feel better. It can be tempting to placate your care partner with such a comment when you don't know what else to say or do. Or other people who are uncomfortable walking the difficult path of caring with you may say something similar. However, these Pollyanna-type words do not help in the face of difficult concerns and decisions, and, unfortunately, may leave you or your care partner feeling discounted and alone.

Because of its subtle quality, hope is often undervalued—or even overlooked—as an integral facet of caresharing. Yet maintaining a genuine sense of hope is essential both for your well-being and for the well-being of your care partner, though it can be hard to hold on to. You must also have a realistic view of hope. And the personal definition of hope that you hold, and that your care partner holds, needs to make sense to each of you.

Your level of hope shapes your daily outlook and your future prospects. Hope can help you move positively from today toward tomorrow—not through rose-colored lenses but with reality firmly in place. Hope can give you the expectation that you have the strength to confront and deal with whatever lies ahead. Like a searchlight that shines even when darkness threatens to envelop you, hope can be a beacon in rough times.

Life is full of challenges, and in the caresharing setting especially, you might feel as if way too many burdens have been dumped on you and your care partner. But even when caresharing seems almost unmanageable, I believe it is possible to maintain a sense of hope. I am a realist, and by saying this, I am in no way minimizing all the dilemmas you face in caring for and about another. However, there is a paradox in hope, in that it may be best achieved during times of adversity. The writings of people such as Anne Frank and Viktor Frankl, who both wrote with great personal hope even in the midst of the terrible things that they faced during the Holocaust, attest to the resiliency of hope.

Hope is both a spiritual tool and a constant process. It is not something you "possess" or gain when you resolve issues once and for all. Rather, hope fluctuates back and forth over time, often meaning that you will take one step forward, two steps back, over and over again. Hope is also a process that bridges the past with the future, and in the dance of caresharing, it is very closely interwoven with interdependency and reciprocity.

When you truly come to grips with the fact that you do not do caring alone, you can open yourself to the power of hope as a reciprocal process. Even when an illness or the formidable challenges of care overwhelm you or your care partner, hope can enter as a small shaft of light in the presence of others whom you trust and know you can rely on. Other people can help you keep a flexible outlook on life and lead you back to being hopeful. Other people can help restore your ability to "bounce back." And within

189

the caresharing partnership, you and the one you are caring for can help each other rebound from hopelessness to hopefulness.

As you consider the factors that make for realistic hope for you and your care partner, it is important to remember that there is no "one size fits all" approach to maintaining hope, nor is there only one kind of hope. Physician Jerome Groopman makes a strong case for the ways that hope can be surprising in the complexities of illness and disability. The narratives in his book *The Anatomy of Hope: How People Prevail in the Face of Illness* describe amazing situations, including his own, where hope has sustained people in often miraculous ways. His clear admonition is to take care not to unduly limit the parameters of hope.

On this caresharing journey, consider the value of hope in your own situation as you plan ahead and make decisions about life, cope with illness or disability, or perhaps face the impending death of the one you are caring for. Sometimes these "big" concerns seem to require more hope than you can muster at the moment. Even in these hard situations, you may find hope by considering the small successes and changes in the daily life of the one for whom you are caring.

In the pages that follow, I will offer many practical suggestions for your journey of hope. Some will resonate with you; others may have little relevance to you. Use what seems to apply to your situation and leave the rest, remembering as you read that hope is a one-step-at-a-time process in the circumstances you face.

DEFINITIONS OF HOPE

Because hope covers a very broad spectrum of thoughts and emotions, it has been defined in many different ways. It is both a noun and a verb, a phenomenon and a process. It can be complicated to explain and even more difficult to maintain, and the explanations may vary from situation to situation. Theologians and psychologists, nurses and health care workers, and individuals faced with a wide variety of daunting experiences have identified hope in numerous ways. There is no one right way to think about hope, and you and your care partner bring your unique perspectives to the understanding of hope. Here are some insights about hope to consider.

HOPE CHANGES OVER TIME

Hope may go through changes during the course of an illness or disability, and what you hope for may be transformed along the way. If your care partner has a chronic illness or is very frail, you and they may rethink your assumptions of what the "good life" is. The busyness of life's activities pales in significance when you know you have only a short time to share with the one you love. Your relationship becomes more important than any projects or trips or material acquisitions.

When someone is given a diagnosis of a terminal illness, I've seen an understandable progression of hope. At first, they might hope that a cure will be found before they die. In realizing that this may not be a reality for them, they may change their hope to wanting to be alive long enough to see a grandchild born or celebrate their fiftieth wedding anniversary. Having achieved that, their hope may be that, in their dying, they will have people around them who care about them (or, as some have told me, they may hope to die alone). Later, they may hope to die pain-free. Hope changes because the process they are experiencing is changing them. They have not given up hope, but they see it from a different perspective.

In my work I have often seen this transformation of hope in the bargaining that happens as someone responds to a terminal diagnosis. A similar process can take place when a loved one has dementia: Although possibilities for intimacy and sharing change from what might have been possible earlier in the relationship, there is always hope for connection, if you understand that it may need to be found and expressed in alternative ways.

HOPE IS DIFFERENT THINGS FOR DIFFERENT PEOPLE

In truth, no matter what the disability or disease, there are many ways people experience and express hope. What matters most is an individual's perception and expression of hope. To help you understand what hope "looks like" in your situation, it is worth considering these reflective questions, either along with your care partner or for yourself:

- How does my care partner define hope?
- How do I define it?
- How do I see hope in relationship to my care partner and their situation?

In working with groups seeking to understand the concept of hope, I have often facilitated a "hope exercise." Many participants have come back to tell me that this has been a helpful way of getting in touch with what hope means to them, so I offer it here in a slightly adapted way. You may use it as a tool to help both you and your care partner further understand how you see hope. You can do the exercise on your own, or with each other.

1. Gather some index cards and some pens, markers, crayons, and/or stickers (your materials may depend on your care partner's capabilities).

2. Take a few minutes to imagine the things that give you hope personally.

3. Use words, drawings, or stickers to put your "hope images" on a card. You could use one card for each thought, so you can create a "hope file" of cards, or you could make a "mini-collage" of hope images on one card.

4. If you are doing this exercise with your care partner, describe to each other what your words and images represent. (You may also want to share your images with a support group or a friend who is with you on this caresharing journey.)

5. You could use the cards to create a "hope quilt" on a bulletin board, or lay them out on a table to share with others, or collect them in a "hope file" to pull out on a day when hope is elusive.

6. Consider displaying one card in a prominent place, where it will be a daily visual reminder of what hope means.

FOUR KEY ASPECTS OF HOPE

I am indebted to Carol Farran, Kaye Herth, and Judith Popovich for their excellent research book, *Hope and Hopelessness: Critical Clinical Constructs.* When I first read their work on hope, many thoughts about the difficult-to-understand concept of hope became clearer for me. Their perspectives, bolstered by their research in medical situations, might give you some new ways to reconsider hope in your situation. Dr. Farran, a breast cancer survivor, and her colleagues have identified four central attributes of hope: as an experiential (or existential) process, as a rational thought process, as a relational process, and as a spiritual process.

HOPE IS MAKING SENSE OF WHAT IS HAPPENING

Farran and her colleagues start by describing hope as an "experiential or existential process." Or, to put it another way, hope is ultimately connected with making sense out of what has happened to you and your care partner, and where you are in your life's journey. How you both make sense of suffering is key.

In 1990 I had the privilege of meeting Viktor Frankl at an American Society on Aging meeting and to hear him say, "Despair is suffering without meaning." In his classic book *Man's Search for Meaning,* in which Frankl relates the awful experiences he survived in the concentration camps of World War II, he describes how he found meaning in the goodness of individuals who comforted others and shared what little food they had.

Although most of us are not subjected to such extreme suffering, we do have suffering in our lives nonetheless. You and your care partner may be struggling with chronic pain, or mental anguish, or approaching death. Developing a sense of meaning about what is happening for you can indeed keep you from despairing and help you maintain hope. Frankl's life and work bear testament to this. As part of this process, you also need to believe that what you and your partner are doing is the best that you can, and that what you are doing needs to make sense to *you*, no matter what the final outcome of your situation may be.

HOPE IS DEVELOPING GOALS AND FINDING RESOURCES

Farran and her colleagues describe a second characteristic of hope as a "rational thought process." If you're thinking that *rational* means "it's all in your head," try thinking of *rational* as grounding hope in reality. This way of looking at hope has profound implications for care partners. This turns hope into an active process that includes developing goals, finding resources (internal or external) to meet them, and taking action over time. The process includes the impact of what's happened to people in the past, what's going on now, and how they see their future. Time is an important part of the process of hope, and it is important not to give up on your care partner's goals too soon.

Helping your care partner set reasonable and realistic goals is a major part of keeping hope alive. Considering "what is possible" is a hopeful stance that presumes that more than one option exists in a particular situation. Whether the goal is walking a certain distance in physical therapy, trying a new medication to deal with depression, or working with a counselor on forgiveness issues with estranged family members, helping your care partner establish realistic, attainable goals—and helping them find the assistance needed to carry out those goals—will give them a sense of control over their lives, which far too many care receivers feel has been taken from them.

Helping your care partner think through possibilities and set goals may require the gentle art of negotiation. Interdependence is key; you need to be careful not to make all the decisions. Reciprocity is a crucial part of sorting out what your care partner wants to do and can do, and deciding what help or resources they require to reach their particular aims. If your care partner is someone who has always been "in charge" in their work or home, they may be having an especially difficult time letting others care for them. Building on their sense of mastery or capacity is an important element in keeping their hope alive. The power to make even the smallest choices can strengthen hope, and this empowerment is vital.

Once your care partner has set a goal, they may have to reach deep inside to discover their inner resources to meet that goal. Their humor, faith, "true grit," determination, perseverance, and resilience will become especially important in holding on to hope as they work toward their goal.

Help your care partner identify outside resources (persons and programs) to help along the way. This is not necessarily a matter of finding people to automatically do things for your care partner, but identifying who can be on "standby" to assist when and as they are needed. You might find it helpful to brainstorm with your care partner names of people—in your extended family, community, or faith community—who could be part of a network of external supports. Naming who they are, how they might be able to assist, and when and who will make the request are all details that, if your care partner is able to be a part of planning, will go a long way toward making them feel empowered rather than "taken care of."

Once your care partner has made *one* decision toward hope, being hopeful for the future may be easier. Acting on hopeful behaviors may, in fact, actually change your care partner's feelings about what is transpiring in their lives. Many times I've seen people who act "as if" something were true, and then they start to believe it *is* true. In other words, it is possible to *act* on hope even in situations that may seem hopeless.

HOPE IS STANDING "SHOULDER TO SHOULDER"

The third finding of Farran and her team is that hope is a "relational process." This is something I have seen often in my social work career: People who share with others with real compassion, no matter what their role or relationship, are key to hope. I have learned the importance of purposeful relationships where people connect in a genuine and personal way.

Time after time, when I have become painfully aware that there was nothing tangible I could do for another, I have been surprised to hear that person tell me how helpful I have been. I am convinced that it was because I was *there*. The simple act of accompanying another along the journey, no matter what that path holds, is part of the relational process that leads to hope.

Believing that your caring relationship makes a difference, even when you have little power over your care receiver's illness or disability, can help you both keep heart. Your nurturing and sustaining relationship can be the basis of hope in caresharing, even when other concerns and worries threaten to overwhelm your care partner. Your listening ear and compassionate heart can make a big difference in their level of hopefulness.

I have come to picture hope as standing "shoulder to shoulder" with another. The image comes from a sermon the pastor of our church gave about how we are stronger standing "shoulder to shoulder" than we are if we try to stand alone to face adversity and struggles. As I listened to these words from my vantage point in the choir seats, I watched a member of our parish, who had recently been widowed, lean over in his pew to touch his shoulder to the shoulder of another. This wonderful image has stayed with me as a reminder of how we stand shoulder to shoulder with the people we care about, and with others in our support network. We are all stronger when we have someone to walk with us, to console us in difficult times.

Hope for you and your care partner may be about realizing that you are not in this dance of caresharing alone, that there are others who will walk with you and support you, both in tangible and intangible ways. Hope is trusting that there are such people, and that there will be others, who will accompany you on this long path.

One time I was in a hospital waiting room while my husband was undergoing hand surgery when a new pastoral ministry intern from my church happened by. I told her that I felt at a disadvantage in getting acquainted with her for the first time in this way. She replied, "On the contrary, I like to be with people in the 'holding time.'" She explained that when people were waiting, as I was for the results of surgery, she saw them as being in a holding pattern for their lives.

I was struck by that image and have been increasingly aware of how much of caresharing is living in a "holding time." It's a little like being in a plane in a holding pattern over an airport when it's not able to land. As passengers, we wonder how long it will take, and we are uncertain about how our plans might have to change. As I thought about this idea of "holding," I also thought about containers that hold liquids to keep them from spilling out. I think that is what people who are "with us" in caresharing do for us.

Sometimes you will need physical holding, someone who will give you a big hug or hold you while you cry. Sometimes you will need more tangible "holding" in the support of meals and rides and caregiving help. Even more, you may need to be held up by others in prayer and emotional support. When you can let yourself be held by others, you can experience a renewed sense of hope. Hope can become real in the love of others who, by holding you and standing with you "shoulder to shoulder," give you strength for the future. This is a valuable gift. In those times where you are waiting and wondering about "what happens next," you can draw on this sense of hope, not that everything is necessarily going to be "all right," but that someone will be there with you as you go through whatever you are facing.

HOPE IS BELIEVING IN A POWER BEYOND OURSELVES
In an often-quoted biblical passage used at many weddings, hope is held between faith and love: "And now faith, hope, and love abide, these three" (1 Cor. 13:13). So, too, do faith and love (the spiritual and the relational) provide the support for hope in the dance of caresharing. In Farran and her colleagues' research on hope, they describe the "spiritual or transcendent process" as the fourth attribute of hope. This aspect relates to the faith and beliefs that give us hope for the future.

Theologians have addressed hope as a spiritual process for centuries. For some people, spiritual hope includes a longing for an afterlife where things will be better. When there is faith that something better awaits us in another world, the promise of even an unseen future can bring hope. For others, spiritual hope stems from believing that there is a Power greater than any individual or group of people in charge of the world. And for many of us, knowing that there is a God or Higher Power who cares about us and those we love helps us keep heart.

The hope that comes from faith is important and may well be what keeps us moving each day in caresharing. I particularly value a verse in the Hebrew Bible that reminds me that, even as I grow older, God will carry and save me: "Even when you turn gray I will carry you. I have made, and I will bear; I will carry and will save" (Isa. 46:4). And I am always encouraged by the image of God lifting up the Israelites on eagles' wings: "I bore you on eagles' wings and brought you to myself" (Exod. 19:4). Outside my window in the Pacific Northwest, I often see these strong, majestic birds flying through the valley. The thought of God bearing me up to fly and soar on those great wings is a great reminder of hope. Even when I am too weak to "fly" spiritually and emotionally, I am held up on the wings of an eagle.

However you and your care partner experience the spiritual or transcendent, this is a meaningful aspect of your hope life. Depending on your care receiver's willingness and cognitive abilities, it can be very beneficial for you to explore together your respective beliefs and how they impact your sense of hope. By sharing your faith perspectives, you can each learn from the other. Together, you can explore the beliefs you were taught, how they might have changed for you over the years, and how they might be shifting even now in this caresharing situation. For example, some care receivers have trouble reconciling their long-standing belief that "God is in charge" because that might imply God wants them to be sick. A more hopeful perspective for them might be that God is "taking care of things" on their behalf in their circumstances. Your reciprocal sharing can help you reclaim the spiritual attributes of hope that give you strength for each day.

You and your care partner will experience the ups and downs of hope; that is the nature of the caresharing journey. As you move through the days and weeks ahead, I encourage you to consider how each of these four aspects of hope relates to you: making sense out of what's happening, grounding your hope in reality, sharing compassion, and looking to your faith to stay hopeful. I have taken the liberty of turning these components of hope into a personal creed of hope. You might find it helpful to post these affirmations in a spot where they can remind you and your care partner of ways you can hold onto the "big picture" of hope.

ieve there is meaning in this experience.

lieve there are things I can accomplish today and people
ɔ will help me.

ɘlieve in my family and friends who will love me through
this.

🖉 I believe that a Power greater than this disease or disability is
with me.

KEEPING HOPE ALIVE

The flip side of hope is hopelessness. Sometimes I see carers totally reject hope for someone early in an illness or disability journey. This happens far too often among those caring for people struggling with dementia. And when the carer feels hopeless, it is telegraphed to the person being cared for, nonverbally or verbally. Even if people try to hide it, the sense of resignation that goes along with hopelessness comes out, sometimes in unexpected ways.

Unfortunately, when people feel hopeless, they also make choices that can negatively affect them for the future. Examples abound in people who try to drown their sorrows in alcohol, drugs, or other destructive behaviors. Or in people who say, "What's the use of trying to change anything?" I have seen people with lung cancer or emphysema, who are required to be on oxygen, still continue to smoke. Despite the jeopardy that this puts them in, their attitude is, "Well, I am going to die anyway." Essentially, they have given up.

At the same time, I have known elders and those with disabilities who have been role models of how to keep hope alive, despite all the assaults they have suffered. They have, in fact, helped me shape my own sense of hope. Ingrid, a seemingly frail ninety-year-old with limited vision and hearing, attended a class where I posed the question, "How old is old?" She answered, "Old is when you quit dreaming your dreams, and I haven't quit dreaming yet!"

What hope there is in that line! This very fragile-looking lady wasn't willing to give up her dreams. She was most aware of her limitations, but she was moving beyond them in her emotional and spiritual life. Her spirit and her hope for the future were firmly intact.

You or your care partner may have a sense that you have no control or choices in your lives, and that there is nothing that you can do to make things better. You may feel stuck in your plight. The losses you have sustained may seem too overwhelming to conquer or even to do anything about. Although it is true that you may not be able to change anything about a disease process or chronic illness, there are steps you can take to keep hope and heart alive, both for yourself and for the person you care about.

CULTIVATE REALISTIC HOPE

Hope is about imaging the realizable. It is built on the reservoir of inner strengths that both you and your care partner possess, not on wishful thinking. Unrealistic optimism is not hopeful; it is only a hollow approximation. Unrealistic hope would be to say to a person in hospice care, "I know you will totally recover from your cancer," when it is clear that they will not. From the perspective of realistic hope, you might say instead, "You may be dying, but we will do all we can to keep you pain-free, and we will journey with you."

By the same token, unrealistic *pessimism* may be just as harmful as unrealistic optimism. If you convey to your care partner that something they want to do or accomplish is impossible to achieve, your message may be just as unhelpful as false reassurance. If you "correct" them for their "unrealistic hope," you may be closing the door to a potential source of hope. Their "unrealistic hope" may, in fact, be the very catalyst keeping them alive! If, for example, your care partner is clinging to a seemingly unrealistic idea of how much progress they can make in physical therapy, that skewed idea may be what is keeping them going. And even with the best human predictions—about rates of recovery, treatment outcomes, abilities returning—medical professionals have been incorrect. People receiving care have surprised their professional carers many times by their sheer grit and resiliency. People face and conquer obstacles that no one thought they could master. Miracles do happen. It is also important to keep in mind that, just because something was not possible in the past, this does not mean it is not attainable at the present time or in the future.

I do need to add a word of caution here. Sometimes the sense of "I can do it" can become a double-edged sword. Although perseverance is good, when taken too far, it can get in the way of requesting or accepting aid when it is needed. If your care partner sees themselves as stronger than they actually are, they may attempt to do more than they actually can, sometimes in an attempt to prove to others how capable they are. But by not asking for the assistance they need, they may end up in precarious circumstances, which, in turn, will alarm you and hinder their progress.

As a carer, you walk a fine line between being "realistic" with your care partner and being encouraging. It's a delicate balance. Realistic hope requires that both you and your care partner look at the positive and negative aspects of the situation in which you find yourselves. It requires persistence to keep your eye on the outcome of a better life. It means encouraging those strengths and possibilities that are still available to your care partner. It means building on the strengths that they possess and providing assistance where it is needed. Letting your care partner take the lead in what is realistic for them can go a long way in keeping hope alive.

BE AWARE OF YOUR LIMITS

When you are in a caresharing partnership, because you are already vulnerable to loss, general feelings of hopelessness around you may affect you even more than normal and add to your sense of burden. The worries of the world may lie especially heavily upon you as a caregiver. It is important not to underestimate the power of world events to assault your hope. If you absorb these concerns on top of the concerns you are already facing in caresharing, things can get pretty overwhelming.

Although I'm not suggesting that you ignore world concerns, I am saying that you need to be aware of your limits. You need to remember that there are many people who are doing things to resolve global and local problems; your focus needs to be on what you can do in your caresharing partnership. Your energy needs to be directed toward your care partner and yourself if you are to keep a sense of hope alive and maintain the ability to deal with the things that you can. You need to be reasonable about the scope of what you take on.

FIND BRIDGES TO HOPE

There will be times in the caresharing process when hope wanes for you or your care partner, such as when you feel discouraged by the day's realities or by the results of some new medical report. That is the time to seek out a "bridge to hope," someone from whom you can borrow hope for a while, or something you can do for yourself that will raise your spirits and restore your sense of hope.

Anyone who keeps you connected with hope can be a bridge to hope. You may know someone who is a "natural optimist," someone who is hopeful about life in general. Their natural enthusiasm for life may be just what you need. Or perhaps you know someone who is at a different place in their lives than you are, someone younger and more energetic, who has positive energy to contribute to your particular circumstances. They may be able to step in and help when you feel too weary to walk forward on your own.

You can also find bridges to hope in your faith, your knowledge, and the occurrences of daily life. Be open to the beliefs that resonate in your heart. Look to the things you have learned about life in general, and about yourself and your care partner in particular, that have kept you hopeful in the past. See how even little things, such as the opening of a flower bud or berry plants bearing fruit, can become bridges to hope.

HAVE SOMETHING TO LOOK FORWARD TO
"Hope includes a future story." This is one of five themes of hope that Ted Bowman outlines in his wonderful little workbook on hope, *Finding Hope When Dreams Have Shattered.* For hope to have a future story, you and your care partner both need to have something you can look forward to. When your care partner has an expectation that something will happen in a new day, hope can get them out of bed in the morning. Many times, I've seen care partners who have responsibilities for pets get up in the morning because they are *needed* to care for that pet. (The positive effects of a pet to soothe a person or provide continuity with the past have also been well documented.)

Hope for the future in little things is key. Many people have oversized expectations, and when these things don't materialize, hope can easily crumble, making it that much harder to feel hopeful again. The reality is that most of us find hope in the smaller things of life. I often give the gift of a bulb that will grow in the winter to people who are home-centered. Watching a plant develop can bring joy; needing to water and tend to it can provide a reason to get up.

Hope can happen in tiny increments. It is about creating and holding on to expectations and desires no matter where disability or illness takes you. When was the last time you intentionally sat down and talked with your care partner about what they might look forward to? Or asked them what they might like to see happen so they *could* have something to look forward to? Here are some questions to consider:

- What gives your care partner hope in facing a new day?
- Are there things you could build into a day to help you and your care partner become more hopeful?
- Ask your care partner, "What would make a good day for you?" Once you have a picture of this, see what you might be able to work out to meet this vision of a good day.

Take Care of Body, Mind, and Spirit

Hope and self-care are closely tied together. Although most of this chapter's discussion on hope focuses on helping your care partner so their sense of hope can grow, you also need to take care of your own body, mind, and spirit to keep your own hope alive. These are not luxuries, but necessities. If you are mired in concerns that weigh you down, you can't be hopeful or help your partner cultivate hope. You need to do things that give you a sense of balance in your own life: Keep your mind alert by exploring the things that interest you, exercise and eat right, and do things that keep your spirit alive, whether it is prayer, meditation, reading Scripture or devotional books, or a spiritual practice, such as walking a labyrinth or going on retreat.

Hope and heart are also closely woven together. You need to keep "heart" or you will lose your sense of hope. Let me explain what I mean by that. The Latin root for *heart, cor,* is the root of words such as "courage," "encourage," and "discourage." So, in essence, you keep heart by keeping courage and by encouraging others. It is an interdependent process: As you benefit from others who bolster you, so you, in turn, need to support others in order to keep heart.

I often suggest to caregivers that they take a "heart inventory." Giving some consideration to these questions will help you get a good sense of the current state of your hope and heart. Your responses can help you focus on the strengths in your particular caresharing relationship and renew your hope in the dance of caresharing.

- Why am I a carer?
- Why do I stay in that role?
- How have I grown because of my sharing with my care partner?
- What have I learned?
- What do I look forward to in a positive way?

AN ACTION PLAN
FOR BUILDING ON HOPE

There are many ways to understand hope, but if hope remains an abstract or elusive idea, it is not operational in your own life. As a care partner, it is important to make hope a practical term that you can apply to caresharing on a day-to-day basis. To live in hope, you need to keep on exploring ways to build on hope—for you and for your care partner. Here are some possibilities you might want to consider.

TAKE A "HOPE INVENTORY"

"Is your cup half-full or half-empty?" As common as this metaphorical question is, it is still a useful tool for understanding the way you perceive life. I often suggest to carers that they take a "hope inventory" to gain a clearer picture of how hopeful, or hopeless, they are feeling, and I make the same suggestion to you. Although I know that this may seem like one more thing to do in your busy days of caring, there is something about putting feelings on paper that can pay big dividends. Carers have found that this gives them something concrete to use in their thinking about hope and hopelessness, so I strongly encourage you to try it.

1. Draw two columns, one representing the "cup half-full" stance of feeling hopeful and the other, the "cup half-empty" position of feeling hopeless. (Remember that these categories are not absolute, and some days you will feel more hopeful than others.)

2. Along the side, make six rows, for the larger world around you, your work life, your home life, your relationships (including your care partner), your physical health, and your sense of self-expression (how you present yourself to the world).

	Cup half-full (I feel hopeful)	Cup half-empty (I feel hopeless)
The world around me		
My work life		
My home life		
My relationships		
My physical health		
My sense of self-expression		

3. Then put a checkmark in the columns where you feel there is something hopeful in your life, and mark the areas where you are feeling more hopeless.

This grid will give you a visual picture of the areas where you could build on hope and the areas where you may need to reframe your thinking or look at things from a new perspective. I encourage you to use this information to develop a personal action plan for yourself so you can strengthen your hope. Think of a step you could take to increase the level of your hope in one area, and be as specific as you can about the action you plan to take. Include these details:

- *What* you are going to do?
- *How much* you are going to do?
- *When* you will do it?
- *How many days* a week you will devote to it?

For example, if you see that there is a hope deficit in the area of your physical health, you might decide on a regular exercise plan to help keep your sense of hope alive. Your plan might look something like this:

- *What:* Take a walk, concentrating on nature and all the things that give me hope
- *How much:* Three times a week, for thirty minutes
- *When:* Between 7:00 and 7:30 a.m., before I get ready for work
- *How many days a week:* Monday, Wednesday, and Friday

Taking the time to do this inventory and create a personal action plan will give you a practical picture of the health of your hope and help you build up your sense of hope. Many times I have seen that having a plan in place motivates people far more than just *considering* an idea. You will be far more likely to follow through on your ideas and have success in building up hope if you have thoughtfully written out your plan.

Your care partner may find this "hope inventory" helpful as well. Once you have completed the inventory for yourself, you can walk them through the steps. Be sure not to rush them. Depending on their strength and level of wellness, they may need to do this in stages. You may also need to remind them (and yourself!) that an "action plan" does not need to focus on "big" stuff. A small change can go a long way toward making a "cup" seem more full than empty.

SHARE UPLIFTING VIGNETTES AND INSPIRATIONAL STORIES
Reading hopeful stories is an excellent means of inspiring hope. In *Finding Hope When Dreams Have Shattered,* Bowman calls

these "affirmative stories," and his book offers many stories of persons who have been able to go through difficulties and move on to hope. You may find that uplifting vignettes about other caregivers is a good way to raise your own spirits. Reading inspirational stories and autobiographies of famous persons is one of the things I do to keep my hope alive. Magazines that come from church groups (especially women's groups) often have uplifting true stories of persons dealing with tough situations who have been helped by their spiritual perspective. You can also find many affirmative stories on the websites of organizations that deal with chronic illness, such as the "Stories of Hope" section on the American Cancer Society website (www.cancer.org). A good way to find these stories is to type in an online search engine (such as Google) the phrase "stories of hope," followed by the specific problem or illness you are dealing with, such as "stories of hope cancer," or "stories of hope Alzheimer's," or "stories of hope Parkinson's." The search results will usually give a good list of websites you can check out. One website that has inspirational stories of a more general nature that might be interesting to share with your care partner is www.guidepostsmag.com.

SHARE LIFE STORIES

As I have stressed throughout this book, our stories are powerful. It is especially important to tell our stories and to listen to the stories of others as a means of building up hope. Our stories and our hope are integrally intertwined. I think of the stories of hope I have heard over the years from elders and people struggling with disability or chronic illness, and I know I have grown as a person because of their narratives.

I have also learned that if our stories are to have meaning, we need to talk about things that are meaningful to us and not try to pretend that everything is going well. This is where the community of faith can be of so much assistance: People in pastoral care or spiritual direction roles can hear your heavy stories. Support groups are another place where stories of meaning can be shared, even where others might be blessed by your story because some part of your narrative helps them. When you can tell your story as it truly is, with no omissions or pretensions, to someone who is an open, compassionate listener, you are taking a major step toward keeping hope alive.

KEEP A GRATITUDE JOURNAL

I often suggest to caregivers and care receivers the practice of keeping a gratitude journal. It is a way of naming the small things that bring joy on a daily basis. I invite you to give it try. Each day, write down at least five things you are thankful for. (If your care partner is unable physically to write in a journal, offer to be their scribe.) You can use your journals to build reciprocity in your relationship by making a commitment to share with each other what you are grateful for each day. A gratitude journal can also provide a tangible reference when either of you is having a "cup half-empty" day. It will serve as a reminder that small moments of joy are possible even in the midst of illness and disability, and that there is hope in finding that joy.

KEEP MEMENTOS OF MEANING NEARBY

Mementos of meaning can be any objects that give you hope. They might be personal treasures, favorite pictures of people and places, even a pretty flower you've grown in your garden. Keeping these things near you can help you remember what personally gives you hope. I have several friends who keep small rock collections in bowls. These pretty or unusual rocks they've picked up at various beaches and other places in their travels remind them of sites they've enjoyed and are comforting to touch. I have a rock shaped like a bird that I use as a paperweight on my desk, and sometimes I pick it up just for inspiration.

Ask your care partner which mementos of meaning they would like to have nearby. As they name objects, or if they already have objects sitting on a desk or table, ask them the story behind these objects and what each means to them. This is a good way to help them stay in touch with their core of hope.

PRACTICE PRAYER OR MEDITATION

Practicing the discipline of regular prayer or meditation has helped many care partners navigate their lives with a sense of hope. You might want to make a list of passages in the scriptures of your religious tradition that are meaningful to you and use them to pray, especially when your own words are difficult to find. I often search out biblical passages that emphasize God's unwavering love and care, and I find the practice of praying the Psalms especially beneficial. Verses such as "I wait for [God], my soul waits, and in [the Divine's] word I hope" (Ps. 130:5) remind me of the importance of having hope in God. The well-known Prayer of St. Francis is another prayer that has been personally helpful:

> Lord, make me an instrument of Thy peace;
> where there is hatred, let me sow love;
> where there is injury, pardon;
> where there is doubt, faith;
> where there is despair, hope;
> where there is darkness, light;
> and where there is sadness, joy.

Many people use the Serenity Prayer as a prayer of hope: "God, grant me the serenity to accept the things I cannot change, courage to change the things I can, and wisdom to know the difference." It is a simple prayer to remember when you are feeling overwhelmed, and it can remind you of what is truly important in your life.

Most world religions also have formalized prayers for peace, and you may want to use one of them when you feel too overloaded to pray for yourself and your care partner. Praying for peace on a larger scale can bring peace and hope for a better future on a personal level as well.

Whether you pray a specific prayer about hope, create your own prayer for hope, or quietly meditate on the word *hope,* the intention and action are empowering steps. Reaching out beyond yourself for wisdom and insight from a Higher Power is, in itself, an act of hope.

UTILIZE RITES AND RITUALS

Another way to keep hope alive is to make purposeful use of rites and rituals. In most cultures, social rites and rituals serve several functions. At the national or community level, public rites bring healing and hope after a trauma or tragedy, such as the memorials that take place on September 11 each year. Our patriotic rituals on Memorial Day or the Fourth of July bring hope to many in remembering what their citizenship means to them. In your individual situation, there may be certain religious rites that help you keep hope, such as a Communion service or a Service of Healing. You and your care partner may have other rituals from your tradition that are similar to those. If your care partner cannot get to a service that is important to them, ask people in their faith community for help in bringing the ritual to your care partner.

You might also think about developing your own rituals for keeping hope. A simple ritual that I have used with groups is to hold up a bowl and ask people to imagine that it is filled with hope. (Actually, I have filled it with glitter.) We stand in a circle, and while I'm reading a poem about hope, I deposit a bit of "hope" in each person's small plastic bag. I invite each person to keep their bag in a prominent place where it will remind them of hope.

You could perform a similar ritual with your care partner by filling a small bowl with something soft or pretty or colorful that you have around the house (confetti made out of torn sheets of colored paper would work well) and reading a poem about hope together or to each other. Then each of you could take a pinch of the bowl's contents and put it in a bag or basket you can keep close at hand to remind you of hope on a daily basis.

As you think about rituals that would encourage you and your care partner to maintain a sense of hope, don't overlook the possibility that even small rituals can make a difference. An inspirational quotation on a daily breakfast tray or the lighting of a votive candle at sundown can go a long way toward helping keep hope alive.

LISTEN TO FAVORITE MUSIC

Music can be a powerful tool in sharing hope and heart. Listening to favorite music can ease the temporal cares of the day, give you and your care partner an emotionally intimate connection, and keep you both open to hopefulness. Whether you play a recording, sing a song, or play an instrument, music can "infuse hope into the human soul," as Pope Benedict XVI put it.

When I listen to my favorite pieces of classical music, I often find myself in tears, transformed by the sheer beauty of the experience. Singing hymns of hope (such as some of the older favorites, "Lead Kindly Light Amid the Encircling Gloom," "Great Is Thy Faithfulness," and "Be Still, My Soul") can touch the spirit and revitalize feelings of hopefulness. Keep in mind, too, that music can reach the mind and heart of your care partner where words cannot go.

CONNECT ONLINE

At times, hope can come from technological resources. Twenty years ago, this would have been a surprising statement, but today, as more of us are computer savvy, the Internet offers a broad array of options for sharing information, stories, and, ultimately, hope. Not only is the Web an amazing source for inspirational stories, but it can also be a virtual network of support, especially for those who cannot leave their homes. Although connecting to such resources does have its limits compared to face-to-face contact, some websites can be of great assistance in maintaining hope by giving you a chance to interact with people who are going through what you're going through.

You can search for "online support groups" to find support groups in general, or search for the specific type of support group you are looking for, such as "cancer support groups." Although these virtual support groups may not be as satisfying as meeting in person, they do offer another way to keep the door to hope open, especially for people whose mobility and travel are limited.

One award-winning site for caregivers that is particularly easy to navigate is www.strengthforcaring.com. This website includes practical advice in digestible short articles and offers many ways to help you as a carer build on your strengths. The first-person accounts of real-life issues are especially compelling. They offer glimpses of what others are realistically doing in caring for and about others of all ages, and you may find some hopeful ideas you could use.

FIND TIME TO MAKE SHARING HAPPEN

In the days and weeks and months of caresharing, sometimes there is so much going on (tests, medical treatments, visitors, personal caretaking, meal preparation, and so forth) that time for personal sharing with your care partner can become a rare commodity. Or perhaps the opposite is true: As an illness wears on, there may be more time, but it is a time of boredom and lethargy, and the energy to make time for personal sharing simply wanes. Cobbling out opportunities and making time for sharing to happen in a meaningful way is an important piece in the hope puzzle.

BE OPEN TO THE MOMENT

A significant contributor to hope is the ability to fully experience the quality of the moment. This evolves from the Buddhist concept of mindfulness, which, in essence is being fully aware of what is happening, being fully present to where you are, now, in this time and this space. This can happen in everyday occurrences, such as when you and your care partner take hold of a moment to be grateful for the small gifts in your relationship—a smile, the sharing of humor, holding hands.

This is much like the concept that theologian and spiritual writer Henri Nouwen described in *Here and Now* as "being present" to another: "A friend who cares makes it clear that, whatever happens in the external world, being present to each other is what really matters. In fact it matters more than pain, illness, or even death."

When you have this mind-set and are fully present to the moment, this can be a good time to gently start a conversation with your care partner about how they see hope in their situation, and then wait for their willingness to continue the discussion. They may respond or they may not, but there is always the potential for serious reflection and shared connection in these moments. (If they choose not to talk about hope, don't pressure them. You can raise the issue again at another time.) Whenever these moments happen, listening to and reflecting on the words that your care partner uses to describe their state of hope may assist you in helping them plan for the future.

Prepare a Legacy of Hope

There is a need within all of us to pass along something of worth to the next generation, but I've seen many care partners fear that they have nothing of material or tangible value to leave for their loved one. Documents such as ethical wills, spiritual autobiographies, or loving letters enable care receivers and carers alike to pass along the values and beliefs that have imbued their life with meaning. Writing one of these documents can help your care partner shift to a more hopeful perspective as they distill what is important in their lives and in their stories, and put their thoughts on paper for loved ones who will cherish the ideas and understand their importance. Consider these three tools that might empower your care partner to leave a legacy of hope.

Write an ethical will. Ethical wills are actually a very old Orthodox Jewish tradition, but in more recent years, there has been an increased interest in them as a way to pass along relevant information among generations in the Jewish community. I have seen the benefit of ethical wills as I work with people from many backgrounds and traditions. Two excellent resources about ethical wills include *Ethical Wills: Putting Your Values on Paper* by Barry Baines, and *So That Your Values Live On: Ethical Wills and How to Prepare Them* (Jewish Lights) by Jack Riemer and Nathaniel Stampher. Actually, I first became interested in ethical wills when I heard Stampher speak at a meeting about the increasing interest within the Jewish community in creating these documents. It has become clear to me as I use ethical wills with elders and people with disabilities that they are very helpful tools for the transmission of principles and beliefs.

If you would like to help your care partner create an ethical will, here are some of the basics that such a will might include:

- Begin with some information about your family background and how it has influenced you.
- Include the life lessons and specific teachings you learned from your family, your religious tradition, and your personal experiences. Also include any cultural or family traditions about "the way we do things" that have made an impact on you and that you would like to pass on to the next generation.
- Describe your religious and spiritual values.
- Include your hopes and wishes for the future for the significant people in your life.

- End with your blessings for the people who will be reading your ethical will.

Ethical wills can be formal or informal, very serious or humorous, long or short. Whether simple or ornate, they are a thought-filled way of instilling hope not only in the one writing the document—who is reassured that the pivotal values of their life will be passed on to the next generation—but also in the people receiving the document. They have been given a valuable treasure of love and hope. I have seen the ending blessing sections have a particularly profound effect on people who receive ethical wills from an important person in their lives.

If you'd like further information and suggestions on creating an ethical will, check out both books I've referenced. They offer formats for creating the document as well as numerous examples written by people from many eras.

Write a spiritual autobiography. A spiritual autobiography can help your care partner leave a spiritual inheritance to those they cherish. Essentially, this autobiography is their story about personal (and sometimes community) events that have had an impact on how their spiritual perspective developed, and how their faith and spiritual beliefs have helped, or hindered, them in life. This word picture of their spiritual journey can be a gift for generations to come. Here are several ways to approach a spiritual autobiography:

- Describe major events in your life, such as graduations, marriage, birth of a child, grandparenting, loss of parents, work or losing a job, and reflect on how these affected your faith, your values, your spiritual life, and your moral values.

- Explore crises and barriers to your faith, as well as "mountaintop" experiences.

- Offer your discernment of your calling, mission, and vocation in life.

- Look at the spiritual challenges and growth that took place when your disability or illness began.

- Highlight the important spiritual principles that have become a core part of your perspective on living and dying.

Write loving letters. Something as simple as a loving letter is another helpful, hope-filled tool you might suggest to your care partner. They might want to think of it as their "last conversation" with those they love. They could thank someone for a certain kindness or let someone know how much they admire that person. They might want to express gratitude or appreciation for a particular act or thank someone for "just being who you are." The letter might include specific things they have appreciated about family and friends, such as "I have always enjoyed your spunk and your wonderful sense of humor that pulled us through difficult times," or "Your unflinching belief in me when I took on difficult projects was always a huge help to me." The letter could also end with words of blessing to those who remain. Although your care partner may want to share their letter while they are still living, such a document is truly a comfort for the future.

SEEK OUT JOY

Partners in caresharing relationships—especially those who realize that there may be little time left in life—have often reminded me of the importance of seeking out joy wherever it can be found. Appreciating a sunset, listening to a cherished piece of music, enjoying the fragrance of a favorite garden flower, or sharing a moment of closeness and intimacy all have the potential to bring happiness and a sense of hope.

A personal example brought home the importance of joy to me. In his fifties, my husband was severely injured in an industrial accident that severed part of one of his fingers and "froze" the use of several other fingers on his hand. As we sat in the examining room, the doctor evaluated the functions that my husband might be able to perform within the new limits he faced.

The physician asked us, "What gives you joy in your life?"

After we had closed our gaping mouths—for neither of us had ever been asked that question by a medical practitioner before—my husband mentioned that he had enjoyed playing the piano. In fact, he played quite well, but obviously the fingering was going to be difficult due to the injury.

Then the doctor asked, "How can you adapt what gives you joy to take into account your limits?"

What a powerful question!

In a caresharing partnership, even if you need to do a lot of adapting, possibilities for joy are present. Indeed, learning to fully experience whatever joy may be possible may be the best of all means for instilling hope. You might pursue this by asking your care partner directly, "What gives you joy in your life?" You might want to use other words for *joy,* such as *pleasure, great happiness,* or *bliss,* but however you phrase it, it is an important question.

Another related, and very necessary, question might be, "And if you have to make some adaptations to enjoy that, how you might do it? How can I help?" Beloved things or activities might need to be adapted to current limitations. For example, a couple who used to garden together shared flowers in a vase in the room where the cared-for person was staying. A mother and daughter who used to attend symphony concerts together listened to a recording of their favorite musicians at home. You might want to place pictures of special places and people nearby for someone who cannot travel or see their loved ones because of ill health or distance.

Sometimes just sharing curiosity about something can bring a sense of joy. Doing simple things, such as cutting open an apple sideways and marveling at the star pattern made by the seeds and enjoying the Creator's minor miracle, can open a small window of hope. Or taking a seed and watching it take root and bud (I like to use avocado seeds because they are so large) can create a spark of joy and bring a sense of hopefulness.

When it comes to joy, the interdependent steps of the dance of caresharing weave together. As a caregiver, you might need to help the person you are caring for experience a sense of satisfaction or pleasure. At other times, the one you are caring for may awaken your sense of joy with their delight in something as simple as a beautiful sky and warm sun on their face.

You may need to be creative to provide the opportunities for joy. Or you may need to set boundaries so that the happiness of playing with grandchildren or with a beloved pet does not over-tax the person being cared for. But by working together, you and your care partner can share joy even in the most restrictive circumstances.

The office where I write has stars and constellations affixed to the ceiling, left by the young girl who occupied the room before I inhabited it. These stars absorb the light from the day and the lamps, and after the lights have been turned out, they glow in the dark. I rather enjoy these pinpoints of light as I close up the computer files and turn out the lights at night. The stars in "my sky" remind me of the way hope works. The small illuminations of joy and love and connection that we receive as we live our lives light up the hope that will keep glowing during our darker times. I like to think of those stars of hope as refracted light from the people who have reflected hope to us. When things block the light and get in the way of being hopeful, the stored illumination from our spiritual beliefs and friends shine on to keep the dark of hopelessness at bay.

As I wrap up this book on the dance of caresharing, my hope is that you keep your spirit, and the spirit of the person for whom you care, alive and well. Keep on developing goals for your life. Keep on seeing the blessings that your care partner can share with you, and you with them, in a reciprocal relationship. Keep open to the unexpected from your care partner; be willing to keep being surprised. Keep looking for and building on hope.

Hope shines through in little ways. You cannot force it, but you can allow it into your heart and soul. And it is in hope that you will find healing, meaning, and balance in this dance of caresharing.

In closing, I want to share a favorite story of hope that lifts me every time I remember it. Agnes was an older lady who had progressed far along in dementia. She would walk back and forth in the halls of the nursing home where she lived, often fidgeting with the buttons on her sweater. Her son Jim visited her daily, and he would walk patiently with her or would take her out for "finger food," such as her favorite burger and fries. One night after he had left the facility, I encountered Agnes and I inquired about the man who had just left. I asked her, "Do you know who that was?" She replied, "No, but I know he was a kind man."

As we have journeyed together through the pages of this book, we have touched on many facets of caresharing. I hope you have been able to take in the message that you are not alone on this path. You and your care partner have much to share in a relationship of love and respect. To know that you are with someone who is a kind and compassionate person is an incredible gift that you can both give and receive. To reach out together to others in your network of support, and be received with understanding and help, reinforces the value of interdependency. To learn new things about yourself and your care partner, and to value the wisdom each has to offer, is a rich experience of discovery. To share soul to soul is a powerful experience of the sacred in all of life.

As you and your care partner continue to dance the steps of caresharing together, may you find hope in the compassion that lives on in the kind hearts of every person in your caresharing network. May you feel connected and empowered. And may Love surround you with care.

POSTLUDE

In the pages of this book, we have explored many facets of the caresharing situation, and I hope you have been able to exchange some new information and ideas about caresharing with your care partner. I also hope both of you have been able to discern the wisdom that each has to offer and have found some encouragement and hope in the process.

You may want to take what you have learned and talk about it with others, in a support group or a community of faith. There is also a good deal of interest in research on caregiving at the national level, and there is now an opportunity to share your particular experiences with the broader caregiver community.

Dr. Rhonda Montgomery and Dr. Karl Kosloski have been researching caregiving for many years, and out of their work a registry of carers called the League of Experienced Family Caregivers (LEFC) has been formed through the University of Wisconsin–Milwaukee Center on Age and Community. The League is seeking caregivers who are willing to help others by sharing their experiences. By gathering and cataloging this information, LEFC hopes to help create better supports and resources for caregivers throughout the country.

If you are interested in sharing your knowledge and insight about the caregiving journey, you can call the LEFC project at

1-800-410-2586 or go to their website, www.familycaregivers. uwm.edu. You don't have to be a computer expert to participate in this ongoing effort. Although the website does contain many resources and current information about caregiving, you can also participate through interviews by telephone or mail-in responses. You would be furthering the important research being done by Montgomery and Kosloski on caregiving, and you would be serving as a mentor for the caregivers of the future.

SUGGESTIONS FOR FURTHER READING

Baines, Barry K. *Ethical Wills: Putting Your Values on Paper.* 2nd ed. Cambridge, Mass.: DaCapo Press, 2006.

Bell, Virginia, and David Troxel. *A Dignified Life: The Best Friends Approach to Alzheimer's Care, A Guide for Family Caregivers.* Deerfield Beach, Fla.: Health Communications, 2002.

Black, Kathy, and Heather Murray Elkins, eds. *Wising Up: Ritual Resources for Women of Faith and Their Journey of Aging.* Cleveland: Pilgrim Press, 2005.

Bowman, Ted. *Finding Hope When Dreams Have Shattered.* St. Paul, Minn.: Ted Bowman, 2001.

Callanan, Maggie, and Patricia Kelley. *Final Gifts: Understanding the Special Awareness, Needs, and Communications of the Dying.* New York: Bantam Books, 1997.

Farran, Carol, Kaye Herth, and Judith Popovich. *Hope and Hopelessness: Critical Clinical Constructs.* Thousand Oaks, Calif.: Sage Publications, 1995.

Feil, Naomi. *The Validation Breakthrough: Simple Techniques for Communicating with People "Alzheimer's Type Dementia."* Baltimore: Health Professions Press, 2002.

Fischer, Kathleen. *Forgiving Your Family: A Journey to Healing.* Nashville: Upper Room Books, 2005.

———. *Winter Grace: Spirituality for the Later Years.* Nashville: Upper Room Books, 1998.

Ford, Marcia. *The Sacred Art of Forgiveness: Forgiving Ourselves and Others through God's Grace.* Woodstock, Vt.: SkyLight Paths Publishing, 2006.

Frankl, Viktor. *Man's Search for Meaning.* Boston: Beacon Press, 2006.

Groopman, Jerome. *The Anatomy of Hope: How People Prevail in the Face of Illness*. New York: Random House, 2004.

Hargrave, Terry. *Families and Forgiveness: Healing Wounds in the Intergenerational Family*. New York: Brunner/Mazel, 1997.

Hellen, Carly R. "Being, Doing, and Belonging: Upholding the Sense of Self with Meaningful Activities." *Alzheimer's Care Quarterly* 1, no. 1 (2000): 42–43.

Kitwood, Thomas. *Dementia Reconsidered: The Person Comes First*. Buckingham, UK: Open University Press, 1997.

Laurenhue, Kathy. *Getting to Know the Life Stories of Older Adults: Activities for Building Relationships*. Baltimore: Health Professions Press, 2007.

Luskin, Frederic. *Forgive for Good: A Proven Prescription for Health and Happiness*. New York: HarperCollins, 2003.

Lustbader, Wendy. *Counting on Kindness: The Dilemmas of Dependency*. New York: The Free Press, 1991.

———. *What's Worth Knowing*. New York: Jeremy P. Tarcher, 2001.

McKim, Donald, ed. *God Never Forgets: Faith, Hope, and Alzheimer's Disease*. Louisville: Westminister John Knox Press, 1997.

Nouwen, Henri J. M. *Here and Now: Living in the Spirit*. New York: Crossroads Publishing, 2002.

———. *The Wounded Healer: Ministry in Contemporary Society*. Garden City, N.Y.: Doubleday, 1972.

Peerman, Gordon. *Blessed Relief: What Christians Can Learn from Buddhists about Suffering*. Woodstock, Vt.: SkyLight Paths, 2008.

Post, Stephen. *The Moral Challenge of Alzheimer's Disease*. Baltimore: Johns Hopkins University Press, 1995.

Remen, Rachel Naomi. *My Grandfather's Blessings: Stories of Strength, Refuge, and Belonging*. New York: Riverhead Books, 2000.

Riemer, Jack, and Nathaniel Stampher. *So That Your Values Live On: Ethical Wills and How to Prepare Them*. Woodstock, Vt.: Jewish Lights Publishing, 1991.

Taylor, Terry. *A Spirituality for Brokenness: Discovering Your Deepest Self in Difficult Times*. Woodstock, Vt.: SkyLight Paths, 2009.

Westberg, Granger. *Good Grief: A Constructive Approach to the Problem of Loss*. 35th ed. Minneapolis: Augsburg-Fortress, 1997.

Wright, Lauren Tyler. *Giving—The Sacred Art: Creating a Lifestyle of Generosity*. Woodstock, Vt.: SkyLight Paths, 2008.

ACKNOWLEDGMENTS

There are many people I want to thank for the birth of this book in its many starts and stops along the way, as life intervened and made the writing difficult:

The many elders and their families who have taught me so much over the years. Especially my Aunt Toni, who always nurtured and believed in me and who died during the writing of this book. I learned so much and was so nurtured by her for more than sixty-one years of my life.

My "power" support group of professional woman who have been together for more than fifteen years, and who have believed in me and my quest to get some ideas together about families and caring: Mary Liz Chaffee, Nancy Edquist, Bonnie Genevay, Denise Klein, and Wendy Lustbader.

The Reverend Don Koepke, my Lutheran colleague, who read a very early draft, offered some major reframing, and urged me to keep going on this book because it was so needed.

Dr. Stephen Sapp, colleague and dear friend, who has conducted so many workshops with me that have become part and parcel of this book, for bailing me out more than once as I pondered and wrote.

All of my students, who, for more than thirty years, always challenged me to tell them why I said the things I did.

Acknowledgments

The women in my parish who kept urging me on. They have been care partners and offered many suggestions.

My weekly walking buddy and nurse colleague Sheila Hunt-Witte, who dragged me into self-care over my protests during the writing of this book.

My long supportive life partner, Larry D. Richards. So many things got put on hold during this time of book development and writing. I am grateful for his love over these forty-plus years in reminding me of the reciprocity of relationships and that we are truly not alone in this life.

But most of all I have to thank my wonderful editors at SkyLight Paths Publishing, Marcia Broucek and Emily Wichland, who alternately held my hand and kept pushing me, always believing in me and the project even when I was ready to give up myself.

Prayer / Meditation

Sacred Attention: A Spiritual Practice for Finding God in the Moment
by Margaret D. McGee
Framed on the Christian liturgical year, this inspiring guide explores ways to develop a practice of attention as a means of talking—and listening—to God.
6 x 9, 144 pp, HC, 978-1-59473-232-4 **$19.99**

Women Pray: Voices through the Ages, from Many Faiths, Cultures and Traditions
Edited and with Introductions by Monica Furlong
5 x 7¼, 256 pp, Quality PB, 978-1-59473-071-9 **$15.99**

Women of Color Pray: Voices of Strength, Faith, Healing, Hope and Courage
Edited and with Introductions by Christal M. Jackson
Through these prayers, poetry, lyrics, meditations and affirmations, you will share in the strong and undeniable connection women of color share with God.
5 x 7¼, 208 pp, Quality PB, 978-1-59473-077-1 **$15.99**

Secrets of Prayer: A Multifaith Guide to Creating Personal Prayer in Your Life *by Nancy Corcoran, CSJ*
This compelling, multifaith guidebook offers you companionship and encouragement on the journey to a healthy prayer life. 6 x 9, 160 pp, Quality PB, 978-1-59473-215-7 **$16.99**

Prayers to an Evolutionary God
by William Cleary; Afterword by Diarmuid O'Murchu
Inspired by the spiritual and scientific teachings of Diarmuid O'Murchu and Teilhard de Chardin, reveals that religion and science can be combined to create an expanding view of the universe—an evolutionary faith.
6 x 9, 208 pp, HC, 978-1-59473-006-1 **$21.99**

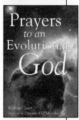

The Art of Public Prayer, 2nd Ed.: Not for Clergy Only *by Lawrence A. Hoffman*
6 x 9, 288 pp, Quality PB, 978-1-893361-06-5 **$19.99**

Prayer / M. Basil Pennington, OCSO

Finding Grace at the Center, 3rd Ed.: The Beginning of Centering Prayer *with Thomas Keating, OCSO, and Thomas E. Clarke, SJ; Foreword by Rev. Cynthia Bourgeault, PhD*
A practical guide to a simple and beautiful form of meditative prayer.
5 x 7¼, 128 pp, Quality PB, 978-1-59473-182-2 **$12.99**

The Monks of Mount Athos: A Western Monk's Extraordinary Spiritual Journey on Eastern Holy Ground *Foreword by Archimandrite Dionysios*
Explores the landscape, the monastic communities and the food of Athos.
6 x 9, 352 pp, Quality PB, 978-1-893361-78-2 **$18.95**

Psalms: A Spiritual Commentary *Illus. by Phillip Ratner*
Reflections on some of the most beloved passages from the Bible's most widely read book. 6 x 9, 176 pp, 24 full-page b/w illus., Quality PB, 978-1-59473-234-8 **$16.99**
HC, 978-1-59473-141-9 **$19.99**

The Song of Songs: A Spiritual Commentary *Illus. by Phillip Ratner*
Explore the Bible's most challenging mystical text.
6 x 9, 160 pp, 14 b/w illus., Quality PB, 978-1-59473-235-5 **$16.99**

Or phone, fax, mail or e-mail to: SKYLIGHT PATHS Publishing
Sunset Farm Offices, Route 4 • P.O. Box 237 • Woodstock, Vermont 05091
Tel: (802) 457-4000 • Fax: (802) 457-4004 • www.skylightpaths.com
Credit card orders: (800) 962-4544 (8:30AM–5:30PM ET Monday–Friday)
Generous discounts on quantity orders. SATISFACTION GUARANTEED. Prices subject to change.

Children's Spirituality

Adam & Eve's First Sunset: God's New Day
by Sandy Eisenberg Sasso; Full-color illus. by Joani Keller Rothenberg 9 x 12, 32 pp, Full-color illus., HC,
978-1-58023-177-0 **$17.95** *For ages 4 & up (A book from Jewish Lights, SkyLight Paths' sister imprint)*

Because Nothing Looks Like God
by Lawrence Kushner and Karen Kushner; Full-color illus. by Dawn W. Majewski
Invites parents and children to explore the questions we all have about God.
11 x 8½, 32 pp, Full-color illus., HC, 978-1-58023-092-6 **$17.99**
For ages 4 & up (A book from Jewish Lights, SkyLight Paths' sister imprint)
Also available: **Teacher's Guide,** 8½ x 11, 22 pp, PB, 978-1-58023-140-4 **$6.95** *For ages 5–8*

But God Remembered: Stories of Women from Creation to the
Promised Land   *by Sandy Eisenberg Sasso; Full-color illus. by Bethanne Andersen*
A fascinating collection of four different stories of women only briefly mentioned in biblical tradition and religious texts.
9 x 12, 32 pp, Full-color illus., Quality PB, 978-1-58023-372-9 **$8.99**; HC, 978-1-879045-43-9 **$16.95**
For ages 8 & up (A book from Jewish Lights, SkyLight Paths' sister imprint)

Cain & Abel: Finding the Fruits of Peace
by Sandy Eisenberg Sasso; Full-color illus. by Joani Keller Rothenberg
A sensitive recasting of the ancient tale shows we have the power to deal with anger
in positive ways. "Editor's Choice" —American Library Association's *Booklist*
9 x 12, 32 pp, Full-color illus., HC, 978-1-58023-123-7 **$16.95** *For ages 5 & up (A book from
Jewish Lights, SkyLight Paths' sister imprint)*

Does God Hear My Prayer?
by August Gold; Full-color photos by Diane Hardy Waller
Introduces preschoolers and young readers to prayer and how it helps them
express their own emotions.
10 x 8½, 32 pp, Full-color photo illus., Quality PB, 978-1-59473-102-0 **$8.99** *For ages 3–6*

The 11th Commandment: Wisdom from Our Children   *by The Children of America*
"If there were an Eleventh Commandment, what would it be?" Children of many
religious denominations across America answer this question—in their own drawings and words. "A rare book of spiritual celebration for all people, of all ages,
for all time." —*Bookviews*   8 x 10, 48 pp, Full-color illus., HC, 978-1-879045-46-0 **$16.95**
For all ages (A book from Jewish Lights, SkyLight Paths' sister imprint)

For Heaven's Sake   *by Sandy Eisenberg Sasso; Full-color illus. by Kathryn Kunz Finney*
Heaven is often found where you least expect it.   9 x 12, 32 pp, Full-color illus., HC,
978-1-58023-054-4 **$16.95** *For ages 4 & up (A book from Jewish Lights, SkyLight Paths' sister imprint)*

God in Between   *by Sandy Eisenberg Sasso; Full-color illus. by Sally Sweetland*
A magical, mythical tale that teaches that God can be found where we are.
9 x 12, 32 pp, Full-color illus., HC, 978-1-879045-86-6 **$16.95** *For ages 4 & up (A book from Jewish
Lights, SkyLight Paths' sister imprint)*

God's Paintbrush: Special 10th Anniversary Edition
Invites children of all faiths and backgrounds to encounter God through moments
in their own lives. 11 x 8½, 32 pp, Full-color illus., HC, 978-1-58023-195-4 **$17.95** *For ages 4 & up*
(A book from Jewish Lights, SkyLight Paths' sister imprint)
Also available: **God's Paintbrush Teacher's Guide** 8½ x 11, 32 pp, PB, 978-1-879045-57-6 **$8.95**

God's Paintbrush Celebration Kit: A Spiritual Activity Kit for Teachers and
Students of All Faiths, All Backgrounds 9½ x 12, 40 Full-color Activity Sheets & Teacher Folder
w/ complete instructions, HC, 978-1-58023-050-6 **$21.95**
Additional activity sheets available:
8-Student Activity Sheet Pack (40 sheets/5 sessions), 978-1-58023-058-2 **$19.95**
Single-Student Activity Sheet Pack (5 sessions), 978-1-58023-059-9 **$3.95**
Also available: **I Am God's Paintbrush** (A Board Book)
by Sandy Eisenberg Sasso; Full-color illus. by Annette Compton
5 x 5, 24 pp, Full-color illus., Board Book, 978-1-59473-265-2 **$7.99** *For ages 0–4*

Children's Spirituality

Remembering My Grandparent: A Kid's Own Grief Workbook in the Christian Tradition *by Nechama Liss-Levinson, PhD, and Rev. Molly Phinney Baskette, MDiv* 8 x 10, 48 pp, 2-color text, HC, 978-1-59473-212-6 **$16.99** *For ages 7 & up*

Does God Ever Sleep? *by Joan Sauro, CSJ*
A charming nighttime reminder that God is always present in our lives.
10 x 8½, 32 pp, Full-color photos, Quality PB, 978-1-59473-110-5 **$8.99** *For ages 3–6*

Does God Forgive Me? *by August Gold; Full-color photos by Diane Hardy Waller*
Gently shows how God forgives all that we do if we are truly sorry.
10 x 8½, 32 pp, Full-color photos, Quality PB, 978-1-59473-142-6 **$8.99** *For ages 3–6*

God Said Amen *by Sandy Eisenberg Sasso; Full-color illus. by Avi Katz*
A warm and inspiring tale that shows us that we need only reach out to each other to find the answers to our prayers.
9 x 12, 32 pp, Full-color illus., HC, 978-1-58023-080-3 **$16.95**
For ages 4 & up (A book from Jewish Lights, SkyLight Paths' sister imprint)

How Does God Listen? *by Kay Lindahl; Full-color photos by Cynthia Maloney*
How do we know when God is listening to us? Children will find the answers to these questions as they engage their senses while the story unfolds, learning how God listens in the wind, waves, clouds, hot chocolate, perfume, our tears and our laughter.
10 x 8½, 32 pp, Full-color photos, Quality PB, 978-1-59473-084-9 **$8.99** *For ages 3–6*

In God's Hands *by Lawrence Kushner and Gary Schmidt; Full-color illus. by Matthew J. Baek*
9 x 12, 32 pp, Full-color illus., HC, 978-1-58023-224-1 **$16.99** *For ages 5 & up (A book from Jewish Lights, SkyLight Paths' sister imprint)*

In God's Name *by Sandy Eisenberg Sasso; Full-color illus. by Phoebe Stone*
Like an ancient myth in its poetic text and vibrant illustrations, this award-winning modern fable about the search for God's name celebrates the diversity and, at the same time, the unity of all the people of the world.
9 x 12, 32 pp, Full-color illus., HC, 978-1-879045-26-2 **$16.99**
For ages 4 & up (A book from Jewish Lights, SkyLight Paths' sister imprint)

Also available in Spanish: **El nombre de Dios**
9 x 12, 32 pp, Full-color illus., HC, 978-1-893361-63-8 **$16.95**

In Our Image: God's First Creatures
by Nancy Sohn Swartz; Full-color illus. by Melanie Hall
A playful new twist on the Genesis story—from the perspective of the animals. Celebrates the interconnectedness of nature and the harmony of all living things.
9 x 12, 32 pp, Full-color illus., HC, 978-1-879045-99-6 **$16.95**
For ages 4 & up (A book from Jewish Lights, SkyLight Paths' sister imprint)

Noah's Wife: The Story of Naamah
by Sandy Eisenberg Sasso; Full-color illus. by Bethanne Andersen
This new story, based on an ancient text, opens readers' religious imaginations to new ideas about the well-known story of the Flood. When God tells Noah to bring the animals of the world onto the ark, God also calls on Naamah, Noah's wife, to save each plant on Earth.
9 x 12, 32 pp, Full-color illus., HC, 978-1-58023-134-3 **$16.95**
For ages 4 & up (A book from Jewish Lights, SkyLight Paths' sister imprint)

Also available: **Naamah:** Noah's Wife (A Board Book)
by Sandy Eisenberg Sasso; Full-color illus. by Bethanne Andersen
5 x 5, 24 pp, Full-color illus., Board Book, 978-1-893361-56-0 **$7.99** *For ages 0–4*

Where Does God Live? *by August Gold and Matthew J. Perlman*
Helps children and their parents find God in the world around us with simple, practical examples children can relate to.
10 x 8½, 32 pp, Full-color photos, Quality PB, 978-1-893361-39-3 **$8.99** *For ages 3–6*

Folktales

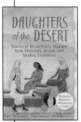

Abraham's Bind & Other Bible Tales of Trickery, Folly, Mercy and Love by Michael J. Caduto
New retellings of episodes in the lives of familiar biblical characters explore relevant life lessons.
6 x 9, 224 pp, HC, 978-1-59473-186-0 **$19.99**

Daughters of the Desert: Stories of Remarkable Women from Christian, Jewish and Muslim Traditions by Claire Rudolf Murphy,
Meghan Nuttall Sayres, Mary Cronk Farrell, Sarah Conover and Betsy Wharton
Breathes new life into the old tales of our female ancestors in faith. Uses traditional scriptural passages as starting points, then with vivid detail fills in historical context and place. Chapters reveal the voices of Sarah, Hagar, Huldah, Esther, Salome, Mary Magdalene, Lydia, Khadija, Fatima and many more. Historical fiction ideal for readers of all ages. Quality paperback includes reader's discussion guide.
5½ x 8½, 192 pp, Quality PB, 978-1-59473-106-8 **$14.99**
HC, 978-1-893361-72-0 **$19.95**

The Triumph of Eve & Other Subversive Bible Tales
by Matt Biers-Ariel
These engaging retellings of familiar Bible stories are witty, often hilarious and always profound. They invite you to grapple with questions and issues that are often hidden in the original texts.
5½ x 8½, 192 pp, Quality PB, 978-1-59473-176-1 **$14.99**
Also available: **The Triumph of Eve Teacher's Guide**
8½ x 11, 44 pp, PB, 978-1-59473-152-5 **$8.99**

Wisdom in the Telling
Finding Inspiration and Grace in Traditional Folktales and Myths Retold
by Lorraine Hartin-Gelardi
6 x 9, 192 pp, HC, 978-1-59473-185-3 **$19.99**

Religious Etiquette / Reference

How to Be a Perfect Stranger, 4th Edition: The Essential Religious Etiquette Handbook Edited by Stuart M. Matlins and Arthur J. Magida
The indispensable guidebook to help the well-meaning guest when visiting other people's religious ceremonies. A straightforward guide to the rituals and celebrations of the major religions and denominations in the United States and Canada from the perspective of an interested guest of any other faith, based on information obtained from authorities of each religion. Belongs in every living room, library and office. Covers:
African American Methodist Churches • Assemblies of God • Bahá'í • Baptist • Buddhist • Christian Church (Disciples of Christ) • Christian Science (Church of Christ, Scientist) • Churches of Christ • Episcopalian and Anglican • Hindu • Islam • Jehovah's Witnesses • Jewish • Lutheran • Mennonite/Amish • Methodist • Mormon (Church of Jesus Christ of Latter-day Saints) • Native American/First Nations • Orthodox Churches • Pentecostal Church of God • Presbyterian • Quaker (Religious Society of Friends) • Reformed Church in America/Canada • Roman Catholic • Seventh-day Adventist • Sikh • Unitarian Universalist • United Church of Canada • United Church of Christ
6 x 9, 432 pp, Quality PB, 978-1-59473-140-2 **$19.99**

The Perfect Stranger's Guide to Funerals and Grieving Practices: A Guide to Etiquette in Other People's Religious Ceremonies Edited by Stuart M. Matlins
6 x 9, 240 pp, Quality PB, 978-1-893361-20-1 **$16.95**

The Perfect Stranger's Guide to Wedding Ceremonies: A Guide to Etiquette in Other People's Religious Ceremonies Edited by Stuart M. Matlins
6 x 9, 208 pp, Quality PB, 978-1-893361-19-5 **$16.95**

Judaism / Christianity / Interfaith

Exploring Muslim Spirituality: An Introduction to the Beauty of Islam
by Hussein Rashid Moves beyond basic information to explore what Islam means to a believer—written by a believer. 6 x 9, 192 pp (est), Quality PB, 978-1-59473-277-5 **$16.99**

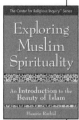

Getting to the Heart of Interfaith
The Eye-Opening, Hope-Filled Friendship of a Pastor, a Rabbi and a Sheikh
by Pastor Don Mackenzie, Rabbi Ted Falcon and Sheikh Jamal Rahman
Offers many insights and encouragements for individuals and groups who want to tap into the promise of interfaith dialogue. 6 x 9, 192 pp, Quality PB, 978-1-59473-263-8 **$16.99**

Hearing the Call across Traditions: Readings on Faith and Service
Edited by Adam Davis; Foreword by Eboo Patel Explores the connections between faith, service and social justice through the prose, verse and sacred texts of the world's great faith traditions. 6 x 9, 352 pp, HC, 978-1-59473-264-5 **$29.99**

How to Do Good and Avoid Evil: A Global Ethic from the Sources of Judaism *by Hans Küng and Rabbi Walter Homolka; Translated by Rev. Dr. John Bowden*
Explores how Judaism's ethical principles can help all religions work together toward a more peaceful humankind. 6 x 9, 224 pp, HC, 978-1-59473-255-3 **$19.99**

The Changing Christian World: A Brief Introduction for Jews
by Rabbi Leonard A. Schoolman 5½ x 8½, 176 pp, Quality PB, 978-1-58023-344-6 **$16.99**
(A book from Jewish Lights, SkyLight Paths' sister imprint)

Christians and Jews in Dialogue: Learning in the Presence of the Other *by Mary C. Boys and Sara S. Lee; Foreword by Dorothy C. Bass* 6 x 9, 240 pp, Quality PB, 978-1-59473-254-6 **$18.99**

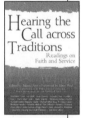

Disaster Spiritual Care: Practical Clergy Responses to Community, Regional and National Tragedy *Edited by Rabbi Stephen B. Roberts, BCJC, & Rev. Willard W.C. Ashley, Sr., DMin, DH*
6 x 9, 384 pp, HC, 978-1-59473-240-9 **$40.00**

InterActive Faith: The Essential Interreligious Community-Building Handbook
Edited by Rev. Bud Heckman with Rori Picker Neiss; Foreword by Rev. Dirk Ficca
6 x 9, 304 pp, Quality PB, 978-1-59473-273-7 **$16.99**; HC, 978-1-59473-237-9 **$40.00**

The Jewish Approach to God: A Brief Introduction for Christians
by Rabbi Neil Gillman, PhD 5½ x 8½, 192 pp, Quality PB, 978-1-58023-190-9 **$16.95**
(A book from Jewish Lights, SkyLight Paths' sister imprint)

The Jewish Approach to Repairing the World (*Tikkun Olam*): A Brief Introduction for Christians *by Rabbi Elliot N. Dorff, PhD, with Reverend Cory Willson* 5½ x 8½, 256 pp, Quality PB 978-1-58023-349-1 **$16.99** *(A book from Jewish Lights, SkyLight Paths' sister imprint)*

The Jewish Connection to Israel, the Promised Land: A Brief Introduction for Christians *by Rabbi Eugene Korn, PhD* 5½ x 8½, 192 pp, Quality PB, 978-1-58023-318-7 **$14.99**
(A book from Jewish Lights, SkyLight Paths' sister imprint)

Jewish Holidays: A Brief Introduction for Christians *by Rabbi Kerry M. Olitzky and Rabbi Daniel Judson* 5½ x 8½, 176 pp, Quality PB, 978-1-58023-302-6 **$16.99**
(A book from Jewish Lights, SkyLight Paths' sister imprint)

Jewish Ritual: A Brief Introduction for Christians
by Rabbi Kerry M. Olitzky and Rabbi Daniel Judson 5½ x 8½, 144 pp, Quality PB, 978-1-58023-210-4 **$14.99**
(A book from Jewish Lights, SkyLight Paths' sister imprint)

Jewish Spirituality: A Brief Introduction for Christians *by Rabbi Lawrence Kushner*
5½ x 8½, 112 pp, Quality PB, 978-1-58023-150-3 **$12.95** *(A book from Jewish Lights, SkyLight Paths' sister imprint)*

A Jewish Understanding of the New Testament *by Rabbi Samuel Sandmel;*
Preface by Rabbi David Sandmel 5½ x 8½, 368 pp, Quality PB, 978-1-59473-048-1 **$19.99**

Modern Jews Engage the New Testament: Enhancing Jewish Well-Being in a
Christian Environment *by Rabbi Michael J. Cook, PhD* 6 x 9, 416 pp, HC
978-1-58023-313-2 **$29.99** *(A book from Jewish Lights, SkyLight Paths' sister imprint)*

Talking about God: Exploring the Meaning of Religious Life with Kierkegaard, Buber, Tillich and Heschel *by Daniel F. Polish, PhD*
6 x 9, 160 pp, Quality PB, 978-1-59473-272-0 **$16.99**; HC, 978-1-59473-230-0 **$21.99**

We Jews and Jesus: Exploring Theological Differences for Mutual Understanding
by Rabbi Samuel Sandmel; Preface by Rabbi David Sandmel
6 x 9, 192 pp, Quality PB, 978-1-59473-208-9 **$16.99**

Sacred Texts—SkyLight Illuminations Series

Offers today's spiritual seeker an enjoyable entry into the great classic texts of the world's spiritual traditions. Each classic is presented in an accessible translation, with facing pages of guided commentary from experts, giving you the keys you need to understand the history, context and meaning of the text.

CHRISTIANITY

The End of Days: Essential Selections from Apocalyptic Texts—
Annotated & Explained *Annotation by Robert G. Clouse*
Helps you understand the complex Christian visions of the end of the world.
5½ x 8½, 224 pp, Quality PB, 978-1-59473-170-9 **$16.99**

The Hidden Gospel of Matthew: Annotated & Explained
Translation & Annotation by Ron Miller Takes you deep into the text cherished around the world to discover the words and events that have the strongest connection to the historical Jesus. 5½ x 8½, 272 pp, Quality PB, 978-1-59473-038-2 **$16.99**

The Infancy Gospels of Jesus: Apocryphal Tales from the Childhoods of Mary and Jesus—Annotated & Explained
Translation & Annotation by Stevan Davies; Foreword by A. Edward Siecienski, PhD
A startling presentation of the early lives of Mary, Jesus and other biblical figures that will amuse and surprise you. 5½ x 8½, 176 pp, Quality PB, 978-1-59473-258-4 **$16.99**

The Lost Sayings of Jesus: Teachings from Ancient Christian, Jewish, Gnostic and Islamic Sources—Annotated & Explained
Translation & Annotation by Andrew Phillip Smith; Foreword by Stephan A. Hoeller
This collection of more than three hundred sayings depicts Jesus as a Wisdom teacher who speaks to people of all faiths as a mystic and spiritual master.
5½ x 8½, 240 pp, Quality PB, 978-1-59473-172-3 **$16.99**

Philokalia: The Eastern Christian Spiritual Texts—Selections Annotated & Explained *Annotation by Allyne Smith; Translation by G. E. H. Palmer, Phillip Sherrard and Bishop Kallistos Ware*
The first approachable introduction to the wisdom of the Philokalia, the classic text of Eastern Christian spirituality. 5½ x 8½, 240 pp, Quality PB, 978-1-59473-103-7 **$16.99**

The Sacred Writings of Paul: Selections Annotated & Explained
Translation & Annotation by Ron Miller Leads you into the exciting immediacy of Paul's teachings. 5½ x 8½, 224 pp, Quality PB, 978-1-59473-213-3 **$16.99**

Saint Augustine of Hippo: Selections from *Confessions* and Other Essential Writings—Annotated & Explained
Annotation by Joseph T. Kelley, PhD; Translation by the Augustinian Heritage Institute
Provides insight into the mind and heart of this foundational Christian figure.
5½ x 8½, 288 pp, Quality PB, 978-1-59473-282-9 **$16.99**

Sex Texts from the Bible: Selections Annotated & Explained
Translation & Annotation by Teresa J. Hornsby; Foreword by Amy-Jill Levine
Demystifies the Bible's ideas on gender roles, marriage, sexual orientation, virginity, lust and sexual pleasure. 5½ x 8½, 208 pp, Quality PB, 978-1-59473-217-1 **$16.99**

Spiritual Writings on Mary: Annotated & Explained
Annotation by Mary Ford-Grabowsky; Foreword by Andrew Harvey
Examines the role of Mary, the mother of Jesus, as a source of inspiration in history and in life today. 5½ x 8½, 288 pp, Quality PB, 978-1-59473-001-6 **$16.99**

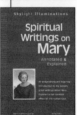

The Way of a Pilgrim: The Jesus Prayer Journey—Annotated & Explained
Translation & Annotation by Gleb Pokrovsky; Foreword by Andrew Harvey
This classic of Russian Orthodox spirituality is the delightful account of one man who sets out to learn the prayer of the heart, also known as the "Jesus prayer."
5½ x 8½, 160 pp, Illus., Quality PB, 978-1-893361-31-7 **$14.95**

Sacred Texts—continued

MORMONISM

The Book of Mormon: Selections Annotated & Explained
Annotation by Jana Riess; Foreword by Phyllis Tickle Explores the sacred epic that is cherished by more than twelve million members of the LDS church as the keystone of their faith. 5½ x 8½, 272 pp, Quality PB, 978-1-59473-076-4 **$16.99**

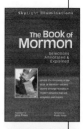

NATIVE AMERICAN

Native American Stories of the Sacred: Annotated & Explained
Retold & Annotated by Evan T. Pritchard Intended for more than entertainment, these teaching tales contain elegantly simple illustrations of time-honored truths. 5½ x 8½, 272 pp, Quality PB, 978-1-59473-112-9 **$16.99**

GNOSTICISM

Gnostic Writings on the Soul: Annotated & Explained
Translation & Annotation by Andrew Phillip Smith; Foreword by Stephan A. Hoeller
Reveals the inspiring ways your soul can remember and return to its unique, divine purpose. 5½ x 8½, 144 pp, Quality PB, 978-1-59473-220-1 **$16.99**

The Gospel of Philip: Annotated & Explained
Translation & Annotation by Andrew Phillip Smith; Foreword by Stevan Davies
Reveals otherwise unrecorded sayings of Jesus and fragments of Gnostic mythology. 5½ x 8½, 160 pp, Quality PB, 978-1-59473-111-2 **$16.99**

The Gospel of Thomas: Annotated & Explained
Translation & Annotation by Stevan Davies; Foreword by Andrew Harvey
Sheds new light on the origins of Christianity and portrays Jesus as a wisdom-loving sage. 5½ x 8½, 192 pp, Quality PB, 978-1-893361-45-4 **$16.99**

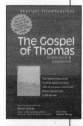

The Secret Book of John: The Gnostic Gospel—Annotated & Explained
Translation & Annotation by Stevan Davies The most significant and influential text of the ancient Gnostic religion. 5½ x 8½, 208 pp, Quality PB, 978-1-59473-082-5 **$16.99**

JUDAISM

The Divine Feminine in Biblical Wisdom Literature
Selections Annotated & Explained
Translation & Annotation by Rabbi Rami Shapiro; Foreword by Rev. Cynthia Bourgeault, PhD
Uses the Hebrew Bible and Wisdom literature to explain Sophia's way of wisdom and illustrate Her creative energy. 5½ x 8½, 240 pp, Quality PB, 978-1-59473-109-9 **$16.99**

Ethics of the Sages: *Pirke Avot*—Annotated & Explained
Translation & Annotation by Rabbi Rami Shapiro Clarifies the ethical teachings of the early Rabbis. 5½ x 8½, 192 pp, Quality PB, 978-1-59473-207-2 **$16.99**

Hasidic Tales: Annotated & Explained
Translation & Annotation by Rabbi Rami Shapiro
Introduces the legendary tales of the impassioned Hasidic rabbis, presenting them as stories rather than as parables. 5½ x 8½, 240 pp, Quality PB, 978-1-893361-86-7 **$16.95**

The Hebrew Prophets: Selections Annotated & Explained
Translation & Annotation by Rabbi Rami Shapiro; Foreword by Rabbi Zalman M. Schachter-Shalomi
Makes the wisdom of these timeless teachers accessible. 5½ x 8½, 224 pp, Quality PB, 978-1-59473-037-5 **$16.99**

Tanya, the Masterpiece of Hasidic Wisdom: Selections Annotated & Explained *Translation & Annotation by Rabbi Rami Shapiro; Foreword by Rabbi Zalman M. Schachter-Shalomi* Clarifies one of the most powerful and potentially transformative books of Jewish wisdom. 5½ x 8½, 240 pp, Quality PB, 978-1-59473-275-1 **$16.99**

Zohar: Annotated & Explained
Translation & Annotation by Daniel C. Matt; Foreword by Andrew Harvey
Brings together the most important teachings of the Zohar, the canonical text of Jewish mystical tradition. 5½ x 8½, 176 pp, Quality PB, 978-1-893361-51-5 **$15.99**

Sacred Texts—continued

ISLAM

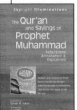

Ghazali on the Principles of Islamic Spirituality
Selections from *Forty Foundations of Religion*—Annotated & Explained
Translation & Annotation by Shaykh Faraz Rabbani and Aaron Spevack, PhD
Makes the core message of this influential spiritual master relevant to anyone seeking a balanced understanding of Islam.
5½ x 8½, 208 pp (est), Quality PB, 978-1-59473-284-3 **$16.99**

The Qur'an and Sayings of Prophet Muhammad
Selections Annotated & Explained
Annotation by Sohaib N. Sultan; Translation by Yusuf Ali, Revised by Sohaib N. Sultan
Foreword by Jane I. Smith
Presents the foundational wisdom of Islam in an easy-to-use format.
5½ x 8½, 256 pp, Quality PB, 978-1-59473-222-5 **$16.99**

Rumi and Islam: Selections from His Stories, Poems, and Discourses—
Annotated & Explained
Translation & Annotation by Ibrahim Gamard
Focuses on Rumi's place within the Sufi tradition of Islam, providing insight into the mystical side of the religion.
5½ x 8½, 240 pp, Quality PB, 978-1-59473-002-3 **$15.99**

EASTERN RELIGIONS

The Art of War—Spirituality for Conflict
Annotated & Explained
by Sun Tzu; Annotation by Thomas Huynh; Translation by Thomas Huynh and the Editors at Sonshi.com; Foreword by Marc Benioff; Preface by Thomas Cleary
Highlights principles that encourage a perceptive and spiritual approach to conflict.
5½ x 8½, 256 pp, Quality PB, 978-1-59473-244-7 **$16.99**

Bhagavad Gita: Annotated & Explained
Translation by Shri Purohit Swami; Annotation by Kendra Crossen Burroughs
Presents the classic text's teachings—with no previous knowledge of Hinduism required.   5½ x 8½, 192 pp, Quality PB, 978-1-893361-28-7 **$16.95**

Dhammapada: Annotated & Explained
Translation by Max Müller, revised by Jack Maguire; Annotation by Jack Maguire
Contains all of Buddhism's key teachings, plus commentary that explains all the names, terms and references.   5½ x 8½, 160 pp, b/w photos, Quality PB, 978-1-893361-42-3 **$14.95**

Selections from the Gospel of Sri Ramakrishna
Annotated & Explained
Translation by Swami Nikhilananda; Annotation by Kendra Crossen Burroughs
Introduces the fascinating world of the Indian mystic and the universal appeal of his message.   5½ x 8½, 240 pp, b/w photos, Quality PB, 978-1-893361-46-1 **$16.95**

Tao Te Ching: Annotated & Explained
Translation & Annotation by Derek Lin; Foreword by Lama Surya Das
Introduces an Eastern classic in an accessible, poetic and completely original way.
5½ x 8½, 208 pp, Quality PB, 978-1-59473-204-1 **$16.99**

STOICISM

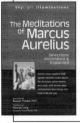

The Meditations of Marcus Aurelius
Selections Annotated & Explained
Annotation by Russell McNeil, PhD; Translation by George Long, revised by Russell McNeil, PhD
Ancient Stoic wisdom that speaks vibrantly today about life, business, government and spirit.   5½ x 8½, 288 pp, Quality PB, 978-1-59473-236-2 **$16.99**

Spirituality of the Seasons

Autumn: A Spiritual Biography of the Season
Edited by Gary Schmidt and Susan M. Felch; Illustrations by Mary Azarian
Rejoice in autumn as a time of preparation and reflection. Includes Wendell Berry, David James Duncan, Robert Frost, A. Bartlett Giamatti, E. B. White, P. D. James, Julian of Norwich, Garret Keizer, Tracy Kidder, Anne Lamott, May Sarton.
6 x 9, 320 pp, 5 b/w illus., Quality PB, 978-1-59473-118-1 **$18.99**

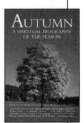

Spring: A Spiritual Biography of the Season
Edited by Gary Schmidt and Susan M. Felch; Illustrations by Mary Azarian
Explore the gentle unfurling of spring and reflect on how nature celebrates rebirth and renewal. Includes Jane Kenyon, Lucy Larcom, Harry Thurston, Nathaniel Hawthorne, Noel Perrin, Annie Dillard, Martha Ballard, Barbara Kingsolver, Dorothy Wordsworth, Donald Hall, David Brill, Lionel Basney, Isak Dinesen, Paul Laurence Dunbar. 6 x 9, 352 pp, 6 b/w illus., Quality PB, 978-1-59473-246-1 **$18.99**

Summer: A Spiritual Biography of the Season
Edited by Gary Schmidt and Susan M. Felch; Illustrations by Barry Moser
"A sumptuous banquet.... These selections lift up an exquisite wholeness found within an everyday sophistication." — ★ *Publishers Weekly* starred review
Includes Anne Lamott, Luci Shaw, Ray Bradbury, Richard Selzer, Thomas Lynch, Walt Whitman, Carl Sandburg, Sherman Alexie, Madeleine L'Engle, Jamaica Kincaid.
6 x 9, 304 pp, 5 b/w illus., Quality PB, 978-1-59473-183-9 **$18.99**
HC, 978-1-59473-083-2 **$21.99**

Winter: A Spiritual Biography of the Season
Edited by Gary Schmidt and Susan M. Felch; Illustrations by Barry Moser
"This outstanding anthology features top-flight nature and spirituality writers on the fierce, inexorable season of winter.... Remarkably lively and warm, despite the icy subject." — ★ *Publishers Weekly* starred review
Includes Will Campbell, Rachel Carson, Annie Dillard, Donald Hall, Ron Hansen, Jane Kenyon, Jamaica Kincaid, Barry Lopez, Kathleen Norris, John Updike, E. B. White.
6 x 9, 288 pp, 6 b/w illus., Deluxe PB w/ flaps, 978-1-893361-92-8 **$18.95**

Spirituality / Animal Companions

Blessing the Animals: Prayers and Ceremonies to Celebrate God's Creatures, Wild and Tame *Edited and with Introductions by Lynn L. Caruso*
5¼ x 7¼, 256 pp, Quality PB, 978-1-59473-253-9 **$15.99**; HC, 978-1-59473-145-7 **$19.99**

Remembering My Pet: A Kid's Own Spiritual Workbook for When a Pet Dies
by Nechama Liss-Levinson, PhD, and Rev. Molly Phinney Baskette, MDiv; Foreword by Lynn L. Caruso
8 x 10, 48 pp, 2-color text, HC, 978-1-59473-221-8 **$16.99**

What Animals Can Teach Us about Spirituality: Inspiring Lessons from Wild and Tame Creatures *by Diana L. Guerrero* 6 x 9, 176 pp, Quality PB, 978-1-893361-84-3 **$16.95**

Spirituality—A Week Inside

Come and Sit: A Week Inside Meditation Centers
by Marcia Z. Nelson; Foreword by Wayne Teasdale
6 x 9, 224 pp, b/w photos, Quality PB, 978-1-893361-35-5 **$16.95**

Lighting the Lamp of Wisdom: A Week Inside a Yoga Ashram
by John Ittner; Foreword by Dr. David Frawley
6 x 9, 192 pp, 10+ b/w photos, Quality PB, 978-1-893361-52-2 **$15.95**

Making a Heart for God: A Week Inside a Catholic Monastery
by Dianne Aprile; Foreword by Brother Patrick Hart, OCSO
6 x 9, 224 pp, b/w photos, Quality PB, 978-1-893361-49-2 **$16.95**

Waking Up: A Week Inside a Zen Monastery
by Jack Maguire; Foreword by John Daido Loori, Roshi
6 x 9, 224 pp, b/w photos, Quality PB, 978-1-893361-55-3 **$16.95**; HC, 978-1-893361-13-3 **$21.95**

Spirituality

Creative Aging: Rethinking Retirement and Non-Retirement in a Changing World *by Marjory Zoet Bankson*
Offers creative ways to nourish our calling and discover meaning and purpose in our older years. 6 x 9, 160 pp, Quality PB, 978-1-59473-281-2 **$16.99**

Laugh Your Way to Grace: Reclaiming the Spiritual Power of Humor
by Rev. Susan Sparks A powerful, humorous case for laughter as a spiritual, healing path. 6 x 9, 144 pp (est), Quality PB, 978-1-59473-280-5 **$16.99**

Living into Hope: A Call to Spiritual Action for Such a Time as This
by Rev. Dr. Joan Brown Campbell; Foreword by Karen Armstrong
A visionary minister speaks out on the pressing issues that face us today, offering inspiration and challenge. 6 x 9, 192 pp (est), HC, 978-1-59473-283-6 **$21.99**

Claiming Earth as Common Ground: The Ecological Crisis through the Lens of Faith *by Andrea Cohen-Kiener; Foreword by Rev. Sally Bingham*
Inspires us to work across denominational lines in order to fulfill our sacred imperative to care for God's creation. 6 x 9, 192 pp, Quality PB, 978-1-59473-261-4 **$16.99**

The Losses of Our Lives: The Sacred Gifts of Renewal in Everyday Loss
by Dr. Nancy Copeland-Payton
Reframes loss from the perspective that our everyday losses help us learn what we need to handle the major losses. 6 x 9, 192 pp, HC, 978-1-59473-271-3 **$19.99**

Bread, Body, Spirit: Finding the Sacred in Food
Edited and with Introductions by Alice Peck 6 x 9, 224 pp, Quality PB, 978-1-59473-242-3 **$19.99**

Creating a Spiritual Retirement: A Guide to the Unseen Possibilities in Our Lives
by Molly Srode 6 x 9, 208 pp, b/w photos, Quality PB, 978-1-59473-050-4 **$14.99**

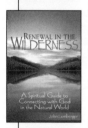

Finding Hope: Cultivating God's Gift of a Hopeful Spirit
by Marcia Ford; Foreword by Andrea Jaeger 8 x 8, 176 pp, Quality PB, 978-1-59473-211-9 **$16.99**

Honoring Motherhood: Prayers, Ceremonies and Blessings
Edited and with Introductions by Lynn L. Caruso 5 x 7¼, 272 pp, HC, 978-1-59473-239-3 **$19.99**

Jewish Spirituality: A Brief Introduction for Christians *by Lawrence Kushner*
5½ x 8½, 112 pp, Quality PB, 978-1-58023-150-3 **$12.95** *(A book from Jewish Lights, SkyLight Paths' sister imprint)*

Journeys of Simplicity: Traveling Light with Thomas Merton, Bashō, Edward Abbey, Annie Dillard & Others *by Philip Harnden*
5 x 7¼, 144 pp, Quality PB, 978-1-59473-181-5 **$12.99**; 128 pp, HC, 978-1-893361-76-8 **$16.95**

Keeping Spiritual Balance As We Grow Older: More than 65 Creative Ways to Use Purpose, Prayer, and the Power of Spirit to Build a Meaningful Retirement
by Molly and Bernie Srode 8 x 8, 224 pp, Quality PB, 978-1-59473-042-9 **$16.99**

Money and the Way of Wisdom: Insights from the Book of Proverbs
by Timothy J. Sandoval, PhD 6 x 9, 192 pp, Quality PB, 978-1-59473-245-4 **$16.99**

Next to Godliness: Finding the Sacred in Housekeeping
Edited by Alice Peck 6 x 9, 224 pp, Quality PB, 978-1-59473-214-0 **$19.99**

Renewal in the Wilderness: A Spiritual Guide to Connecting with God in the Natural World
by John Lionberger 6 x 9, 176 pp, b/w photos, Quality PB, 978-1-59473-219-5 **$16.99**

Soul Fire: Accessing Your Creativity
by Thomas Ryan, CSP 6 x 9, 160 pp, Quality PB, 978-1-59473-243-0 **$16.99**

A Spirituality for Brokenness: Discovering Your Deepest Self in Difficult Times
by Terry Taylor 6 x 9, 176 pp, Quality PB, 978-1-59473-229-4 **$16.99**

Spiritually Incorrect: Finding God in All the *Wrong* Places *by Dan Wakefield; Illus. by Marian DelVecchio* 5½ x 8½, 192 pp, b/w illus., Quality PB, 978-1-59473-137-2 **$15.99**

A Walk with Four Spiritual Guides: Krishna, Buddha, Jesus, and Ramakrishna
by Andrew Harvey 5½ x 8½, 192 pp, 10 b/w photos & illus., Quality PB, 978-1-59473-138-9 **$15.99**

The Workplace and Spirituality: New Perspectives on Research and Practice
Edited by Dr. Joan Marques, Dr. Satinder Dhiman and Dr. Richard King
6 x 9, 256 pp, HC, 978-1-59473-260-7 **$29.99**

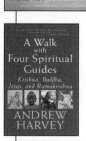

Spirituality & Crafts

Beading—The Creative Spirit: Finding Your Sacred Center through the Art of Beadwork *by Rev. Wendy Ellsworth*
Invites you on a spiritual pilgrimage into the kaleidoscope world of glass and color.   7 x 9, 240 pp, 8-page color insert, 40+ b/w photos and 40 diagrams
Quality PB, 978-1-59473-267-6 **$18.99**

Contemplative Crochet: A Hands-On Guide for Interlocking Faith and Craft *by Cindy Crandall-Frazier; Foreword by Linda Skolnik*
Illuminates the spiritual lessons you can learn through crocheting.
7 x 9, 208 pp, b/w photos, Quality PB, 978-1-59473-238-6 **$16.99**

The Knitting Way: A Guide to Spiritual Self-Discovery
by Linda Skolnik and Janice MacDaniels Examines how you can explore and strengthen your spiritual life through knitting.
7 x 9, 240 pp, b/w photos, Quality PB, 978-1-59473-079-5 **$16.99**

The Painting Path: Embodying Spiritual Discovery through Yoga, Brush and Color *by Linda Novick; Foreword by Richard Segalman*
Explores the divine connection you can experience through art.
7 x 9, 208 pp, 8-page color insert, plus b/w photos
Quality PB, 978-1-59473-226-3 **$18.99**

The Quilting Path: A Guide to Spiritual Discovery through Fabric, Thread and Kabbalah *by Louise Silk*
Explores how to cultivate personal growth through quilt making.
7 x 9, 192 pp, b/w photos and illus., Quality PB, 978-1-59473-206-5 **$16.99**

The Scrapbooking Journey: A Hands-On Guide to Spiritual Discovery
by Cory Richardson-Lauve; Foreword by Stacy Julian   Reveals how this craft can become a practice used to deepen and shape your life.
7 x 9, 176 pp, 8-page color insert, plus b/w photos, Quality PB, 978-1-59473-216-4 **$18.99**

The Soulwork of Clay: A Hands-On Approach to Spirituality
by Marjory Zoet Bankson; Photos by Peter Bankson
Takes you through the seven-step process of making clay into a pot, drawing parallels at each stage to the process of spiritual growth.
7 x 9, 192 pp, b/w photos, Quality PB, 978-1-59473-249-2 **$16.99**

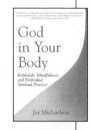

Kabbalah / Enneagram
(Books from Jewish Lights Publishing, SkyLight Paths' sister imprint)

God in Your Body: Kabbalah, Mindfulness and Embodied Spiritual Practice
by Jay Michaelson 6 x 9, 272 pp, Quality PB, 978-1-58023-304-0 **$18.99**

Cast in God's Image: Discover Your Personality Type Using the Enneagram and Kabbalah
by Rabbi Howard A. Addison 7 x 9, 176 pp, Quality PB, 978-1-58023-124-4 **$16.95**

Ehyeh: A Kabbalah for Tomorrow *by Dr. Arthur Green*
6 x 9, 224 pp, Quality PB, 978-1-58023-213-5 **$16.99**

The Enneagram and Kabbalah, 2nd Edition: Reading Your Soul
by Rabbi Howard A. Addison 6 x 9, 192 pp, Quality PB, 978-1-58023-229-6 **$16.99**

The Gift of Kabbalah: Discovering the Secrets of Heaven, Renewing Your Life on Earth
by Tamar Frankiel, PhD 6 x 9, 256 pp, Quality PB, 978-1-58023-141-1 **$16.95**

Kabbalah: A Brief Introduction for Christians
by Tamar Frankiel, PhD 5½ x 8½, 176 pp, Quality PB, 978-1-58023-303-3 **$16.99**

Zohar: Annotated & Explained *Translation & Annotation by Daniel C. Matt*
Foreword by Andrew Harvey 5½ x 8½, 176 pp, Quality PB, 978-1-893361-51-5 **$15.99**

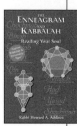

Spiritual Poetry—The Mystic Poets

Experience these mystic poets as you never have before. Each beautiful, compact book includes a brief introduction to the poet's time and place, a summary of the major themes of the poet's mysticism and religious tradition, essential selections from the poet's most important works, and an appreciative preface by a contemporary spiritual writer.

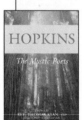

Hafiz
The Mystic Poets
Preface by Ibrahim Gamard

Hafiz is known throughout the world as Persia's greatest poet, with sales of his poems in Iran today only surpassed by those of the Qur'an itself. His probing and joyful verse speaks to people from all backgrounds who long to taste and feel divine love and experience harmony with all living things.

5 x 7¼, 144 pp, HC, 978-1-59473-009-2 **$16.99**

Hopkins
The Mystic Poets
Preface by Rev. Thomas Ryan, CSP

Gerard Manley Hopkins, Christian mystical poet, is beloved for his use of fresh language and startling metaphors to describe the world around him. Although his verse is lovely, beneath the surface lies a searching soul, wrestling with and yearning for God.

5 x 7¼, 112 pp, HC, 978-1-59473-010-8 **$16.99**

Tagore
The Mystic Poets
Preface by Swami Adiswarananda

Rabindranath Tagore is often considered the Shakespeare of modern India. A great mystic, Tagore was the teacher of W. B. Yeats and Robert Frost, the close friend of Albert Einstein and Mahatma Gandhi, and the winner of the Nobel Prize for Literature. This beautiful sampling of Tagore's two most important works, *The Gardener* and *Gitanjali*, offers a glimpse into his spiritual vision that has inspired people around the world.

5 x 7¼, 144 pp, HC, 978-1-59473-008-5 **$16.99**

Whitman
The Mystic Poets
Preface by Gary David Comstock

Walt Whitman was the most innovative and influential poet of the nineteenth century. This beautiful sampling of Whitman's most important poetry from *Leaves of Grass,* and selections from his prose writings, offers a glimpse into the spiritual side of his most radical themes—love for country, love for others and love of Self.

5 x 7¼, 192 pp, HC, 978-1-59473-041-2 **$16.99**

Journeys of Simplicity
Traveling Light with Thomas Merton, Bashō, Edward Abbey, Annie Dillard & Others
by Philip Harnden

Invites you to consider a more graceful way of traveling through life. PB includes journal pages to help you get started on your own spiritual journey.

5 x 7¼, 144 pp, Quality PB, 978-1-59473-181-5 **$12.99**
5 x 7¼, 128 pp, HC, 978-1-893361-76-8 **$16.95**

Spiritual Practice

Laugh Your Way to Grace: Reclaiming the Spiritual Power of Humor
by Rev. Susan Sparks A powerful, humorous case for laughter as a spiritual, healing path. 6 x 9, 144 pp (est), Quality PB, 978-1-59473-280-5 **$16.99**

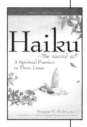

Haiku—The Sacred Art: A Spiritual Practice in Three Lines
by Margaret D. McGee Introduces haiku as a simple and effective way of tapping into the sacred moments that permeate everyday living.
5½ x 8½, 192 pp, Quality PB, 978-1-59473-269-0 **$16.99**

Dance—The Sacred Art: The Joy of Movement as a Spiritual Practice
by Cynthia Winton-Henry Invites all of us, regardless of experience, into the possibility of dance/movement as a spiritual practice.
5½ x 8½, 224 pp, Quality PB, 978-1-59473-268-3 **$16.99**

Spiritual Adventures in the Snow: Skiing & Snowboarding as Renewal for Your Soul *by Dr. Marcia McFee and Rev. Karen Foster; Foreword by Paul Arthur* Explores snow sports as tangible experiences of the spiritual essence of our bodies and the earth. 5½ x 8½, 208 pp, Quality PB, 978-1-59473-270-6 **$16.99**

Recovery—The Sacred Art: The Twelve Steps as Spiritual Practice
by Rami Shapiro; Foreword by Joan Borysenko, PhD Uniquely interprets the Twelve Steps of Alcoholics Anonymous to speak to everyone seeking a freer and more God-centered life. 5½ x 8½, 240 pp, Quality PB, 978-1-59473-259-1 **$16.99**

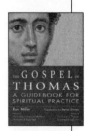

Everyday Herbs in Spiritual Life: A Guide to Many Practices
by Michael J. Caduto; Foreword by Rosemary Gladstar
7 x 9, 208 pp, 20+ b/w illus., Quality PB, 978-1-59473-174-7 **$16.99**

Divining the Body: Reclaim the Holiness of Your Physical Self *by Jan Phillips*
8 x 8, 256 pp, Quality PB, 978-1-59473-080-1 **$16.99**

The Gospel of Thomas: A Guidebook for Spiritual Practice
by Ron Miller; Translations by Stevan Davies 6 x 9, 160 pp, Quality PB, 978-1-59473-047-4 **$14.99**

Hospitality—The Sacred Art: Discovering the Hidden Spiritual Power of Invitation and Welcome *by Rev. Nanette Sawyer; Foreword by Rev. Dirk Ficca*
5½ x 8½, 208 pp, Quality PB, 978-1-59473-228-7 **$16.99**

Labyrinths from the Outside In: Walking to Spiritual Insight—A Beginner's Guide
by Donna Schaper and Carole Ann Camp
6 x 9, 208 pp, b/w illus. and photos, Quality PB, 978-1-893361-18-8 **$16.95**

Practicing the Sacred Art of Listening: A Guide to Enrich Your Relationships and Kindle Your Spiritual Life *by Kay Lindahl* 8 x 8, 176 pp, Quality PB, 978-1-893361-85-0 **$16.95**

Running—The Sacred Art: Preparing to Practice *by Dr. Warren A. Kay; Foreword by Kristin Armstrong* 5½ x 8½, 160 pp, Quality PB, 978-1-59473-227-0 **$16.99**

The Sacred Art of Bowing: Preparing to Practice
by Andi Young 5½ x 8½, 128 pp, b/w illus., Quality PB, 978-1-893361-82-9 **$14.95**

The Sacred Art of Chant: Preparing to Practice
by Ana Hernández 5½ x 8½, 192 pp, Quality PB, 978-1-59473-036-8 **$15.99**

The Sacred Art of Fasting: Preparing to Practice
by Thomas Ryan, CSP 5½ x 8½, 192 pp, Quality PB, 978-1-59473-078-8 **$15.99**

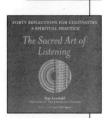

The Sacred Art of Forgiveness: Forgiving Ourselves and Others through God's Grace
by Marcia Ford 8 x 8, 176 pp, Quality PB, 978-1-59473-175-4 **$16.99**

The Sacred Art of Listening: Forty Reflections for Cultivating a Spiritual Practice
by Kay Lindahl; Illustrations by Amy Schnapper 8 x 8, 160 pp, b/w illus., Quality PB, 978-1-893361-44-7 **$16.99**

The Sacred Art of Lovingkindness: Preparing to Practice
by Rabbi Rami Shapiro; Foreword by Marcia Ford 5½ x 8½, 176 pp, Quality PB, 978-1-59473-151-8 **$16.99**

Sacred Speech: A Practical Guide for Keeping Spirit in Your Speech
by Rev. Donna Schaper 6 x 9, 176 pp, Quality PB, 978-1-59473-068-9 **$15.99**
HC, 978-1-893361-74-4 **$21.95**

Soul Fire: Accessing Your Creativity
by Thomas Ryan, CSP 6 x 9, 160 pp, Quality PB, 978-1-59473-243-0 **$16.99**

Thanking & Blessing—The Sacred Art: Spiritual Vitality through Gratefulness
by Jay Marshall, PhD; Foreword by Philip Gulley 5½ x 8½, 176 pp, Quality PB, 978-1-59473-231-7 **$16.99**

About SKYLIGHT PATHS Publishing

SkyLight Paths Publishing is creating a place where people of different spiritual traditions come together for challenge and inspiration, a place where we can help each other understand the mystery that lies at the heart of our existence.

Through spirituality, our religious beliefs are increasingly becoming a part of our lives—rather than *apart* from our lives. While many of us may be more interested than ever in spiritual growth, we may be less firmly planted in traditional religion. Yet, we do want to deepen our relationship to the sacred, to learn from our own as well as from other faith traditions, and to practice in new ways.

SkyLight Paths sees both believers and seekers as a community that increasingly transcends traditional boundaries of religion and denomination—people wanting to learn from each other, *walking together, finding the way.*

For your information and convenience, at the back of this book we have provided a list of other SkyLight Paths books you might find interesting and useful. They cover the following subjects:

Buddhism / Zen	Global Spiritual	Monasticism
Catholicism	Perspectives	Mysticism
Children's Books	Gnosticism	Poetry
Christianity	Hinduism /	Prayer
Comparative	Vedanta	Religious Etiquette
Religion	Inspiration	Retirement
Current Events	Islam / Sufism	Spiritual Biography
Earth-Based	Judaism	Spiritual Direction
Spirituality	Kabbalah	Spirituality
Enneagram	Meditation	Women's Interest
	Midrash Fiction	Worship

Or phone, fax, mail or e-mail to: SKYLIGHT PATHS Publishing
Sunset Farm Offices, Route 4 • P.O. Box 237 • Woodstock, Vermont 05091
Tel: (802) 457-4000 • Fax: (802) 457-4004 • www.skylightpaths.com
Credit card orders: (800) 962-4544 (8:30AM–5:30PM ET Monday–Friday)
Generous discounts on quantity orders. SATISFACTION GUARANTEED. Prices subject to change.

For more information about each book,
visit our website at www.skylightpaths.com